The Justice of Mercy

Law, Meaning, and Violence

The scope of Law, Meaning, and Violence is defined by the wide-ranging scholarly debates signaled by each of the words in the title. Those debates have taken place among and between lawyers, anthropologists, political theorists, sociologists, and historians, as well as literary and cultural critics. This series is intended to recognize the importance of such ongoing conversations about law, meaning, and violence as well as to encourage and further them.

Series Editors: Martha Minow, Harvard Law School
                    Austin Sarat, Amherst College

The Justice of Mercy

LINDA ROSS MEYER

The University of Michigan Press

Ann Arbor

Copyright © by the University of Michigan 2010

All rights reserved

Published in the United States of America by

The University of Michigan Press

Manufactured in the United States of America

♾ Printed on acid-free paper

2013   2012   2011   2010   4   3   2   1

A CIP catalog record for this book is available from the British Library.

Library of Congress Cataloging-in-Publication Data

Meyer, Linda, 1962–

    The justice of mercy / Linda Ross Meyer.

      p.   cm. — (Law, meaning, and violence series)

    Includes bibliographical references and index.

    ISBN 978-0-472-11745-1 (cloth : alk. paper)

    ISBN 978-0-472-02455-1 (e-book)

    1. Law—Philosophy.   2. Justice.   3. Mercy.   4. Kant, Immanuel,
1724–1804.   I. Title.

K250.M49   2010

340'.11—dc22   2010020149

For my teachers

Contents

Acknowledgments

This book is the work of an embarrassing number of years. The problem of finding a place for mercy within law is *the* question for me, and I suspect it always will be. But, being finite, I doubt that I will ever answer all the questions I have, so I can only proffer this effort as "what I have learned so far."

As with any deeply personal work that stretches over decades, I could never begin to acknowledge all the colleagues, teachers, students, research assistants, friends, and family members who have given me ideas and references, challenged and changed my thinking, patiently read and clarified my prose, and supported, encouraged, nagged, and, most important, shown me grace and mercy in so many ways. I thank my family, Jeff, Cara, and Zane; the extended Meyer/Olson/Wachholz/Pearson/Helyar/Knappenberger clan; and my close friends and colleagues, especially Ian Ayres, Roger Berkowitz, Jennifer Brown, Marianne Constable, Jennifer Culbert, Jeremy Elkins, Neal Feigenson, Ann Hopkins, Steve Latham, Shai Lavi, Doug and Melissa Logan, Greg Loken, Bill Odle, Trisha Olson, Austin Sarat, Sylvia Schafer, Marty Slaughter, Max Simmons, and Martha Umphrey. All read and/or discussed this project with me, whether they liked to or not, enriching and refining it. In a very important sense, this book is not really mine, but I will claim it anyway, if only to take responsibility for its flaws.

A special thanks goes to Marianne Constable, Mark Antaki, Roger Berkowitz, Neal Feigenson, Jeff Meyer, Marty Slaughter, and Jill Stauffer, who selflessly gave extensive time and made superb comments on early drafts of this book. I also wish to thank Dean Brad Saxton and my students and colleagues at Quinnipiac University, who supported this project financially, patiently listened to years of presentations about mercy, and gave me insightful, generous, and constructive comments on earlier pieces of this project, especially Brian Bix, Jennifer Brown, Neal Feigenson, Steve Gilles, Carrie Kaas, Stan Krauss, Leslie Lax, Leonard Long, Andrew Lolli, Heather McKay, Jeff Meyer, Sandy

Meiklejohn, David Rosettenstein, Emily Graner Sexton, Amy Solomito, and Gail Stern. This project also benefited greatly from invitations to present portions of it at Amherst College, Suffolk University, and at the University of Tel Aviv, for which I am indebted to Austin Sarat, Nasser Hussain, Nir Eisikovits, Shai Lavi, and the participants in the workshops they organized, who were all so generous with their reading, their comments, and their time. I thank Austin Sarat, Melody Herr, Martha Minow, Jim Reische, Kevin Rennells, and the editorial board and reviewers at Michigan, who thought this project worthwhile and allowed it to be a book. Finally, I would like to thank my teachers who inspired this quest and to whom this book is dedicated, especially Llona Steele, Carol Brandert, J. Michael Young, Warner Morse, Beth Schultz, David Lieberman, Robert Post, Philippe Nonet, John Wachholz, and Ron and Nancy Olson.

Portions of this book have been adapted from the following essays:

"The Merciful State," in *Forgiveness, Mercy, and Clemency,* ed. Austin Sarat and Nasser Hussain (Stanford: Stanford University Press, 2007). Copyright 2007 by the Board of Trustees of the Leland Stanford Jr. University, all rights reserved. By permission of the publisher, www.sup.org.

"Between Reason and Power: Experiencing Legal Truth," *University of Cincinnati Law Review* 67 (1999): 727. Copyright *University of Cincinnati Law Review.* Used with permission.

"Herbert Morris and Punishment," *Quinnipiac Law Review* 22 (2003): 109. Used with permission.

"Miscarriages of Mercy?" in *When Law Fails: Making Sense of Miscarriages of Justice,* ed. Charles Ogletree Jr. and Austin Sarat, Charles Hamilton Houston Series on Race and Justice (New York: New York University Press, 2009). Used with permission.

"The New Revenge and the Old Retribution: Insights from Monte Cristo," in *Studies in Law, Politics, and Society,* vol. 31, ed. Austin Sarat and Patricia Ewick (Oxford: Elsevier, 2003). Used with permission of Emerald Group Publishing Limited.

"Eternal Remorse," in *Studies in Law, Politics, and Society,* vol. 36, ed. Austin Sarat, special vol., *Toward a Critique of Guilt: Perspectives from Law and the Humanities,* ed. Matthew Anderson (Oxford: Elsevier, 2005). Used with permission of Emerald Group Publishing Limited.

Introduction

But how canst thou spare the wicked if thou art wholly just and supremely just? For how does the wholly and supremely just do something that is not just? . . . We can find no reason to explain why, among men who are equally evil, thou does save some, and not others, through thy supreme goodness, and does condemn the latter, and not the former, through thy supreme justice.[1]

The problem of "justifying" mercy is old,[2] but it has resurfaced recently in light of truth and reconciliation commissions and other transitional justice methods, debates over discretion in the federal sentencing guidelines, debates over the executive's clemency powers,[3] and debates over "restorative justice" alternatives to traditional, state-imposed retributive punishment.[4] We wonder whether a reconciliation that does not involve punishment can be just; we wonder whether an executive is ever right to pardon out of compassion; we wonder whether judges should have discretion to sentence leniently in cases where defendants are remorseful, evoke compassion, have dependents, are ill, or are community heroes.

As the preceding quotation illustrates, St. Anselm articulated the problem as well as any contemporary writer: if God is all-just, then how can he be at the same time merciful? For if he is merciful, then he treats like cases unlike and is thereby unjust. Mercy, for Anselm, is the grace that lightens or eliminates deserved punishment. Justice is treating like alike, according to desert. To be both just and merciful, then, would seem to be logically impossible.

Within the retributive punishment tradition that understands punishment as some form of "just deserts," nearly all of the current philosophical literature on mercy either seeks to discredit mercy's place in public punishment or seeks to find a limited place for it "to the side" of regular forms of retribution.[5] The most common arguments of this kind are (1) that mercy has a place only as a form of equity, when needed to give retributive principles more play than is possible within the strict legal rules;[6] (2) that mercy as forgiveness has a place in "private" relationships but not usually in the context of public punishment—except perhaps in very limited circumstances in which victims have given the government the "go ahead" to forgive;[7] (3) that mercy may have a limited role of reestablishing peace in cases where justice is impossible or unworkable;[8] or (4) that mercy as compassion may be useful as an emotional state to better discern justice (determining, rather than reducing, just punishment).[9]

Efforts to advocate theories of punishment that give pride of place to mercy as forgiveness and reconciliation[10] have not yet been given a complete conceptual and philosophical grounding within mainstream philosophical traditions.[11] They are instead often advocated on policy or utilitarian grounds as the best we can do within the realm of the possible, given the practical limitations of *real* justice.[12] Mercy as an act of reducing or eliminating just punishment, in other words, must be (at most) an exceptional, not central, part of the legal system.

The main hurdle for reconciliatory theories, as it has been since Anselm, is the threefold retributivist objection that mercy is demeaning, inegalitarian, and unjustifiable. As Justice Clarence Thomas said, "A system that does not hold individuals accountable for their harmful acts treats them as less than full citizens. In such a world, people are reduced to the status of children or, even worse, treated as though they are animals without a soul."[13] This book tries to dig out the roots of retributivism to address these objections.

A different way of eliminating the mercy problem—one that I do not discuss in this book—is to reject retributivism's premises and to define punishment in utilitarian terms, by arguing that we should exact whatever penalty best reduces overall suffering from criminal activity. Desert, in such a model, is just a side constraint or no constraint at all: if the greater suffering caused by crime could be eliminated by the lesser suffering of punishing a few innocent people, well, why not do this, except to the extent that it might create more suffering in the long term by undermining public confidence in the penal system? Lenity, in utilitarian terms, would be just another value factored into an analysis of social benefits: if a lenient sentence prevents more crime or causes less suffering overall than a heavier sentence, then lenity is appropriate. However, utilitarian theories of punishment have various difficulties,[14] the keenest of which is a variant of Justice Thomas's Kantian objection: utilitarian theories treat defendants as objects to be manipulated by incentives and penalties, rather than persons capable of making moral choices.

If one takes the Kantian view that defendants ought not be treated as objects to be manipulated by sticks and carrots but must be understood as persons making autonomous moral choices and deserving punishment when they make selfish ones, employing lenity as a "carrot" seems demeaning and wrong. We should not do right selfishly, to get a benefit; doing right is itself a requirement of unselfishness. For these reasons, this book treats mercy as a problem within a framework of retributive punishment and says little about utilitarian theories. The challenge is to confront retributivism's Kantian account of moral personhood directly.

Hence, to defend mercy requires an argument about why reason pace Kant is not the ground of responsibility, ethics, and community. I will argue that reason cannot be such a ground because reason itself requires a prior stance of being with others. In doing so, I flip the accepted relationship between justice and mercy on its head. Instead of mercy being the antithesis or exception to law or, at best, a practical compromise, mercy takes over as the ground of justice, the basis on which justice itself is possible. The philosophical understanding of moral personhood switches from a kind of simplified Kant that has become legal catechism—what I call *kanticism*—which purports to ground current retributive approaches to sentencing, to an understanding derived from the later Kant of the *Critique of Judgment,* Martin Heidegger, and Emmanuel Levinas. Switching our philosophical lens shows a very different account of the relationship between justice and grace and, derivatively, between punishment and mercy.

The goal of this book is to let mercy appear in a different light and to speak to both the analytic and continental philosophical traditions from a starting place laid out by their common ancestor, Kant. Part 1, comprised of chapters 1–4, undertakes the task of seeing mercy and punishment—and, consequently, law—from a different philosophical perspective.

Chapter 1 explains the problem caused by our reliance on kanticism. The central problem is that, in our kanticism, we believe that reason comes *before* our connection to each other, as a necessary "glue" linking person to person, a condition of the possibility of ethical community. Because mercy does not follow rules of reason and cannot be universalized, we believe it to be in conflict with the possibility of community, destabilizing our reason-mediated relations with each other and denying us our place within a "kingdom of ends." Yet reason itself, thought as a system of perfectly articulated universal rules, is not within our grasp, and we are left chasing shadows, unable to cross the unfathomable distance between one person and another.

Chapter 2 moves to a new philosophical starting place and introduces Heidegger and Levinas. These thinkers switch the problem around: ethical community is the given, and reason is derivative. We do not need reason as the glue of community; we are already *with* others. Mercy, as a compassionate gift to an undeserving guilty person, no longer is destabilizing or contrary to human nature but reflects the human situation: we are at core those who receive the gift of world and others without deserving that gift. We do not *earn* community through choosing to be reasonable; it is already given. Law changes, too. It is understood no longer as universal rules of reason but as a tradition that guides us by analogy, not deduction. Law is no longer syllogism but common law—a provisionally stated "holding" that can be refined and revised as the rule hits the road in future cases. The ability to *see* the "distinction with a difference" between cases is perceptive, not deductive—a way of already being in tune with others and with one's world. As with community, the perception of likeness or difference that guides legal analysis comes *before* rules and enables us to articulate them. This "givenness" is at the heart of both mercy and law: it is a "gift" that we neither earned nor made nor deserved but that enables both law and community.

Chapter 3 sketches out how punishment theory is implicated in the problems with kanticism. Retributivism thinks of punishment as restoring us to ethical community by repairing the maxims of our actions to be fully universalized laws, applicable to ourselves as well as others. The retributive story is that, as we experience the rebound of our own imperfect rule, the rule is perfected and we are thereby restored to solidarity with others as reasonable persons. The problem we discover is that there is no human standpoint from which such a universal rule can be established. Retributivism is therefore not a possibility for us.

Chapter 4 is the heart of this book and introduces a theory of punishment and mercy from our different philosophical starting place. Wrong is no longer the irrational but the indifferent, no longer a failure to live up to our nature as rational but a failure to live up to our nature as "with others." Punishment is no longer the universalizing of a maxim but the pain of a shared remembering of one's self-alienation from the connection and responsibility for others. The pain of this experience seeks resolution in a settlement or sacrifice that will rekindle trust and ethical community for the future. This "settlement" or possible future is not "deserved" but is the return of our own being-with. In this way, punishment becomes inextricably linked with mercy as an "undeserved" leniency. Punishment culminates in an unsecured, undeserved settlement or compromise that takes an unguaranteed risk of being-with and proffers trust for a future, rather than settling accounts with the past. Punishment is the restoration of being-with, rather than the restoration of reason.

In part 2, comprising chapters 5 and 6 and the conclusion, I play out this new view of mercy in more concrete legal contexts of pardon and sentencing, using both legal and narrative examples. My methodology in these chapters matches the philosophical insights gained in part 1. For this reason, I do not try to construct *rules* of mercy that I then apply to various contexts. Instead, consistent with the idea that law is *given* by tradition and perception in a way that is temporally extended, incomplete, and based in common-law reasoning, I try to tease an account of mercy out of the concrete contexts already provided in the legal and cultural materials I study. I examine these "cases" to try to learn something about how mercy *already is at work* in our legal system. Viewed through the lens of being-with, we perceive our legal system differently; some practices that we usually consider exceptional come to seem central, and others that seemed central move to the background. Philosophical study, like the common law, becomes a matter of reading these past cases and articulating provisional "holdings" that partially illuminate a way forward, by seeing patterns and family resemblances in what is already there in our tradition. Because we are human and finite, we cannot pretend to articulate universal principles that will hold for all time. We must be content to feel our way forward by drawing on the richness of what has come before.

Chapter 5 addresses the question of when pardons might or might not be appropriate and how we can think about these ethical questions from a non-Kantian perspective. Chapter 6 addresses the question of whether there are unforgivable crimes and what mercy might mean in such cases. The conclusion builds on two novels—Alexandre Dumas' *Count of Monte Cristo* and J. M. Coetzee's *Disgrace*—that are usually read as triumphs of retributive justice. I read these novels to dramatize the fault lines of retributivism and to reflect on how punishment can be understood anew as a shared memory of wrong that calls for mercy as a nondemeaning, undeserved settlement. Even in these stories, as in the law generally, I find mercy already at work.

PART ONE

CHAPTER 1

Beyond Kanticism to Being-with

Justice is usually understood as acting according to reason, and reason is conceived as a system of logically consistent rules. This "reason" of ours is the glue of community, giving us "reason" to treat each other fairly and to order our mutual affairs according to rules rather than whim. Without reason, we fear a return to a brutal state of nature, in which life is a battle zone between needy, violent people. This chapter will show how this conception of justice as reason and of community as requiring the "glue" of reason is bound up in an incomplete and dogmatic understanding of Kantian philosophy, a kind of Kantian catechism, or "kanticism."

Given this understanding of justice, if we take mercy, in its most basic sense, as giving a person less punishment than he or she deserves or, in a deeper and broader sense, as a gift or grace—giving another a benefit that is undeserved and to which the other has no right—the disjunction between mercy and law seems obvious by definition. Mercy, or grace, is unlawful, outside the rules, beyond rights.

This ideal of justice as a system of rules is deeply embedded in our legal system. Reason is the touchstone for law. Irrational laws are unconstitutional; irrational people are not criminally responsible. Differences in treatment must be either explained as reasonable or eliminated. "Interest," "feeling," or "opinion" is not universal and therefore not a reason; selfish prudence is not a reason.

Law students imbibe these assumptions from the first day of law school. When asked a question like, "Should the Nazis be allowed to march in Skokie?" students learn not to say "I feel . . ." or "In my opinion . . ." or "Well, it just depends on your personal views" or "It depends on whether the trial judge is a Republican." Reasons, not "personal points of view" or political predictions, must be given and analyzed. Students also learn not to give post hoc empirically contingent answers to doctrinal conundrums—such as "If it turns out that the march causes more suffering to the residents of Skokie than canceling it causes the Nazis, then the trial court was wrong to allow it" or "If it turns out that canceling the march resulted in a 10 percent drop in peaceful protests across the country, then the trial court was wrong to cancel it"—because what counts as a relevant consideration and what threshold of likelihood will be deemed critical must be decided by reason in advance, before the empirical sciences can be deployed to determine whether those considerations exist or not.

Compared with other forms of discourse, law seems strange. Why can a plaintiff's lawyer not simply point out to the trial judge that to rule in his opponent's favor would create a grave risk of reversal by appellate Judge Z, who always rules in favor of accident victims—even if the lawyer can back up his prediction by meticulous empirical research? Why can a judge not give damages to injured plaintiffs explicitly on the ground that causation takes too much time and money to establish? Why can a jury not convict and incapacitate a defendant on the ground that he or she is statistically likely to commit crimes anyway, even if he or she has not yet done so? Why should a judge not judge on an ad hoc basis, without issuing inefficient, time-consuming opinions and struggling to articulate rules? Why should a judge not randomly distribute convictions, so as to increase information costs for criminals and deter crime?[1] Why should society not judge judges on how beneficial their rulings turn out to be for our collective social welfare?

As others have pointed out, law resists colonization by the social sciences[2] and retains its rationalist catechism—its "kanticism." Our continuing allegiance to reasoned justification demands that law be rule-bound, nonarbitrary, and universal and that legal decision makers make decisions based on preexisting rules about what features of the situation are legally relevant, not on their own "subjective" predictions of other judges' actions, their evaluation of the efficacy of various policies, their predilections, their self-interest, or their analysis of public opinion polls. Law, Ronald Dworkin says, is about principle, not policy.[3] Why do we limit law in this way? For no further utilitarian reason—just because that is what acting on the basis of reason requires. As a form of kanticism, the law is in many respects fundamentally nonutilitarian.

The utilitarian and social scientific approaches are not the only ones law's kanticism rejects. Law also rejects the personal and the private. Jurors are not to allow emotion to sway their decisions; public officials are not to let personal concerns or affinities interfere with their public decisions; nepotism is wrong, bribes are wrong, vigilantism is wrong, and so on. Law must be public, universal, and reasonable. Emotion, understood as mere inclination and based in a self-interest, individual perspective, or self-reference that cannot apply to all alike, is irrelevant and distracting to the obligation to do one's duty.

It is because of the kanticism of our legal system that we tend to treat mercy as the mad woman in the attic of law. Mercy does not treat like cases alike, cannot be analyzed as a right subject to an obligation, is associated with emotions and personal relationships, is historically based in hierarchy rather than equality, and is not governable by rules. Its nature appears to run counter to that of law, which we conceive to be impersonal and egalitarian and universal.

To find an approach to law that acknowledges mercy and reconciliation is to question the very grounding of law in reason. This search requires a return to Kant's text, to untangle the roots of the dichotomy between emotion and reason, the roots of reason and autonomy as the ground of both responsibility and community, the roots of the insistence on universal law as a paradigm, and the roots of the categorical nature of imperatives of reason, impervious to the pragmatic claims of imagined futures or the contingent relationship of the parties.

I. THE KANTICISM OF LAW

The kanticism of law can be located most easily in Kant's *Groundwork of the Metaphysics of Morals.*[4] The *Groundwork* sets out a series of connected propositions that are deeply embedded in our legal system. Kant's argument for making reason the foundation of ethics (and community) goes as follows:

For Kant, human will is only free of causal necessity if it is an exercise of reason, for reason follows its own principles of logic and consistency, and the claims of logic are not affected by the arbitrary power of nature's relations of cause and effect. If all men are mortal and Socrates is a man, then I must acknowledge Socrates is mortal, regardless of barometric pressure, global warming, or my uncontrollable upwelling of sympathy and admiration for Socrates. As only our ability to reason frees us from causal necessity, only reason is truly completely within our power, and only reason can be the basis on which we can be responsible: "Everything in nature works according to laws. Reasonable [*vernunftiges*] beings alone have the faculty of acting according *to the conception* of laws, that is according to principles, *i.e.,* have a *will*" (Kant, *Groundwork,* 40). Once the will is isolated from "every impulse which could arise to it from obedience to any law [of nature], there remains nothing but the universal conformity of its actions to law [as such], which alone is to serve the will as a principle, i.e. I am never to act otherwise than so that I could also will that my maxim should become a universal law" (ibid., 27). Hence, the first statement of Kant's categorical imperative can be restated as "Always act in accordance with reason." The good will, the ethical will, the free will, is at the same time the reasonable, consistent, rule-bound will.

I judge the worth of my actions by their "good will"—that is, the reasons actuating them (in Kant's language, the "maxim of the action")—not by the contingent results that follow. Results depend too much on nature's causal forces that are beyond my control. I cannot be responsible for what is not within my power; therefore, I am responsible not based on results but only for doing my rational best based on what I, using appropriate diligence, knew at the time I acted. It is right for me to save a child from being run over by a car, even if the child grows up to be Hitler. Conversely, attempted murder is a serious crime, even if no one is hurt. The rightness of the act should be determined by its reason, not its consequences. Reason is the end in itself, that which is always good.

If we accept that reason is an end in itself, then it must be so whether it is my own reason or someone else's, for reason requires me to treat like cases alike. Hence Kant derives the second statement of the categorical imperative, which can be stated as "Treat reason, whether in yourself or others, as an end in itself and not a means only." Here, then, reason becomes not only the basis of freedom and responsibility but the basis of community. I recognize the other as "like" me when the other is also capable of reason (even if nonhuman). My obligations to the other are the same as those I have toward myself, so I must treat the reason in others as I treat the reason in myself. I may no more kill (without adequate justification) than risk my life (without adequate justification). Without the mutual recognition of reason, there is no connection with the other. Reason is, in our kanticism, the "glue" that binds us together and creates community.

The logical requirement of consistency requires not only that we respect others who have reason but that we act only on universally applicable principles. We test the rightness of our thinking by determining whether it can be applied to all like cases. Reason demands that our law be universal. We cannot make unjustified exceptions for ourselves, our friends, our families. We cannot make exceptions for "just this once." If a principle seems exceptionable in some set of circumstances, we must state why it is exceptionable in categorical terms that can then be folded back into the statement of our rule. For example, if our first-cut rule is "No late papers" but it seems wrong not to accept a paper from a student who came down suddenly with a collapsed lung, then we must restate our rule to apply to all like cases: "No late papers except in cases of sudden and serious illness." The categorical and universal applicability of rules of reason requires that no case be unique.

Finally, this mutuality of reason that links us together can form a larger statelike ethical community of reasonable beings through a "kingdom of ends" in which reasonable beings come together and work out reasonable laws for themselves. These laws, based in reason, will necessarily be consistent and harmonious, forming the basis of an ethical community and an ideal state. This is the third statement of the categorical imperative: "Now since it is by laws that ends are determined as regards their universal validity, hence, if we abstract from the personal differences of rational beings, and likewise from all the content of their private ends, we shall be able to conceive all ends combined in a systematic whole (including both rational beings as ends in themselves, and also the special ends which each may propose to himself), that is to say, we can conceive a kingdom of ends, which on the preceding principles is possible" (Kant, *Groundwork,* 62).

Our commitment to reason, moreover, lends us a spark of the divine. We rise above the squalor of dependence, passivity, and heteronomy to govern ourselves: "And it is just in this that the paradox lies; that the mere dignity of a man as a rational creature, without any other end or advantage to be attained thereby, in other words, respect for a mere idea, should yet serve as an inflexible precept of the will, and that it is precisely in this independence of the maxim on all such springs of action that its sublimity consists; and it is this that makes every reasonable subject worthy to be a legislative member in the kingdom of ends: for otherwise he would have to be conceived only as subject to the physical law of his wants" (Kant, *Groundwork,* 68). We substitute our own law of reason, like the divine will (ibid., 41), for the natural "physical law of our wants." We overcome our own creatureliness and become, at least in concept, demigods.

This kanticism is deeply embedded in the principles and practices of our law. Judges proceed from case to case by stating universal principles that explain their result as consistent with past precedent.[5] Rules of decision must be stated with some level of generality: a decision cannot apply to just one case or for just one time. Herbert Wechsler's concept of "neutral principles" of constitutional law[6] tried to capture this idea, but even apart from Wechsler, the standard judicial practice requires, above all, a demonstration of the consistency of the decision at bar with prior cases or else a reasoned explanation of why the precedent was wrong and the explication of a new basis for decisions into the future. Legal principles must transcend the case in place and in time, reaching back into the past and vaulting into the future with a single line of logic.

Unlike our empirical knowledge of the world, reason is not bounded by the forms of intuition—by space or time. In reason, we reach for an Archimedean standpoint of certainty, logic, and what is always true, everywhere and whenever. Hence, the retroactivity of judicial decisions imagines that the "reasons" for the rule were there all along to be discovered. The decision is explained by its reasons, and we expect the loser either to acknowledge the rightness of the reasoning or to reasonably point out its flaws on appeal. In a Kant-like kingdom of ends, if we reach the most reasonable answer, we should all finally be brought into agreement, regardless of our personal losses or suffering.

Our substantive law also reflects these Kantian commitments. In criminal law, we accord irresponsibility with insanity—with the absence of the ability to reason. Regardless of emotional turmoil or temptation, we usually assume that if one can reason, one is responsible under the law: logic is impervious to natural causes, and the reasonable will is ipso facto the free will. The traditional M'Naghten rule defining insanity reflects this: if you know the nature and quality of your act and you know right from wrong, then you are not insane, regardless of your emotional or volitional state.[7] In other words, if you can form the major and minor premise of a syllogism (e.g., "Murder is wrong" and "This is murder"), then the conclusion ("Therefore, this is wrong") necessarily follows. We may mitigate (e.g., in the case of voluntary manslaughter) or excuse (e.g., in the case of duress) out of a recognition of human weakness, but these doctrines are the exceptions in the law and are traditionally carefully barricaded by restrictive categories (imminent threats to life or certain kinds of wrongful provocation).

In criminal law, we have come to care more about mens rea than result, with desert primarily defined in terms of culpability rather than the extent of harm caused.[8] One who does great harm innocently, under traditional doctrines of criminal law (leaving to one side the highly debated public welfare crimes) is not criminally responsible. Inchoate crimes (attempt, conspiracy, solicitation) are, under Model Penal Code principles at least, punished as severely as completed crimes, despite the fact that no harm need occur. As Meir Dan-Cohen puts it, "The core of criminal law doctrine, centered around the concept of mens rea and the variety of criminal excuses, probably comes closer than any other set of social practices to an instantiation of the Kantian conception of the responsible human subject as the noumenal self, characterized exclusively by a rational free will unencumbered by character, temperament, and circumstance."[9]

In constitutional law, due process and equal protection doctrine require that laws have a "rational basis," apply equally across like cases, and accord autonomy and respect to citizens. Nonutilitarian rights claims are framed by both judges and litigants around Kantian categories of autonomy, equality, respect, and rational treatment.

In tort law, negligence is defined as not avoiding what a "reasonable person" would avoid and is determined by what could be known at the time of the action, not what we discover later. There is no liability in negligence for dangers one had no reason to know about at the time one acted, regardless of how much harm results. Strict liability remains a source of academic debate and dissension insofar as it challenges and resists the kanticism paradigm.

Our contract paradigm accords binding force to agreements reached by parties who are presumed to be equal, rational, and autonomous. Exceptions to this paradigm are still exceptional, and the presumption of equal, free, and reasonable parties remains, though it may be overcome in particular cases.

Finally, in the very rituals of law—the solemn marble courtrooms; the fashionless, timeless black robes; the elevated bench; the pediment carvings of gods and goddesses; the calm and orderly procedure—we reflect our sense that law is to ennoble us, to elevate us to the realm of reason out of the squalor of the street, apart from nature's rule of "physical wants" and apart from time itself. Law promises us better, nobler, eternal, and higher selves.

In short, then, Kant's principles serve as the "glue" of an ideal ethical community and the foundational assumptions of law and its practice. If, indeed, reason and its universal law are the "glue" that create our community and our legal system, mercy threatens it, for it would seem to undermine the very bases of our connection to each other as "like": reason, responsibility, and consistent and equal treatment. More upsetting, perhaps, mercy seems to undermine our aspirations to achieve something nobler than mere scrabbling after our own interests. In fact, it seems to pander to our weakness, absolving us of responsibility and therefore dignity, "sublimity," and near divinity. Mercy seems a cop-out, demeaning us and demoralizing us instead of calling us to struggle ever harder for *real* justice. Our kanticism is a powerful dream of humanity as only a little lower than the angels, and that lends law both nobility and authority. Mercy brings us down.

II. KANT'S CRITIQUE OF JUDGMENT

The *Groundwork*, so influential in law, does not, however, complete Kant's own thought. It is part of a larger corpus. When we look at the *Groundwork* in context, we see that it may not be the central Kantian text for judgment or law after all.[10]

Kant devoted his life to exploring the special character and limits of human knowledge. The *Critique of Pure Reason* sets strict limits on "pure" reason. Carefully delineating those areas of knowledge where we can have certainty, it exposes the contingent and empirical and merely phenomenal nature of most of our knowledge of the world. Scientific investigation is always only of effects, not causes—its knowledge affected by its own methods of investigation and ways of perceiving. We cannot, therefore, claim to be able to know nature with a priori certainty, nor can we know ourselves, as objects of nature. Our empirical knowledge is always contingent, in progress, and partial.

By confining our knowledge of nature within appropriate boundaries, Kant says, he "den[ies] *knowledge,* in order to make room for *faith.* . . . The preconception that it is possible to make headway in metaphysics without a previous criticism of pure reason, is the source of all that unbelief, always very dogmatic, which wars against morality."[11] Kant here expresses concern that the pretensions of earlier philosophers to, for example, prove the existence of God through reason alone had led to the discredit of both faith and philosophy, leaving ethics as well as religion in need of ground and at risk of falling to the skepticism of pure empiricism. Kant insists that our always-incomplete *knowledge* of nature makes possible the *faith* that human nature is something other than the effect of natural causes: human action, language, and culture are not just a pattern of brain chemicals or survival adaptations; they only *appear* to be, from the scientific standpoint. The physiological and psychological picture of humanity may be only phenomenon, not truth.

Freed from the reductionism of science, Kant could explore in his second critique, the *Critique of Practical Reason,* the rational preconditions of human action that ground the ethical demands of reason—that are true for all reasonable beings, not just humans—including the notion of free will necessary for responsibility. In the *Groundwork,* a kind of prologue to the *Critique of Practical Reason,* Kant characterizes human life as caught between the law of reason and the law of nature. We have our feet in two worlds, the rational and the natural. We are called by reason to ethical duties, duties conceived in an empirical vacuum, which, for us, are arduous and unpleasant given the friction of our natural impulses and desires. Hence, morality is felt as "duty." Our freedom as moral actors comes only in the often difficult and unpleasant service to reason. Yet, to give in to our natural selves, our emotions and desires, makes us little more than objects, pushed by forces beyond our control into perpetual war with each other and with ourselves—one person's power pitted against another's, one moment's passion defeating the passion of another moment.

In his third critique, the *Critique of Judgment,* Kant tries to work through the rift between reason and nature. Here, Kant is concerned precisely with *human* knowledge of the application of rational principles to *this* world, or, as he called it, "judgment." Judgment is a uniquely human function, not applicable to reasonable creatures generally. Only humans need to bring universal principles to bear on experience, because only humans have both universal principles and experience. So this work tries to span the gap between reason and nature, explain the connection between reason and the senses. If we are concerned not about the rational basis of law in general but about human law in particular, we should be looking to Kant's third critique, not the *Groundwork.*

The three critiques together cover the traditional topics of philosophy: the ground of the True, the Good, and the Beautiful. Yet what does a work on the nature of aesthetic judgment have to do with law? Hannah Arendt, for one, seized on this work as the core of Kant's political philosophy and believed that it held the seeds of the completion of her own work, explaining why political truth is found between reason and nature and involves uncertainty and emotion.[12]

Judgment, according to Kant, is the faculty of "thinking the particular as contained under the Universal."[13] He differentiates judgment from the capacity or faculty of understanding (*Verstand*)—that is, the ability to categorize and analyze experience by formulating concepts ("chair," "table," "mammal," etc.). He also differentiates judgment from the capacity or faculty of reason (*Vernunft*)—that is, the ability to deduce the logical and necessary preconditions of human action, meaning, and experience.[14] Finally, he differentiates judgment from perception—the senses that provide the raw data of experience. Judgment unites perception with the understanding, making it possible to connect sensation to rules or concepts formulated by the understanding. In other words, judgment *applies* the categories and concepts of understanding to the data of experience. Judgment, however, as Kant argues in his *Critique of Pure Reason,* cannot itself be brought under a rule (no methodology for judging can be specified), because "this in turn, for the very reason that it is a rule, again demands guidance from judgment" (177). For this reason, Kant continues, judgment "is a peculiar talent which can be practiced only, and cannot be taught . . . A physician, a judge, or a ruler may have at command many excellent pathological, legal, or political rules, even to the degree that he may become a profound teacher of them, and yet, none the less, may easily stumble in their application. For although admirable in understanding, he may be wanting in natural power of judgment" (177–78).

Judgment cannot be rule-based, because it is tied to perception. Judgment must recognize the patterns in perception that connect it with a general rule. As in traditional law school examinations, one must "spot the issue." "Spotting an issue" requires isolating bits of experience, sifting the relevant from the irrelevant, and judging whether the case, properly refined, is sufficiently "like" other paradigm cases to be classed under the same rule. This judgment of relevance and likeness, analogy and disanalogy, relies more on perception than proposition and cannot be governed by rules.[15]

Hence, even when a principle is easily specified by the understanding, its application may be difficult. (Kant calls this employment of judgment "determinant judgment," where the rule is specified in advance and judgment is to "pick out" an example that fits the rule [Kant, *Judgment*, 17].) Such cases present themselves to lawyers all the time, and law professors refine the art in their final exams with such questions as "Are plastic pink flamingos in one's yard 'capital improvements' within the meaning of the rule?" or "Does jokingly calling out 'Fire!' in a crowded theater amount to felony murder if a member of the crowd is trampled?" Even though Kant believes that the moral law is given by reason, its applications are not. The principles of ethics, like a priori knowledge generally, cannot give us much help in the nitty-gritty of application. Philosophy cannot make us good or supplant the good instincts and judgment of the unphilosophical community member.[16]

The conditions of good judgment are even trickier to define in the case of "reflective judgments," or "pattern-finding" judgments—that is, cases in which "only the particular be given for which the universal has to be found" (Kant, *Judgment*, 17). Because reflective judgment is pattern-finding, not application-finding, it must respect the limits of empirical knowledge Kant sets out in the *Critique of Pure Reason* for discovery of other natural laws. Our attempt to articulate the patterns we see are then only provisional, like the hypotheses of science. We can only *assume* that the world has patterns and makes sense; from our human point of view, we can never be sure.

Judgment also relies on the imagination, a faculty, related to perception, that can "arrest" the flow of experiential input so that judgment can do its job of comparing and contrasting and fitting the particular to the universal. Imagination holds experience before us and shows objects that are absent, "gathering together the manifold of intuition" (Kant, *Judgment,* 64). The imagination stops us in front of an experienced truth, so that we have time and attention to take it in. Imagination gives us space to think, makes us "passive" in order to give us a chance to perceive order and sense in our experience. This is the arresting quality of art, which enrapts us, focuses our attention, draws out from the manifold the important and significant and holds it up for our contemplation. Imagination is also responsible for seeing the analogies that "enlarge[] the concept itself in an unbounded fashion" and "bring[] the faculty of intellectual Ideas (the Reason) into movement"; that is, "by a representation more thought . . . is occasioned than can [in the concept] be grasped or made clear" (Kant, *Judgment,* 199). Metaphors and analogies "arouse more thought than can be expressed in a concept determined by words" and "enliven the mind by opening out to it the prospect into an illimitable field of kindred representations" (199–200).

Our desire for order, pattern, form, and simplicity, for a world that makes sense as though it were designed by an intellect like our own, is the aesthetic core of judgment. Kant notes that when we discover such unities, we experience spontaneous pleasure and satisfaction, common to all human beings (*Judgment,* 26–29). The solving of a difficult problem, the sensation of the proverbial "lightbulb going on" in our heads, good triumphing over evil, and, more purely and primitively, for Kant, the simple pleasure in "form," pattern, and natural beauty are experiences that confirm our faith in a reasonable world and make us feel at home in it, as reasonable beings who, by our own natural inclinations, try to make things make sense. Hence, the basis for aesthetic judgment in any field is the thought-based and humanly universal sensation of pleasure in, as Kant calls it, purposiveness, or *Zweckmässigkeit,* which arises when our perceptions of the world seem to fit with the tidy structure of our own reason making. *Zweck* is also *zu-Weg*—"on a way," a path to, a direction or pointing toward that leads from one thing to another, connecting the unconnected and bringing things in the world together for us, "gathering the manifold."

Kant finds this sensation in its purest form in the appreciation of the beautiful, as it is the form of judgment that is least entangled with other faculties of understanding and reason and that needs no conceptual element (*Judgment,* 238–39). According to Kant, pleasure arises in the contemplation of the beautiful merely from the form of the object being compared in imagination to the form of our understanding. Beautiful, in other words, is a world that makes sense.

Imagination brings to light analogies, stories, metaphors, and maxims that allow us humans, along with others who share our love of sense making, to experience the satisfaction in the accord of imagination and understanding, the world and the mind, that Kant calls beauty. Reason alone cannot do this; it can speak only in universals. It can provide only the idea of truth but no intuition of it, no "feel" for how it fits into the world. For creatures who understand through the senses as well as through reason, truth *appears* only in art.

It is clear from Kant's introduction to the *Critique of Judgment* that we are to take the account of beauty as comprising the aesthetic taste necessary for good judgment in any field where the universal must be linked to particulars, including science and morality. Just as science "prefers" simpler explanations to the more complex, law, in its search for analogies and disanalogies, has an aesthetic sense guiding it "on a way," too—toward integrity, fairness, stability, or fit, for example. Justice is an aesthetic. Judgment is an art.

Taste for any of these qualities cannot be reduced to concepts or rules. "Integrity" is not reducible to logical consistency, for example. (Dworkin has to make reference to a chain novel to explain it, after all.)[17] A sense that a punishment "fit" the crime requires narrative or metaphoric fitness, not the literal "eye for an eye" of exact correspondence. An attempt to "fit" cases together in a line of precedent also depends on analogical judgments, not logical ones. To return to our "No late papers" rule and its exception for "sudden and serious illnesses," how did we know that our rule required such an exception? Our judgment of "fit"—or, in this case, lack of fit—came *before* we formulated the exception.

Hence, the first problem with our kanticism is that we have mistaken the *Groundwork*'s "universal laws" of reason as clear, easy principles we can arrive at through reasoned deliberation alone. From the perspective of the *Critique of Judgment,* the application and adumbration of our categorical imperative to "be reasonable" requires good judgment, judgment that is aesthetic, that is not rule-bound but provisional, and that is tied up with our emotional and sensual experience of the world. Even Kant's moral emotion of *Achtung*—which is usually translated as "respect" but which comes closer to "awe"—comes to take on an aesthetic tone: we love the law because we are the kind of beings who must be reasonable, who must try to make sense of the world. Justice is an aesthetic urge, a need, a desire for a world that fits us.

If sense and reason are no longer divided but united, then law is not necessarily timeless rule following or an absence of all emotion but something much more sensory and temporal—"on a way." Already we begin to see that the opposition between law (the absolute, reasoned rule) and mercy (the particular, emotional exception) is in many ways un-Kantian after all. If our kanticism is not Kantian, then perhaps we have gotten it wrong.

III. THE LIMITS OF OUR KANTICISM

We see now that judgment is not as simple as the syllogistic application of rules to facts, even according to Kant. Our ability to do law is governed not by reason (pure and timeless and universal) but by judgment (analogical, pattern-finding, tied to perception). After a more complete understanding of Kant's work on judgment, our assumption that reason is the "glue" of law and community comes to seem much more just that—an assumption.

Knowing Another (and Ourselves) as Reasonable

By the logic of the *Groundwork,* we are logically committed to acknowledge ethical duties to ourselves and others after we see (1) that we ourselves reason and (2) that others reason. However, both of these propositions are empirical, not given a priori. The best we can say about the first is that we cannot get on with our lives at all unless we assume it to be true. If I really believed that my argument here were a determined product of my upbringing and brain chemicals, why would I bother making it? How could it mean anything? In other words, we cannot think without assuming we can think. But Kant points out in the *Critique of Pure Reason* that we cannot know ourselves empirically through a Cartesian "inward investigation" any more than we can know anything else in our empirical world. Even if our "reason" is for us a grounding and necessary assumption we must make to get on, there is no reason to think that anyone else out there is reasonable. I cannot know with certainty how your mind works (or even whether you have a mind). Reason, whether our own or another's, is just a very convenient empirical assumption. In the end, then, our kanticism is grounded on an article of faith: that we reason. Reason as the glue of ethics, law, and community, then, comes unstuck. Why should we believe in it?

The Universal Law

Much of our kanticism also relies on the idea of a universal law of reason, applicable across time and space to all like cases. The method of law is often characterized as an effort to articulate such a rule, or to legislate the perfect self-justifying and perfectly drafted statute that would need no further gloss but could be applied by its plain language to any relevant case and achieve a just result. Such a statute would be a true Kantian universal law of reason, with all the nuances of its application spelled out ahead of time (i.e., outside of time), including all the necessary and only the sufficient considerations.

Who could draft such a statute, applicable across time and space, perfectly tailored to any conceivable fact pattern, every consideration mapped out with perfect forethought? Well, of course, only God could; that is, it could only be done by a philosopher's god—perfectly reasonable, perfectly articulate, perfectly logical, and knowing everything timelessly, always in advance. We humans, however, are not timeless, all-knowing, and we do not have a language that can ride on the back of every particular. Our language employs clumsy, general, ambiguous terms that clump and smash differences into heaps of such logical detritus that logicians have wished to scrap it entirely. Moreover, our language is, like the humans that think in it, evolving all the time, changing its denotations and connotations, reinventing itself, improvising, compromising. Just take a look in the *Oxford English Dictionary.*

How could I possibly act so as to make the maxim of my action a universal law of reason? How could I possibly be such a god? The answer, as Kant knows very well, is that I cannot. I have only a painful duty to try to reach these heights of logical consistency, and I have an aesthetic need to make sense of a manifold, crazy, kaleidoscopic world.

From this perspective, human life is doomed and tragic: justice is an illusion, a mirage that disappears every time we think we are getting close.[18] If this is so, it is not mercy that must be an exceptional, unusual, impossible thing, a thing that would undermine community and responsibility—it is law.

This unsettling thought leads us to another aspect of Kant's *Critique of Judgment.* Besides beauty, which is the sensation of pleasure in the fit between our minds and our world, there is the sublime. The sublime is the antithesis of beauty: it is the feeling of disjunction between ourselves and the world, the feeling of not being at home in the world, a feeling that the world is beyond our power to comprehend (*Judgment,* 101–32). In the experience of beauty, we learn to love disinterestedly,[19] whereas in the experience of the sublime, we learn to esteem the good even when it is painful. We call sublime the soldier who faces death "for nothing" but out of duty; we call sublime the awe that the rugged, uninhabitable mountains inspire. The alien nature of the world, which thwarts us and dwarfs us and could cause us suffering, also inspires awe (*Achtung*), that same emotion of reason that motivates us to do our duty. Kant explains this sense of awe as an intimation that because we are different from the world, not in harmony with it, we have a different destination. Our reason, which is stymied by the immense, chaotic, and incomprehensible, is foregrounded and highlighted by its very contrast with what is chaotic and inhospitable in our experience of the world. We cherish it more dearly when we sense its difference from its surroundings and its fragile inexorability.

At the same time, the sublime, in its immensity and incomprehensibility, gives us intimations of infinity, an idea that we intuit through reason, but one for which our concepts, imagination, and understanding are inadequate. We can have the bare idea of infinity, but we do not have it within our grasp. The fact that we can have this idea puts us, in this one respect, in a privileged place. We can think thoughts that are greater than the highest mountains, deeper than the deepest seas, more lasting than granite, more powerful than hurricanes. We can have an idea of the physically impossible, the morally adamant. The immensity of nature cannot dwarf the mind, and in that thought, Kant argues, we have awe for our own humanity and come, ourselves, close to sublimity.

In the *Critique of Judgment,* the awe that motivates us to do our duty comes to be an aspect of the sublime, experienced when we find we do not fit into the world, when duty is hard, when tragedy lays waste to our expectations, when the world fails to make sense. Justice, then, becomes a shadow toward which we strive and of which we are in awe, but it does not fit neatly into our world. It is the exceptional, the sublime, and it evades our grasp, though we respect it and reach for it nonetheless. The very gulf between the world and our moral ideas highlights the nobility of those moral ideas. This nobility appears even, or perhaps especially, in our always-tragic failure to meet those demands.

IV. STARTING IN ANOTHER PLACE

Digging into our kanticism suggests that reason is not the solid, commonplace ground we thought it was but a shadow and a promise, or a fleeting hope. Is there another way of conceiving of humans and of human solidarity that does not depend on reason, now remote and nearly outside our reach; another place to start to find the responsibility and community necessary for law? This question is a critical one, for nihilism looms behind it. Without the "glue" of reason, the distance between "individuals" becomes unbreachable, and a "we" cannot find any purchase, any place of mutual understanding or "objectivity." Justice becomes just one person's "opinion" or "personal political choice." If we cannot find a different account, then we are doomed to chase shadows of justice, to vil-lify our world as ever unjust: Nothing that is can be good enough. Nothing that is can be worthy. Nothing is.

This is why Nietzsche both feared and proclaimed the death of God and why he struggled so hard to find a new ground for human meaning, law, ethics, and community. Without it, he believed, we were doomed to care less and less for the "merely" finite, the "merely" human. With no heavenly guarantee of meaning on earth, with justice and reason impossible to achieve, what, then, is or was the point of anything? There is no law, no justice, no beauty, no truth, no Zweckmässigkeit, no way leading anywhere.

Nietzsche hoped to reestablish our concern for our imperfect world, through a powerful remaking of it, a positing of new values in place of the old. But this "merely positing" of law makes law a matter of whim. How can we re-spect it? How could it have moral authority?[20] (How could moral authority it-self have moral authority if we just make it up?) If law is the commands of those with the power to coerce obedience, as the gunman writ large, how can it ob-ligate us or have the character of an "ought"?

Nietzsche's attempt to find this new ground in sheer human will is the place we occupy today, in so many ways. It is the death of our ideal of law as reason,[21] of course, and the rise of law as merely "posited," law as policy, law as power, law as the gunman writ large. From this perspective, the difference between law and mercy vanishes: both are exercises of sheer power, equally contingent and un-bound by obligation or reason. Law is the (present) will of the people, mercy the whim of the judge. We can talk about both in the language of mutual ad-vantage or efficiency: the line between reason and inclination is erased. Au-thority and obligation are whatever we (with the power to say) say they are. What we say is only what we say now. What those in power say later makes now as if it never has been. What is good is what we prefer now, and now, and now. "Law" shifts and shimmies with might and market.[22] Nothing binds us. Noth-ing is timeless or universal or obligatory. Nothing is lawful (in the old sense) at all. Mercy and law lose their peculiar meaning for us completely, swept away and consumed in a tide of ever-changing preferences, a voracious all-consum-ing willing.

So our kanticism is precarious at best, and the "citadel" of law as reason is seriously undermined, though it still resists, to some extent, the siege of law as public opinion poll, law as efficient preference satisfaction, or law as incentive to reach a state of efficient preference satisfaction. Criminal law, for example, still holds us to very old ideas of responsibility, obligation, and mens rea that transcend time and policy, but even the ideals of criminal law are often belied by the realities.[23] We need to see what is deeper than reason and necessary for it to be, and I wish to suggest that this deeper ground is closely tied to the old debate between mercy and law. What if the ground of law is not our willing or our making or our deserving but a gift or mercy that is already there for us to find? Would that give us back a true sense of the obligatory in law—the essential ingredient that makes law not just a (very large) gunman's order? The old debate between law and mercy was decided in favor of law.[24] What would happen if mercy won instead? The implications may reach farther than the outcome of sentencing decisions.

CHAPTER 2

Before Reason: Being-in-the-World-with-Others

What if reason is not the ground of community or the essence of being human? This chapter outlines a different starting place. Instead of assuming we attain community and responsibility only through our efforts to overcome inclination and pursue reason, as the enlightenment philosophers did,[1] what if we assume that the world and others are "given" to us already? What if reason is not necessary as the "glue" of community; what if our relation with others comes even before reason? If community and responsibility are not something we "deserve" only when and insofar as we make the effort of will to be reasonable, if community and responsibility are given even before reason, then perhaps law itself is an undeserved gift, a kind of mercy.

Several modern thinkers converge on such a Copernican revolution in our understanding of the nature of being human, moving away from a Kantian self constituted by reason and self-will.[2] I will draw primarily on Heidegger here, because he makes clear the full implications of a shift away from reason to a "given" and provides a phenomenology of this new human self as *being-in-the-world-with-others*. I will also explore a similar turn in Levinas.

Heidegger and Levinas both turn the traditional antagonism between law and mercy on its head. For both, the relationship with others is a given, an "always-already," not something that is mandated or mediated by the logic of treating like reasonable beings alike. This simple change holds extremely significant consequences for the problem of mercy in sentencing. If we do not need reason as glue, then granting (unreasonable and undeserved) mercy may not destroy the ground of community after all but may instead reflect and recognize the lopsided risk and vulnerability that is at the heart of community. Mercy can be understood as this undeserved gift of mutual vulnerability— *com-passion* (feeling-with, being receptive or passive-with, suffering-with). We are already at each others' mercy: we rely on the gift of others' opening to us— a gift that we do not deserve, because it is already there before any choice or action on our part is possible. We have a responsibility for others that we did not choose, a susceptibility to others that we did not create. We are always already called to respond, always already "guilty," always already receiving the gift of others.

As this chapter hopes to sketch it, mercy—even as we usually understand it, as an undeserved gift to the guilty from another to whom he is responsible—is the basis of both our union with each other and our understanding of the world, and justice and law come only on the basis and out of this primal mercy. For this always already-given mercy, we could use a word that emphasizes its "givenness" and call it "grace." Mercy at the more prosaic level of punishment and sentencing, then, need not be understood as the demeaning treatment of another as less than a fully responsible person that denies full membership in humanity. It can instead be understood as an instance of the recognition and reunion of the basic grace of mutual interrelationship from which we start and a humble tender of the gift of future possibility of being-with. In short, merciful sentencing is no longer contrary to human nature but in accord with it.

I. HEIDEGGER: FROM REASON TO BEING-IN-THE-WORLD

Heidegger suggests that to be human is not primarily to reason but, as he puts it, to be in the world and with others. We are, in his terminology, *Dasein* (being there) or the ones who are open to Being.[3] While enlightenment philosophers from Descartes through Kant were preoccupied by how the mind could be sure of its knowledge of the world, Heidegger steps behind that question to ask what sort of a being could ask such a question. It could only be asked, answers Heidegger, by a being who experiences anything at all. To think is already to be concerned and to encounter and therefore to be already engaged with a world. We are already outside ourselves, says Heidegger, so the very question of how the "subject" can know an "object" contains a misdescription of the way we are.

> Being-in is not a "property" which Dasein sometimes has and sometimes does not have, and *without* which it could *be* just as well as it could with it. It is not the case that man "is" and then has, by way of an extra, a relationship-of-Being

towards the "world"—a world with which he provides himself occasionally . . . Taking up relationships toward the world is possible only *because* Dasein, as Being-in-the-world, is as it is.[4]

Not only does the enlightenment tradition misdescribe the basic nature of being human, but the question of how a "subject" can know an "object" also assumes the possibility of a perspective from *outside* the "subject" and its "object," from which to gauge whether and when knowledge is possible. Who says that the subject cannot know the object? Who has this outside perspective? As Heidegger puts it, "What higher court is to decide *whether* and *in what sense* there is to be any problem of knowledge other than that of the phenomenon of knowing as such and the kind of Being which belongs to the knower?"[5] Only a higher intelligence that can get out of the inside of the subject to know the difference between the subject and object can tell if there is a problem with knowledge: the positing of an "inside" and an "outside" presupposes an Archimedean standpoint of a being that is not already inside, that is, of a philosopher's god.

Heidegger is taking on again the Kantian task of thinking through *human* knowledge as such: "The question of whether there is a world at all and whether its Being can be proved, makes no sense if it is raised by *Dasein* as Being-in-the-World; and who else would raise it?"[6] "Knowing" must be understood as the knowing of *Dasein.* The world, as well as our connection with it, is a *given,* not a problem. There is no universal, timeless, purely rational standpoint, except as an abstraction that is already grounded in our concrete experience with the world.

Our knowledge is temporal, based on what lets itself be known—what of its own appears to us. We no longer have to choose between a universe whose truth is "guaranteed" by a philosopher's god who created it and therefore knows objects "as they truly are" (Descartes) and a universe that we "merely posit" and create for ourselves through our own will (Nietzsche). Instead, thought and world are both finite, appearing in time, given to us. Knowing and truth concern what appears to us, not what is "in itself" apart from us.

Thinking from a finite human standpoint means that things have sense for us not when they are disconnected "substances" with "properties," not when they are "ideas" in the mind of God, but when they are in a world in relation to other things. Thinking is our already being in a world—that is, concerned with things around us, enmeshed in a web of relationships among things that show up for us as we engage with them and work with them, from past experience to future possibility. Just as the legal term *strict scrutiny* takes on sense for us not after merely looking up a definition of it in *Black's Law Dictionary* but in seeing how it plays out in myriads of court decisions, we "get" our world not through theoretical knowledge but in practice. The preeminence of practical knowledge is as true for our understanding of people as it is for our understanding of things.

This has several aspects and consequences. First, our fundamental knowledge of each other is practical, personal, and imbedded in context: it is a "knowing how" to be with others, not the abstracted knowledge of others as objects-of-science that hides the thing-in-itself. I know how to cajole, joke, tease, infuriate, admire, frighten, and ignore others before I know anything of psychology or psychiatry—indeed, even before I can talk. But the point is not just developmental but philosophical. These abstracted sciences of human behavior are only possible on the basis of this prior knowledge of "how" to be with. Only on the basis of our practical knowledge can we discern and abstract and delimit the relevant categories of scientific investigation. We can pick out features from the messy "background" noise and define, for example, "childhood" or "fantasy" as relevant and sufficiently discrete categories of investigation only because we already know so much about human beings in context and in practice.[7]

Second, action and passion are not dualities but interdependent. We are able to act only because we are also "passively" open, receptive, impassioned, and aware. Heidegger's term for this is *Befindlichkeit* (literally, "where we find ourselves"), often translated as "state of mind," "mood," or "attunement." We are as we are because we already are in a world and affected by and attentive to that world and each other. Emotion is not an outside force pushing us around, as Kant conceives "inclination," but an experience that opens us to new possibilities of understanding.[8]

> We do not "have" a body; rather, we "are" bodily . . . Every bodily state involves some way in which the things around us and the people with us lay a claim on us or do not do so. When our stomachs are "out of sorts" they can cast a pall over all things. What would otherwise seem indifferent to us suddenly becomes irritating and disturbing; what we usually take in stride now impedes us . . . Here it is essential to observe that feeling is not something that runs its course in our "inner lives." It is rather that basic mode of our Dasein by force of which and in accordance with which we are always already lifted beyond ourselves into being as a whole . . . Mood is precisely the basic way in which we are *outside* ourselves. But that is the way we are essentially and constantly.[9]

Third, we are finite. Our knowledge is always based on a heritage we did not create and is cast forward on a future we cannot completely control or anticipate. The if/then structure of logic itself relies on our *already* understanding the "context of involvements" within which the premise can be as it is posited to be. Heidegger helps us understand that to see "something *as something*" is to draw on a past (the *as something*) that is always already there.[10]

Being in the World of Judgment and Legal Reasoning

For law, the key example of the temporality of understanding is common-law reasoning, which tries to figure out how to treat the "case of first impression" by analogical reference to prior categories, holdings, and facts and, in deciding the new case, alters the reach and nuance of the old "rules" by adding to the analogical portfolio for the future.[11] Not only does the past inform the present case, but the decision in the present case changes the past.[12]

For example, take a case of theft from a hotel room. The traditional rule was that hotel owners in these cases were usually held responsible, even if they did nothing careless. Let us assume that this is the "holding" from which we begin to think about a set of new cases, say, thefts from a steamship's sleeping cabin, a sleeping compartment on a train, and rented apartments. Should these cases be treated the same way or differently? How do we decide?

The common-law judge does not (indeed, must not) just "apply" the universal rule of "strict liability for innkeepers." Instead, the judge asks what is relevantly the same or different about the next cases: at the very least, the judge has to ask, Is this really an "innkeeper-like" situation? Maybe we should not be looking at innkeeper cases at all but instead should look at the history of liability for guests staying in private homes? Already, we have made a judgment of "similarity" and picked out a set of past experiences as sufficiently like the ones at hand to shed some light on our decision.

The judge might consider that the history of innkeeping is, to some extent, unique: English innkeepers in earlier times were given special rights to retain guests' goods for payment in exchange for assuming responsibility for their guests' protection from others. We also know that in the uncertainties of early travel, guests were at the mercy of these innkeepers and could not protect themselves. Are these factors still relevant in the cases we must now decide? Does it matter that ships move and inns do not, that shipowners do or do not have the same power to retain the guest's possessions? Does it matter that train sleeping cars are owned by subcontractors who do not control the movement of the train and have to allow noncustomers to walk through their cars? Does it matter that landlords rent for months instead of days, that landlords provide furnishings or do not, that the rooms are shared or not shared, that they lock or do not, that they are expensive or cheap, that the landlord remains on the premises or does not, that the doors are painted red or are not? Which of the infinite number of comparisons or contrasts we *could* make between these cases are we to focus on? What are the *relevant* considerations?

Deciding which of these factors are "relevant" and matter and which are "not relevant" and do not matter is a complex judgment of pattern finding, more perception than deduction. If one decides, for example, that the shipowner is still strictly liable for passenger losses even when not given the innkeeper's rights of distraint, then, in doing so, one has also changed the way in which the earlier innkeeper case may be understood: the right of distraint becomes less important in understanding the sense of the old innkeeper cases than such factors as the powerlessness of the guest to protect himself or the capacity of the innkeeper to take safety measures. Likewise, if we find that the right of distraint makes the innkeeper cases sufficiently different so as to be no guide for us, we highlight the importance of that factor in our reading of the old holding. Thus, the common law reaches back into the tradition for guidance and, in trying to find a pattern to fit the new case, thereby changes how we articulate the "holding" of the old case as well as the one we are currently deciding. The tradition both guides and morphs at the same time. The newly articulated holding, of course, is itself subject to a new understanding when we confront yet another case and reflect on whether a previously unexamined element of the old case is "relevant" or not in the new situation.

Over a series of cases, we find that we come to understand better which features of the case are "relevant" and which are not, and we sometimes formulate a rule on this basis. But even when we formulate a rule, like the ones in legal treatises or common-law compilations, we must still determine whether the rule "applies" to the next case. Is this an "innkeeper liability" case or not? And if it is not, why not? That judgment of "why or why not" changes the contours and connotation and limits of the rule (maybe only a tiny bit or maybe a great deal). So, even in simply deciding which rule fits the case, we have changed the rule. The rules help us index, shuffle, and find our way through the many possible patterns, but they do not stay static.

It is no mystery that common-law case-by-case reasoning works this way when we reflect that language itself also works this way, giving voice to the new by reference to the old and simultaneously changing the connotation of the "old" words, as is the case with the terms *cell phone, facsimile, Internet, Web site, surfing, skyping, texting,* and so on. Words both "hold" relationships and activities and experiences from our personal and cultural past and, at the same time, allow us to encounter and understand what is new. As Heidegger puts it, "Language is the house of Being." If natural language were unambiguous and constructed of necessary and sufficient definitions—that is, if it fit the model of a universal rule—we would be struck speechless all the time, whenever we encounter new combinations and aspects of our world outside the reach of our previous categories. But natural language is metaphorical and analogical, not categorical and logical. Language naturally links a new present with the past through a Wittgensteinian "family resemblance" of situation to situation. As Wittgenstein advises us, we need only think of the diverse objects we call "chairs" or "games."

From this Wittgensteinian perspective on language, there is no context-free meaning, no "standard instance."[13] Meaning is always tied both to the past and to the context in which it lives; what we sometimes call the "plain meaning" of a word is its meaning in a common context—a context we imagine for that word when we see it out of context. The contextuality of language permits any particular to be described in thousands of ways, pointing out this or that relation to other things in the (past) world. The description that language—and, by extension, law—will give to an action or thing will depend on which aspect of it is important or salient to us at the moment (i.e., what we are doing with it, how we are involved with it). My grandmother's old oak rocker is a rocker (when I need to distinguish it from an easy chair), a chair (when I tell the movers what I have), a wooden object (when I am concerned about fire danger or termites), a medium brown with a bit of green (when I am redecorating), a movable (to distinguish it from my landlord's property), an antique (when I think about its value on the market), an heirloom (when I ponder its family history), a thing of beauty (when I look up from my computer to watch the afternoon sun play on it), and a soothing motion (when I want to put my child to sleep). By extension, a fact in a case has analogical importance not intrinsically but in relation to the point of the inquiry. The common-law method, by keeping the focus on the context, sees that the statement of any rule is always tied to the point to which we are at present attending. Any pronouncements not so tied are only "dicta," not "holding." From the perspective of a different situation or inquiry, a new aspect of an old case may assume new importance.

Being in the World of Law and Ethics

How do these foundational considerations play out in the context of law and ethical theory? Heidegger's insight is that the basis of human thought is not deductive reasoning but experience, connectedness, in-touchness, ability to perceive the world and each other and "see" things *as* like and unlike, connected with each other in some relation of relevance or irrelevance from the past into a future. We already see the colors of a painting "as" red, as robes, as paint; we do not have sensory experiences that only later are endowed by reason with meaning.[14] Likewise, we already see each other "as" *Dasein,* "as" friend, foe, neighbor, child, kindly, arrogant, silly, jaunty, spunky, shy, supercilious, profound, concerned, impatient, preoccupied, cruel, enthusiastic, smug, carefree, sincere, spacey, manipulative, compassionate. We read each others' faces, body language, eyes, words, silences, and bearing. From our earliest moments, we speak with eyes, hands, feet. A mother can understand her preverbal child as a reasoning, expressive being, even though the child lacks the ability to formulate words (or rules). We are already "with" each other and outside of ourselves, not caught in a solipsistic prison in which we can doubt the existence of others.

This being-with outside ourselves is prior to any particular emotional experience of sympathy. Being-with is not just a matter of the empirical contingency of whether we happen to be sympathetic or not. From the first, we find ourselves affected by each other, because we are finite, limited, and at risk. We could not be affected (passively attentive) unless we were also finite.

We can be deceived, of course, but only because we are already attentive and connected to others who are constantly throwing us signals and meaningful gestures and words. One cannot be deceived without already conceiving, without having several meanings to untangle, several potential interpretations to unpack. The problem of being deceived by others, then, is not that we can never know the thing-in-itself that lurks in the hearts of men but that we know so much about what might lurk there.[15] This does not imply, however, that we are all the "same" or that we can ever be absolutely transparent to each other. Like the world itself, we encounter others in time, from a familiar past to an unfamiliar future, and from our own place in the web. We see only a little way at a time, and we change, too, through our own encounter with others and world. Personalities are unique not because they are unknowable in principle (though we can never fully know someone else who is constantly changing through time) but because they are not identical—one's experience can only be "like" another's (in some respect) but never the "same" as another's. This is also true of the world—no quiet morning on the marsh is ever the same as another. Each is unique. If we understood the world logically, of course, then all members of a category would be "same." But logic is derivative. We understand the world and others analogically first, and that means through metaphor and resemblance, not identity. Only after we have perceived something as "like" can we categorize it logically as "same."

The implications of Heidegger's views for law and its kanticism can now be made clear. Because the construction of human understanding as logic, reason, or science is an abstraction made possible by the concrete ways in which we "read" each other foundationally, reason is not the glue that binds reasonable beings together as identical equals-in-reason in order to achieve a "kingdom of ends." Instead, community and our knowledge of each other come before any attempt to describe that community in rational terms, to state the contractual terms of that engagement in a rule form amenable to logical manipulation, or even to specify the categories that would make us "same" and therefore "equal." We recognize each other as "fellow" *Daseins* from the outset, not through the mediation of reason's requirement of consistency. We already know how to treat each other—how to be kind or cruel, how to hurt or help, how to provoke a smile or frown. Hence, obligations are not imposed through reason but precede reason. (Even Kant acknowledges this, noting that one need not be a philosopher to be moral but conceding that practical wisdom precedes ethical theory.)[16] We are already tied to each other, bound in community. Our very being who we are is constituted by those ties and bonds. To be sure, we can resist or break those bonds (and thereby, to some extent, resist and break ourselves), but we do not need reason as the "glue" to connect us to each other. The mutual connection is what is already there—a given, a gift, a grace.

From this standpoint, the grounding "categorical imperatives" shift. Instead of being responsible "to the conception of laws" or to "reason," we are responsive to and for each other. Our ties, literally "ob-*ligations*," are personal and particular, not originally, at least, "universal." My duty is *to* someone, and my responsibility is *for* someone and only abstractly and derivatively to reason or the universal law. To restate the categorical imperative in its first mode—act so that the maxim of your action can be a universal law, or, more simply, "be reasonable"—is to recognize that being-in-and-with is now who we are: "Honor your responsibilities to and for others, for they make you who you are."

Equality, too, changes. It is no longer rational formal equality, treating the same the same,[17] where the relevant features of sameness must be abstracted from the individual situation and totted up in a balance sheet. Each case is unique and can only be analogous, but not identical, to another. Connection, not logical consistency, is the foundation. Exclusion or division is the self-negating thought here, for as I said earlier, we resist or break our bonds to others only by breaking ourselves. Including is the imperative thought. So the second statement of the categorical imperative from this new foundation is "To be is to belong (be-along)."

To form laws together as finite creatures is not to legislate reasonable universal rules but to live law out in context, over time, based on preexisting mutual understanding and connection. Government is not founded on an imposition of abstract statements of reason on the world (though we can derivatively, based on experience, make such abstract statements, we still have to decide to which cases they "apply") but is founded on a working out of new connections with others from case to "relevant" case, on the ground, based on where and how we are and have been. Law is not so crucially the positive legislation in the statute books than the ways we have of being together, as legislation gets enforced (or not enforced), worked with (or worked around), applied to this case but not that, and generally fleshed out in practice.[18] Of course, we cannot ignore that many of our ways of being together are never laid down in rules at all but "go without saying."[19] For example, I should not now interrupt this paragraph with a description of my vacation (though if I did something like that, you might take it as a kind of art that breaks rules so as to point them out). So the third restatement of the categorical imperative is "Work through the future together on the basis of the past."

The "being-with" that Heidegger speaks of does not mandate a particular political arrangement. Even liberalism, as we live it out, is a kind of being-with—indeed, the kind of being-with that we often try to practice for the most part in U.S. institutions. Liberalism is a form of being-with that sees part of our obligation to each other as allowing practices of deliberation and debate to take a central place in our responsibilities to and for each other. This deliberation *in practice* itself has highly contextual features that are not immediately explicable on the basis of an abstract rule or justification: for example, in deliberation and debate, I may insult a public official on the basis of his academic performance, but I may not insult my students on the basis of their academic performance. We also have a *practice together* of leaving each other alone in appropriate ways and times and with elaborate and embedded contextual nuances: for example, (some of) you must let me bathe alone, but you need not let me do my grocery shopping alone. Part of our practice of being together suggests that you must treat me "equally" in certain ways and at certain times and with certain exceptions and nuances: for example, you may not pay me less at work because of my gender, but you need not have me over to dinner the same number of times as you do men you know.[20] Of course, we can always ask why the rule of gender equality does not apply here. Our answer *in application* may change the contours of the rule.

There are four key implications of the turn that Heidegger suggests. First, our root, richest, and most reliable form of understanding each other and the world is through concrete practical experience (not abstract logical analysis or science). Second, both personally and politically, we are constituted and enabled in a host of possibilities by the personal bonds and cultural practices we are "given." Third, as finite beings, we neither start from scratch nor reach an "end" but must always be working out law from the past and to the future in practices (incompletely articulated), and our knowledge and "power" to create our polity is neither absolute nor eternal. Fourth, law and the language in which it is written are not susceptible of simple logical application, but application requires experience and judgment grounded in the connections forged by narrative and analogy from the past and pointing into the future.

II. LEVINAS: THE IMPORTANCE OF THE OTHER

Levinas's phenomenology also challenges the primacy of reason. He, too, emphasizes that we are already in connection with others, without the intermediation of reason as "glue." Like Heidegger, he emphasizes that we are open to and connected with each other from the outset, that the openness and connection precede our understanding of reason and justice rather than being created by it. We do not need reason to ground a community; it is not reason that demands that we respect reason in others as well as ourselves. The relationship with others is already there and grounds reason itself.

However, I turn to Levinas here because his understanding of the relation between self and others corrects for some of the misleading inferences often drawn from Heidegger's account of being-with. Because Heidegger is trying to overcome the enlightenment gulf between subject and object that implies the point of view of a philosopher's god, Heidegger emphasizes that it is a mistake to posit a thing-in-itself that we cannot know. This emphasis is often read to imply a "Borgness" of total and transparent interpenetration between me, the world, and others. For this reason, Levinas, among others, has criticized Heidegger for constructing a totalitarian system in which all *Daseins* are the same, know the same, and can read each other and their world completely. On this reading, Heidegger's thought would seem to support the worst forms of communitarianism and even perhaps totalitarianism and Naziism, and, of course, Heidegger's historical ties to the Nazi regime do not help in allaying this objection.

Levinas instead emphasizes the uniqueness of each person and argues that our knowledge of others, while still coming before reason through an immediate perception of connectedness, is only a beginning of a relationship. I cannot know others completely, and the very incompleteness of my knowledge generates, at the same time, a profound call of responsibility and compassion (as I am drawn to others) and a humble respect (as I perceive their uniqueness and difference from me). Hence, Levinas's account of the connection between persons provides an important link between, on the one hand, "primal mercy" as the grace or gift of being-with and, on the other, the everyday, more familiar sense of mercy as compassionate lenity, as well as leaving room for the awe one should feel for what is unique and unknowable about the other. The primal mercy or grace of being-with should generate a responsibility, compassion, awe, and respect for the other that calls for humility in judgment and lenity in assessing blame.

Levinas on the Dangers of Totalizing Conceptions and the Uniqueness of Persons

This book is not the place for a complete adjudication of Levinas's objections to Heidegger. For our purposes in sketching out being-with, Levinas's remonstrances against Heidegger and Levinas's own nuanced understanding of human relationships will be understood not as objections but as a help to fleshing out our understanding of being-with. I will therefore leave aside, to some extent, the interpretive question of whether Levinas's reformulation of person-to-person relationships is consistent or inconsistent with Heidegger's texts.

Levinas rejects any idea of a grand metaphysical solipsism (Aristotle, Spinoza, Hegel). In such a system, he fears, individuals are just part of the bigger picture, alike and transparent, or, as Spinoza would say, merely aspects of God thinking himself. Personality is impossible in such a system; people cannot exist as (different and differentiated) people. Levinas says that Heidegger's complementary relation between *Dasein* and *Sein* is too "totalizing" in this same way. While Heidegger's philosophy breaches the gulf between subject and object that makes any encounter with the world problematic, Levinas thinks that his account goes too far the other way, binding subject and object together in a common world that fails to account for the difference and transcendence of the individual self. For Levinas, Heidegger's *Daseins* are too open, too transparent, to be unique people with their own private worlds, fantasies, thoughts, and experience. Totalizing philosophy, too, for Levinas, has a political danger: in his view, it is tied to totalitarian regimes that lack sufficient deference, reverence, and respect for individual persons.

In Heidegger's defense, one might point out that Being is not a state or thing but a giving (of world, things, others, knowledge) in time. Being itself retreats from our "complete" knowledge precisely because it is the giving, not a giver or what it gives. We pay attention to the world and forget *that it is given.* Moreover, we are finite, knowing things only in and over time, not knowing, as a philosopher's god might, everything for all time. Indeed, especially in the modern age, Being's very "givenness" hides itself from *Dasein* and leads to the illusion that human will creates, controls, and values all that is.[21] Heidegger also repeatedly emphasizes that all revealing is also concealing; there is no complete uncovering of one *Dasein* to another for all time. He might even say that Levinas's refusal to accept Being's connection with *Dasein* is another symptom of modern technological thinking, with a tendency toward totalitarianism that is caused by forgetting there is something other than human will, not by getting lost in a totalizing Being. For Heidegger, the dangers of totalitarianism lie not in our openness to Being but in its closure to us, in the illusion that we can (re)make and control all that is (including ourselves and each other). As the measure of all things, humankind becomes the despot of all things. In our exile from our own proper essence as those to whom Being reveals, we are even likely to lose, corrupt, and enslave ourselves. Hence, for Heidegger, the effort to think Being is itself an act of ethics,[22] an act of remembering our own essence as a *gift* and a *given* and, fundamentally, to come to a place of humility. To let beings, including other *Daseins,* be is to let them unfold before us, not to take them over, remake them, use them, or improve them—as we tend to do in our era of "merely positing" law, when we forget anything that might bind us, limit us, or obligate us.[23]

Levinas seems to acknowledge all of this. But Heidegger's "we" bothers Levinas nonetheless, as does Heidegger's insistence that we (*Daseins*) are at best spectators to the unveiling of world and Being. Levinas wants to insist on preserving the self from submersion into either being-in or being-with.[24] He also wants to insist on the fundamental ethical call to respond to others: others are not merely "unfolding" before us but crying out to us. While I have my doubts about Levinas's claims that being-in is too totalizing, I believe Levinas's emphasis on the call of being-with is helpful and evocative.

The "Face": Levinas's Account of the Prerational Connection to Others

Though Levinas insists on the uniqueness of the self, he agrees that to avoid the solipsism of complete isolation of myself from the "outside"of my consciousness, I am still fundamentally open to others, but in a way different, or at least with different emphasis, than some of Heidegger's descriptions of being-with might indicate. According to Levinas, I have an unmediated, but limited, experience of the other as "face." The "face" is not a literal face, of course, but a philosophical metaphor for the idea that I know immediately that the other I confront is also a personality who experiences, feels, and speaks, even though I cannot presume to know what "is given" to him or her to know. There is no one "clearing" in which my experience of the other occurs or in which medium or light I perceive the face. The "face to face" is, for Levinas, *the* given, an unmediated recognition that the other is, again, to use Heidegger's term, a fellow *Dasein*.[25]

But the perception of "face" is not a perception like that of things, in the sense of "There it is" or "There she is." It is at root an ethical perception of the call and challenge of the other. In this encounter, I am confronted by the other, by a "she" or "he," who cannot be subsumed in a "we," and the other challenges my experienced world precisely because she does not entirely share it or fit within it. The "world" we share must be tendered and negotiated in language, in which I must expose my personality to "you," make myself vulnerable, and give (speak) without hope of recompense (response). Levinas insists that it is through this primary encounter with others that "the world" we are in is given to us—not already through Being, but through our encounter with the other. The encounter with the other is first; the ethical precedes the ontological. Our knowledge of the world comes out of our ethical dialogue with others—as language, history, culture, and even science. The vulnerability and nonreciprocal gift of my response to the other echoes themes in the philosophy of language. As Donald Davidson has said, the first premise of any conversation is a principle of "charity," an assumption that the person one addresses is able to understand and respond meaningfully and that his or her words and actions can be interpreted symbolically, not just causally.[26]

The encounter with the other not only puts me at risk in a nonreciprocal fashion, but, as Levinas puts it in *Totality and Infinity,* also awakens a sense of a lack within myself. Here, Levinas makes us think through Descartes' doubting ego in a different, more phenomenological, way. In Levinas's account of Descartes' thought experiment, I think, and that thought is all I am certain of.

But this very standard of certainty I set for myself is another idea that is always there, from the start, along with and inextricable from my thinking. Hence, I have in myself an idea of perfection, certainty, or, as Levinas puts it, infinity. This idea cannot be based on myself, for I see from the outset, as soon as I think and measure my thinking in comparison with this idea, that I am neither perfect nor infinite. So, Descartes concludes, the idea of infinity must come from outside myself. The "outside myself" that is somehow already there in me from the beginning is the "infinite other" who provides the standard by which I always think and, in thinking, necessarily judge myself lacking.

In Levinas's twist on this thought experiment, I can no longer be "merely" an I, for I come to see that I need the other. To confront the "other" is to know that there is something I do not know and cannot know but that I nonetheless need in order to think, to be me. The other is the ever-mysterious, infinite measure of my own lack and vulnerability, that calls me to engage with the infinite other. The other reveals that I am unjustified, that is, that I have no ground within myself. Hence, I come to see the other as the object of desire—desire for ground, for sense, for understanding. I cannot be just an I, self-standing and self-referential and able to enjoy my own solipsism in perfect freedom; I am an I always in relation to, always with desire for, always in vulnerability and shame before, the infinite other, who I cannot know/subsume (because I can never plumb his or her depths). Though confronting the other as "face" shows me the possibility of murder (for I see the other as embodying a personality I could destroy), I am aware, in the same encounter, of the ethical impossibility of murder (because the longing for the other is now always necessary to me being me—I cannot return to a happy solipsism). My incompleteness, my need for the other, is my responsibility to the call of the other, for which, Levinas says, I need to seek "pardon": "Reaching the other . . . is, on the ontological level, the event of the most radical breakup of the very category of ego, for it is for me to be somewhere else than myself; is to be pardoned, not to be a definite existence";[27] "The welcoming of the Other is ipso facto the consciousness of my own injustice—the shame that freedom feels for itself . . . The Other, whose exceptional presence is inscribed in the ethical impossibility of killing him in which I stand, marks the end of powers. If I can no longer have power over him it is because he overflows absolutely every *idea* I can have of him."[28]

Hence, I see the other with fear and awe, as beyond me, as infinite in his or her difference and yet necessary for me to be me. As Levinas puts it, "The nakedness of the face is *denument*. To recognize the Other is to recognize a hunger. To recognize the Other is to give. But it is to give to the master, to the lord, to him whom one approaches as 'You' [*vous,* not *tu,* you not thou] in a dimension of height."[29] Only if the sacredness of the other's personality remains apart from me is a true relationship of me (accusative, called for) and she or he (nominative, subject) possible.

Though every encounter with another person has this aspect of a primary "address," I understand Levinas in part through the parable of my own experience of my daughter's birth. So much of the pregnancy had been egoistic and, well, literally, belly button gazing. I tracked my body changing, my feelings, my cravings, my imagination of motherhood, my excitement, my worry, my pain, my will to endure it, my triumph in the act of birth. Then, suddenly, there were two eyes looking at me. What had been part of me was now another being, a stranger, completely alien, new, waiting to be encountered in all her uniqueness and trackless expanse of possibilities. I was terrified and yet moved at the same time by a sudden surge of adoration. At once I was called for and called on, my expectations were shattered, and my life and very self-concept were transformed. I was forever after not a me but a "m-other."

Hence, for Levinas, language and reason, our "common ground," do not bind us together but themselves arise from a more primary dynamic ethical relation with the other. We are called by duty before we are able to formulate what the nature of our obligation is. As Levinas puts it again and again, responsibility precedes knowledge. To know another is possible only in part, only derivatively, and only after and on the basis of being called and questioned by the other, made vulnerable and placed at risk to an infinite call of responsibility: "*Toward another* culminates in a *for another,* a suffering for his suffering, without light, that is, without measure."[30]

Levinas and Justice

Because Levinas thinks of the call of the other as an infinite obligation, a responsibility based only on an ability to respond, it is hard for him to reconcile this fundamental and infinite ethical call with law. When a third person enters the scene, I am torn between infinite responsibility and infinite responsibility. Each other calls for everything I can give. Any division of my efforts between two others is an unethical compromise. Levinas's thought creates a tension, then, between ethics and law. Law, for Levinas, seems to be inescapably positivistic, the compromise of a mere "bright-line rule" without ethical justification that negotiates arbitrarily between these infinite calls by establishing rules and limits to responsibility. As Desmond Manderson puts it, "The rules and systems that law makes must betray this ethical consciousness of the imperfection of rules, by reducing and limiting it."[31] As such, law seems in fundamental conflict with ethics, and the best we can hope for is an oscillation between the rule of law and the call of the unique all-requiring other, reenacting the tension between justice and mercy, rather than resolving it. For Levinas, there is yet a trace of the ethical in the legal, in the nagging doubts that tug at us from the particular case. Jill Stauffer writes,

> What is the relation of ethics to justice, or ethics to politics? Levinas calls the relation a necessary one. But he does so in a way that won't answer, to our satisfaction, the question we have about what we ought to *do* about our response to others. To answer that question with any finality would be to commit Levinasian ethics to a system and thereby betray the infinite responsibility for which ethics stands. The relation between ethics and politics is not unidirectional, nor causal or temporal. It is an oscillation, an indecision, a constant balancing, an endless vigilance. That is what justice requires. Institutions of law call what is needed in instances such as these, *judgment*.[32]

Levinas does not have a full account of judgment that can resolve or explain the place of contestation between mercy as the unique (though infinite) call of the other and law as the general rule, treating like alike rather than each uniquely, though he recognizes, as Heidegger does, that primal mercy or grace (understood as our ungrounded and undeserved obligation to the call of an other) must be the ground of justice.[33] Levinas's conception of law, at times, as impermeable "universal rule" rather than the common-law guiding of metaphoric family resemblance may itself be responsible for duplicating the problem of law and mercy, rule and particular, rather than finding a way to bridge the ethical and legal. Here, it seems to me, Levinas can be helped along by emphasizing the temporality of language and thought—and therefore also law.[34]

Common-law reasoning *is* the attempt to know how to respond to the unique case from where we stand in our own imperfectly applicable past experience. But what we often forget is that the call of the particular infuses the decision regarding whether or not the past is relevant or irrelevant and, either way, changes our experience (our past law, rule or practice) in the encounter. Law cannot contain others in logical boxes, because the others shift the boundaries of the boxes in the course of law's "application." Because common-law reasoning strives to remember the cases narratively (in at least some of their uniqueness) and not just the "rules" of the case, injustice can poke out of the past as a chafing lack of fit that may be retrofitted long after the case is "past." We often repudiate old decisions in the course of making new ones, because they no longer "fit" the pattern we see. We repudiate state-mandated prayer, Japanese internment, slavery, segregation, racial purity laws, even as we base decisions today on our sullied past experience. The repercussions of the encounter with the unique are not entirely cut off, even after a case is "decided." The "infinity" of our obligation to the unique other, if understood more temporally as a continuing or future obligation, is still at play in legal judgment, even as it is in ethical judgment. Of course, I still cannot give "everything now" in legal judgment. But the reason I cannot is only partly because of the need to divide my giving among many obligations. I cannot give "everything now" even to one other person, except in the case in which I die for them (and even then I would need additional time to give all I *had* as well as all I am, as well as more time to give all I am capable of giving). Both the giving and the capacity to give change with time and take time. Inside time, we cannot fulfill infinite obligations, even to one. So the failure of law in this respect does not set it apart from the ethical. Obligation is always compromised. The infinite responsibility to the unique other must be reformulated as an obligation that continues *over (through) time* both ethically and legally and is impossible to fulfill *both ethically and legally* in any *now*.

Insofar as Levinas sees a gap between law and ethics from this perspective—law as always compromised, ethics as true infinite responsibility for the unique other—this problem need not re-create an irresolvable tension between law and mercy (understood now from Levinas as our ethical response to the particular and unique), if we have understood law temporally rather than as universal timeless rules that set impermeable limits. But there is another way in which we might understand Levinas's point about the uniqueness of the other and its relation to law (even after we have reconceived law as analogical and temporal rather than as universal rules). To do this, we must infuse both Levinas and Heidegger's insights with what we have already learned from Kant.

III. BEING-IN-THE-WORLD-WITH-OTHERS AS THE UNION OF THE JUDGMENT OF THE BEAUTIFUL AND THE SUBLIME

Taken together, Heidegger and Levinas provide a phenomenology of the human experience that both explains and protests against our tendency to exploit (others and world) and exposes to us our essential openness (being-in/with or face) as in a world and with others. For purposes of our investigation of mercy, both philosophers see reason as derivative, an abstraction coming only after and on the basis of the encounter with world and with others that is already given for no reason. Both see that this preexisting encounter with others grounds all of law and all of reason, and both see that we are "called," obligated, to be with and for others, before any rule can be made or any law imposed. The call of responsibility is to take a nonreciprocal risk in opening ourselves to the gift-we-do-not-deserve of an encounter with others.

We have, then, both the undeserved *gift* of being-in/with and the ungrounded *call* of responsibility. Both the grace of world and the guilt of responsibility are already there. Neither is determined by choice, will, or desert. If we think of mercy as undeserved leniency for one who is guilty—a gift to the guilty—then mercy describes the human condition. This primal mercy is a gift, a grace, a mutual vulnerability, a com-passion, the original being-with that we are, the given and taken-on call of care that demands a response. All of this comes before desert, before choice or contract, before reason, before law. It is the ground of any possibility of human law or justice, and it conditions and allows justice to appear for us.

So far, the two thinkers agree. Mercy—the gift to the guilty—is the lady of the house, the ground of law. The problem comes in understanding Law (i.e., right law, or justice) and judgment (the method of justice). Does justice lie in the "fitting" common-law traditions of the past as heritage, which Heidegger so well describes, or is justice the unmediated response to the singular, embodied, heart-wrenching and infinite cry of the other, which Levinas so well describes? Kant can help us here. I suggest that one way to bring together these accounts of the being of justice is through Kant's understanding of the beautiful and the sublime.[35]

Heidegger emphasizes our primal connection with things, which both shine and hide from us, the given and grace of our being.[36] Levinas emphasizes our primal connection with others, who also both show (face) and hide, a connection that is a longing, a painful vulnerability, a duty for no reason, undefined, a constant risking and giving to others with no guarantee of return. Justice can be understood as the unity of these two ideas.

After our turn to Heidegger and Levinas, justice as the judgment of the "beautiful" is understood no longer as universal rules of reason but, as in later Kant, as the experience of "purposiveness" (*Zweckmässigkeit*), as embedded patterns and ways of being-with that "appear" and grow up as custom when we live and work together. Justice is the "fittingness" of what we do as beings who *are* the kinds of being who are already with others in a world. As Heidegger teaches us, this relatedness is a perceptiveness and a knowing-how, not a theoretical knowing-that—an improvisation on the past that is an art, not a following of rules of reason. The beautiful is the self-illumination of a good poem, sculpture, analogy, narrative, symbol, metaphor, or judicial opinion; it is the organic growing up of ways that enable us, without deliberation or even conscious strategy, to do dishes together, drive on highways together, line up for trains, sing in harmony, hold a classroom discussion, move politely and gracefully from conversation to conversation at a cocktail party, or build houses or roads or lives together as a "good team." In this way, we grow patterns of being together, customs and practices that settle in as law, not through arbitrary, bright-line rules (sometimes not even articulated), but flexibly, through variations and improvisations, sensitive to the particulars of situation and case.

The model for this understanding of law is not universal rules but the common law, working itself out from case to case, each case trailing threads of significance that can be caught up in new webs of analogies, forging new patterns, or left adrift. The key judgments are those of analogy, not deduction, which themselves depend on an elusive sense of "fit" or relevance that cannot be specified in a rule but is "perceived" by judgment. The openness of the common law enables us to work from past to future, understanding new cases in the light of old ones, as does language itself, founding new words on old ones. The common law becomes a kind of etymology of cases through which we can trace the patterns of our past experience and by which we can find likenesses enough, words that fit by metaphor and analogy, to "say" the law provisionally in the new case we now confront and with a view (though imperfect) to other "like" cases we can, from our past, expect to see. Law, like the language in which it lives, is a constellation of "family resemblances" and ways of going on, allowing for incremental change, elaboration, and improvisation on old themes. A good judge, with the *art* of judgment, can unpack and elucidate these patterns for us.

But justice is also the judgment of the "sublime"—the elusive infinity of responsibility; the "perfect" rule that we only have an idea of and that can never be captured in any actual rule; the "call" to respond from over the chasm of individual difference without assuming, presuming, or consuming the other; the sense of unease that makes customs or practices that "used to fit" chafe, bother, and vaguely nauseate us; and even the sudden personal confrontation with the depth and profundity of an other that, regardless of custom or established law, immediately and radically calls from us respect and response. Justice can strike us, sometimes, as we come to confront an other who radically challenges our

categories and customs. A Judge Ruffin who has previously upheld the custom-
ary law of master-slave relations confronts the torture death of a pregnant female slave and is forced to reconsider the meaning, customs, and law of slavery
itself, leaving the rules adrift.[37] As a judge and defendant who come face to face
at a sentencing hearing share a joke, a sudden bond of inexplicable trust and
goodwill is created over an abyss of ethnic, racial, and class difference. These
places where justice strikes us may be places where our traditional, comfortable, incrementally innovative approach to law must make a radical leap of
thought, announce a new principle, depart from the pattern of the past in the
as-yet-inarticulate insight that *this* case is different, that *this* person calls for
more or less than what we have given before.

In justice as the unity of the beautiful and sublime, primal mercy is at play
in the *givenness* of the past traditions that guide us, as well as the *givenness* of
our immediate, passionate, embodied response and perception of the situation
we confront. Mercy is, in short, in the undeserved grace or giveness of our being-in-and-with. But our everyday understanding of mercy also has a special
relation to the judgment of the sublime. In the comfortableness of judgments
of the beautiful or fitting, we tend to forget that our past traditions are given,
because, as Heidegger might put it, when we use our past cultural "case law" as
"tools" of judgment, their Being as a giving retreats from view. Just as we do not
need to think about the history and etymology of each word we use, already
comfortable with the old-leather-glove feel and connotation of our "mother"
tongue, we do not think about how we rely on our perception of relevance or
fit. We simply do our judging without thinking about how we are doing it,
moving from "No late papers" to "No late papers except in cases of sudden serious illness" or from "innkeeper" to "landlord" without even noticing that we
made a judgment of "fit."

But when an individual case threatens to overturn our comfortable sense of
fit, we are struck afresh by our responsibility for the other. We experience this
judgment often as one of "compassion" because of its emotional attunement to
the singular. It is, as yet, inarticulate, incapable of being articulated in the traditions or case law we have at our fingertips. Before it can come to language, however, it comes to presence as a body slam of emotion, as an overwhelming need
to act against established law. Marty Slaughter puts it this way:

Justice "that is simply the operation of law" is tantamount to a justice that has
the self-enclosure of the beautiful. On the other hand, love and mercy lie "beyond" this beautiful totality of legal justice. They are singular and operate as

unjustified exceptions, neither justifiable nor rational, neither universalisable nor part of a rational system. They interrupt the self-encounter of legal justice just as in aesthetics the "sublime" refers to what interrupts the self-enclosure of the beautiful. They are beyond totality, at once the ethical condition but also the sublime excess of justice.[38]

This is the experience of mercy that comes, at times, in criminal sentencing, when an inexplicable bond is created among the judging parties, when a judge is simply "moved" to be merciful, or when a jury nullifies, simply refusing to apply the law. This judgment of mercy can be a judgment of the sublime—a sudden awareness that there is something we have missed, something we do not yet know, a responsibility we have not yet fully encompassed or articulated. This judgment may be the first signal of a sea change in the law—as when sympathy for a particular battered woman's plight comes, later, to change the law of murder. Or it may remain isolated, a case limited to its particular facts. The otherwise inexplicable deference we give to trial courts, executive and administrative officials making "discretionary" decisions on the front lines of the legal system is the law's recognition of the importance of difficult-to-articulate sublime judgment.[39]

The sheer *givenness* of the judgment in such cases, as well as our explicit recognition of that *givenness,* is often what we call mercy. It seems to us an "exceptional" experience, *against* law. But from our new standpoint, we can see that what we experience as "irrational" mercy in such cases is really only the underlying ground of *being-in/with* coming to our explicit attention in the context of sublime judgment. What we do not see is that the same gift of *being-in/with,* the same openness to the particular that is a *gift to the guilty,* the same perceptive compassion, is "hidden" in the "usual" case. We tend to understand the run-of-the-mill case as involving the "mere" application of a rule, though on attentive examination, *the (beautiful) judgment's unmediated perception of "fit" or relevance that grounds the application of any rule is seen to be grounded in the same "given" of singular experience.* This connection between mercy as the "grace" of being-with—that is, as the ground of who we are—and mercy as the "leniency for no reason" of criminal sentencing will be more fully explored in the next chapters. But the relationship here is meant to be a reverse image of the usual assumption of kanticism—that we must treat like cases alike in order to be true to our nature as reasonable beings. Here, the claim is analogous: we must exercise mercy because we are beings whose essence is an undeserved gift of being-with. Being who we are, in other words, requires us to be compassionate, giving, open, risk-taking, and responsive and generous to others—that is, merciful.

IV. RETRACING OUR STEPS

How far this line of thought has taken us becomes apparent when we revisit the way in which the problem of justice and mercy is usually handled. Returning, for a moment, to Anselm's question presented at the beginning of this book's introduction, we see that justice is usually conceived as treating like cases alike, in reason. Mercy on the traditional view, however, is murkier. Sometimes it is understood as leniency or a remitting of punishment. At its grandest, it is the giving of a gift in canceling a debt or a punishment "for no reason." Most scholars try, in various ways, to avert the collision of mercy and justice in this last category of mercy "for no reason." My citations to various authors below illustrate the range of positions that have been taken, but is certainly not the last word on what any particular writer now has to say. Academia is temporal, too, and these writers may have shifted or elaborated their positions in more recent work. Like criminal sentences, a particular piece of writing captures a person at a moment, never for all time.

One tack is to restrict mercy by defining it as equity—allowing mercy to account for cases in which the legal rules are too procrustean and cannot account for individual differences that are morally relevant. One example is Kathleen Dean Moore's work on pardons, which argues that pardoning is appropriate when, despite justiciable reasons to think that a sentence was too harsh, the written (positive) law does not allow a correction.[40] The "rules" of law are only human, after all, and cannot reflect what a truly "universal" law would take into account. Mercy is equity—a gap filler—but it is not a gift, for it is still morally obligatory even if legally discretionary.[41] Yet, as many authors have pointed out, including St. Anselm, such an account of mercy makes it another form of justice.[42]

Other writers try to defend a more discretionary or supererogatory account of mercy. One possibility is that mercy is an "imperfect" obligation; that is, we have a duty to be merciful in general, but no one ever has a corresponding "right" to mercy. Mercy is explicitly, then, a gift. Why is it good to be merciful sometimes? Usually the answer has little to do with the offender. Most theorists of mercy as an "imperfect obligation" concede that mercy is good for the mercy giver's character. A compassionate attitude is more virtuous, in general, than a condemnatory attitude; therefore, we sometimes sacrifice justice for the betterment of the mercy giver, though perhaps not of the receiver.[43] However, others argue that a merciful character may not be better than a just one.[44] Herbert Morris takes issue with the very idea that forgiveness is good for you, arguing that overcoming resentment out of concern for one's own mental health is not forgiveness but, at best, good hygiene and, at worst, self-aggrandizement.[45]

Other writers try to find mercy a place by changing the nature of criminal desert. For example, H. Scott Hestevold tries to argue that mercy comes into play whenever one may choose a more lenient of several penalty options that all fit the desert of the offender.[46] This possibility, however, seems to evaporate in any nuanced account of desert, as others have pointed out.[47] Others argue that mercy may compensate for other misfortunes an offender has suffered, as a kind of cosmic justice.[48] In a similar fashion, R. A. Duff argues that mercy might recognize other considerations that "trump" justice; in his view, a communicative punishment is not appropriate if other issues are more pressing.[49]

Many authors simply give up. They find no place at all for mercy in the context of public punishment, precisely because it conflicts with justice, because only victims (not judges) have "standing" to forgive, or because mercy presupposes a hierarchical relationship, not one of equality.[50] As Lyla O'Driscoll puts it, "We see little virtue in the humiliating and hypocritical benefaction bestowed by an aristocrat on a worthy underling who, unjustly, is unable to assert a legal right to the benefit he desperately needs."[51]

All of the preceding theories base their definitions of mercy on the need to squeeze it into the corners of justice, finding room for it only in the private, the emotional, the personal, the supererogatory. Making mercy the lady of the house, however, changes our focus. The clash between mercy and justice may not be a matter of good analytic housekeeping that properly cloisters off mercy into the private, the emotional, or the "dire circumstances" at the edge of justice. Instead, as N. E. Simmonds argues, "If a paradox is the sign of sickness in the whole body of thought, its premature excision may simply shield us from unsettling truths ... Too swift a desire to tidy up this moral problem and establish a clear set of prescriptions may be unhelpful and damaging."[52] Herbert Morris likewise urges more reflection: "I find myself drawn, when reflecting on forgiveness, to the idea of transcendence, to grace, and I believe [others] may have too quickly moved away from the mystery that lies at the heart of forgiveness."[53] What I have done here is to take seriously this call for more reflection.

In sum, our path has been this: just as we used to understand law as how the nature of being human (reason) is reflected in the context of the government of human community, we should now understand justice (in both its beauty and sublimity) as what we see from a place "given" to us by the fact that we are those who are "with" the world and "with" others. If to be human is to be "called" by others as a given, without further ground, then our responsibility to and for each other is without reason, an undeserved guilt that is also a gift of being-with from which we begin. Mercy or grace, as this gift to the guilty, represents the fundamental ethical obligation—to risk and open oneself to a vulnerable connection with others for no reason, simply because that is who we are. There is no social contract, reason, expectation of return, reciprocal obligation, equality, or universal law except as derivative from this fundamental obligation to give and to accept the gifts that others bring and are. We do not esteem others (and ourselves) because of their "rational nature," nor do we "value" them because they satisfy our preferences in some way; we esteem others because we *are* the kinds of being who esteem, who are grateful and giving, risk-taking and vulnerable, suffering the absence of but always called to the relationship of being-with, just as we are always called to look for and sometimes to see, receive, and wonder at or to miss and lament the loss of the meaning in the world.

Who gives this meaning? Who calls us to be with others? Is there a who? As Kant understood, we cannot know; such matters are beyond human knowledge and are matters for faith, not philosophy. We cannot even meaningfully ask the question without re-creating a god of philosophy, like an Unmoved Mover, Reason, or Will "outside" *Dasein*. Any god we might "posit" or "create" for ourselves cannot bind us. All we can do or think is what we already are—the responding, responsible, vulnerable, suffering, needing, giving, sense-seeking, longing-for ones.

Heidegger uses the German word *Sorge* to refer to the united temporal aspects of *Dasein*.[54] Usually translated as "care" in English, *Sorge* carries, in both languages, the sense of "laden with cares" as well as the sense of "devoted."[55] For both Levinas and Heidegger, the result of conceiving of human being as a longing for and receptivity to meaning and to relationship creates this double sense: we are capable of responsibility ("responding to" what is not ours to control) only insofar as we are also capable of suffering. The two are inextricable. The English translation of *Sorge* as "care" also carries a history. It may be connected both to χάρις (Latin *caritas*, "grace, kindness, joy, love") and, perhaps, to Κῆρα (goddess of death, doom, fate, bane, ruin), perhaps itself related to κῆρ (heart), from which comes κερτόμιος (heart-piercing) and κῆρυξ (herald of sacrifice). The tragic poet Euripides plays on these assonances in saying κέρτομος θεοῦ χαρά, which Liddell and Scott translate as "a joy [of/from] the god to pierce my heart."[56] Our finitude enables us to be open and receptive—responsible, giving, loving—but also suffering, heartaching, "pierced" open by joy or sorrow alike. To circle back to Kant, the place we occupy between reason and nature gives us duty—a uniquely painful, already given and unyielding obligation to others and ourselves, undertaken in awe, which both makes us suffer but also lends human life a certain sublimity. Extending grace to others is not ipso facto ignoble or condescending; it is a humble and courageous risk taking that recognizes the difference of the other and yet seeks to tender oneself to the other. Receiving grace is also no shame or humiliation but the very ground of responsibility—the receptivity and connection with others that enables and calls for response. Both giving and receiving constitute us. You are both my gift and guilt—my mercy. There is no good reason, "desert," or further ground for this foundational giving and receiving; there is no social contract or guarantee of reciprocity. Being-with is simply who we are.

CHAPTER 3

The Failure of Retribution

How does the metaphysical background of primal mercy as *caritas,* grace, and the "given" that comes before reason come to matter to a philosophy of punishment? If we recall that the main objection to mercy, understood in punishment terms as giving an offender less than is deserved, is that mercy is unequal and demeaning of who we are as reasonable creatures, we have already come part of the way to a response to that objection and, from there, to a sense of mercy's proper place in punishment. If our very nature is to be called to take a risk on an other for no reason and to receive the world and others as a gift, then mercy as a giving or receiving of leniency for no reason is no longer demeaning or antithetical to who we are as humans but is at the core of who we are as humans. Responsibility and community are no longer the reward of our herculean efforts to overcome inclination and adhere to reason but are there already, whether or not we "deserve" them. Mercy, as an undeserved gift, is no longer in tension with responsibility, because responsibility no longer depends on desert but is itself a given—a gift of guilt. Moreover, for me, you are "sublime" and not completely within my comprehension, so what I give to you, even as mercy, should not be demeaning to you, denying you full responsibility and personhood. Indeed, as I shall argue, any judgment I form of you is always tentative; mercy as leniency is a form of humility that respects the limits of my judgment and the temporality and changing nature of us both and of our understanding of the world.

But this is only a beginning. Once reason is rethought as not universal but as judgment from the "given" and "giving" of our mutual being-with, and once law is rethought as the temporal and provisional analogical connection from past to future embodied in common-law reasoning, much more still needs to be said about responsibility, desert, and equality in criminal law. We need to take another look at punishment theory to see whether we are still asking the right questions. What becomes of wrong, punishment, and mercy after we flip reason and grace, and how do we connect them with our usual understanding of these terms?

Once we rethink what punishment is, we will see that punishment is not something we can "impose"; it is only something that can happen (or not). We will also understand more clearly why punishment cannot be thought of as deserved pain imposed in response to a wrong. Instead, punishment begins with the pain of remorse, which can happen in the presence of a compassionate witness to the wrong as wrong. Understanding the wrong as wrong and bringing it to language in confession and apology lead to a need for merciful settlement, for a way out of the pain of remorse. Punishment, then, is this movement from remorse to confession and settlement. It cannot be coerced or imposed.

As I articulate in this chapter and in chapter 4, this change is a difference in how we think of punishment, not necessarily in how we institutionalize it. Indeed, if these ideas were not already somehow embedded or foreshadowed in our legal culture and practices, I could not think or articulate them. But I hope to show that by rethinking punishment, we can change the way we understand our existing institutions, highlighting what has been seen as peripheral and de-emphasizing some practices we usually think of as iconic. For example, plea bargaining, the hidden underbelly of sentencing and retributive theory's embarrassment, can, from this new perspective, potentially be understood anew as a place where punishment might happen—as an individualized, merciful settlement of the pain of remorse. But a fuller answer to the question of punishment must await the shift of thought to be made here, and I will return to it at the end of chapter 4. This chapter will engage with traditional and contemporary theories of punishment to sort out which parts of these theories we must leave behind with kanticism and which can point us to a theory more consonant with an understanding of humans as being-in/with.

I. WHAT IS PUNISHMENT? CONSEQUENTIALISM AND KANTICISM IN OUR THEORIES OF PUNISHMENT

We usually start thinking about punishment by dividing theories about it into retribution, deterrence, rehabilitation, and incapacitation. These divisions, however, largely reflect what punishment is *for* but not really what it *is*.[1] We usually see punishment as a tool for achieving something else. Once we begin focusing on what we are trying to achieve, punishment itself disappears from view, like all good tools do.[2] If punishment is for reducing crime, for example, we begin to focus on reducing crime in any way we can—including installing LoJack in cars or better lighting in parking lots. The question of which way of reducing crime counts as punishment runs from view. If punishment is for reducing suffering, we begin to focus on reducing even the suffering caused by punishment itself, and punishment is rejiggered to better fit its use before we even know what it is. Likewise, with punishment that is for deterrence,[3] incapacitation,[4] rehabilitation,[5] communication of norms,[6] curbing free-riders,[7] maximizing republican values,[8] or vindicating and supporting victims,[9] we focus on all ways to deter, incapacitate, rehabilitate, and so on; we fit our "punishments" to these goals, yet we do not call all the ways of achieving the goals "punishment." For example, we may have a parade for the victims to show our solidarity and support, but we do not claim that this is punishment. Which way of achieving these goals is what we call punishment? Punishment as such again escapes us. We begin to think that punishment means nothing in particular— that it is perhaps only violence or pain employed by the government for some (hopefully legitimating) purpose.

Leo Zaibert makes something like this point the basis of his book on punishment and retribution, arguing that it is necessary to construct a necessary and sufficient definition of punishment *before* determining what conditions would justify it. He argues that we must be clear about what punishment is before we can decide how it might be justified. The difficulty with putting it this way, however, is that, like law itself, justification seems to be *part of* what punishment is. Without here reopening the debate between theories of positive law and natural law, the problem is that an unjustified order seems no law at all but merely the "gunman writ large,"[10] since part of the meaning of law is that it obligates, that is, is just. Likewise, an unjustified harm seems no punishment at all but just a harm. Like law, punishment, by definition, at least *purports* to be just, as part of what it is.[11]

Zaibert's attempt to separate definition from justification is instructive. He defines punishment from the perspective of the punisher as an act, believed to be painful, inflicted on the offender in response to a perceived wrong by an angry/resentful blamer.[12] His laudable attempt to avoid both defining punishment by way of a punisher's "intention" and prefiguring a "justification" of punishment in defining it, however, seems to miss something essential to what punishment is. The problem with Zaibert's definition is that there is no link, other than the emotion of the punisher, between the wrong and the harm the punisher imposes. The harm must be imposed not only *in response* to the wrong but *because* of the wrong. Though Zaibert works hard to avoid it, this "because" smuggles in the justifying principle. There must be something about the link between harm 1 and harm 2 that ties them together. Otherwise, we have only harm 1 and then an angry, blaming person inflicting harm 2. The blaming person, in Zaibert's definition, *believes* the punishment is justified (i.e., "the world would be a better place if something happened to B . . . which would somehow offset" the wrong),[13] but that is just the point. It is not really punishment if it does not at least *purport* to be justified.

Looking at punishment as not a tool or piece of equipment for achieving some social goal does not, however, mean looking at it as "unjustified," unless we take justification to require some goal or reason outside of punishment itself, beside which punishment will disappear. Looking at punishment to truly understand its difference from mere violence or harm-for-a-further-purpose requires understanding what sense it makes, what meaning it has. Looking at punishment afresh also means questioning our usual assumption that the punisher's perspective (the subjective perspective) is the right one.

If we think of judgment as an artful unity of our reason with our experience, as Kant's third critique invites us to do, then looking at the judgment involved in punishment as an *art* may make sense. In Heidegger's work on art, he asks, what truth is at work in great art? So we might ask of punishment, what is the work, the meaning, the truth, the sense, of punishment-at-its-best? What happens there, what shows up there, that does not show up in mere harm? What is the happening or event or coming to truth that is punishment? My full answer will come in the next chapter, but I must first consider the traditional retributive answer to the question from our kanticism.

The standard retributivist explanation, from Hegel following Kant, does give us one meaningful account of what punishment-at-its-best is (instead of what it is *for*). The account is a familiar one: If we humans, as creatures of reason, have a categorical imperative to be reasonable, an inexorable duty to follow law rather than nature, reason rather than inclination, then what happens when our "good will" fails? When we follow inclination rather than reason, it is a failure to will, a failure to be in the kingdom of ends, a failure to be fully human. We make ourselves an exception to the rule, and we are thereby cast outside our true nature, alienated from ourselves and others, prisoners of our own solipsism, objects moved by forces of nature, our subjecthood stripped away.

Though our wrong, considered as a harm in the world, is in the past, unreachable for us, our current condition as alienated nonsubjects persists. As Hegel puts it, the continuing actuality of the wrong is in the will of the offender.[14] What remedy is there? How can we regain our place as members of the kingdom of ends? Kant's answer, understood through Hegel's reinterpretation, is that we can stop being exceptions and live under the rule we wrongly willed, as though it were a universal law. The punishment, then, is the rebound of our own act upon us, our suffering the consequences of our own action.

> The penalty which falls on the criminal is not merely *implicitly* just—as just, it is *eo ipso* his implicit will, an embodiment of his freedom, his right; on the contrary, it is also a right *established* within the criminal himself, i.e. in his objectively embodied will, in his action. The reason for this is that his action is the action of a rational being and this implies that it is something universal and that by doing it the criminal has laid down a law which he has explicitly recognized in his action and under which in consequence he should be brought as under his right ... Since that is so, punishment is regarded as containing the criminal's right and hence by being punished he is honoured as a rational being. He does not receive this due of honour unless the concept and measure of his punishment are derived from his own act. Still less does he receive it if he is treated either as a harmful animal who has to be made harmless, or with a view to deterring and reforming him.[15]

Owning/suffering our own action as a universal law brings us back within the kingdom of ends. The offender is no longer an exception, an outcast, an "outlaw." The offender's punishment "is the reconciliation of the criminal with himself, i.e., with the law known by him as his own and as valid for him and his protection; when this law is executed upon him, he himself finds in this process the satisfaction of justice and nothing save his own act."[16] Whether or not an offender subjectively understands his or her punishment this way, objectively, from the Hegelian perspective of world spirit, the offender is reconciled with his or her own humanity. Punishment, then, is the necessary "rebound of our wrong" (and nothing more), which we have a duty to undergo because we are creatures of reason in a kingdom of ends. We then have, as Kant and Hegel tell us, a right to be punished, because we have a right to be honored as reasonable creatures whose actions have meaning and universal import. To fail to punish, to be merciful, is demeaning: it treats the offender as though he or she had no will, had no reason, and "could not help it." The offender remains "irrational," excluded from the kingdom of ends. Punishment, then, is the due (and perhaps even the actualization and spiritual progress) of reason.[17]

The beauty and strength of Hegel's account is that it clarifies both what punishment is and how it relates to a breach of duty. It also matches up with our very strong intuitions that punishment should somehow "fit" the crime and is somehow "due" even when there is no need for deterrence, rehabilitation, victim satisfaction, education, or some other social goal.[18] It shows us punishment as a true "sanction" that sanctifies the offender and makes him or her once again a full member of the community of reason. Hence, the continuing attraction of retribution is that it alone, among all the theories of punishment, says what punishment is and explains why it is necessary to our being who we are (if who we are is conceived as creatures of reason).

This standard account of punishment, however, also makes it very difficult to make a case for mercy. Pardon, leniency, and clemency all seem demeaning—a disrespectful, patronizing, and condescending refusal to give someone her or his full due. As Michael Moore succinctly puts it, "It is elitist and condescending toward others not to grant them the same responsibility and desert you grant to yourself."[19] Kant himself is forced to conclude, "Even if a Civil Society resolved to dissolve itself with the consent of all its members . . . the last Murderer lying in the prison ought to be executed before the resolution was carried out."[20] In this account of punishment, we hear the taunt of Dostoevsky's Grand Inquisitor: "Respecting him less, Thou wouldst have asked less of him. That would have been more like love, for his burden would have been lighter. He is weak and vile."[21]

So how can we respond to Hegel and Kant and the Grand Inquisitor? First, we can take note of the difficulties brought up earlier that are inherent in Kantian metaphysics itself.

1. Respecting moral personhood requires the empirical knowledge that there are, indeed, other reasonable beings out there. Since, according to Kant, we cannot even have empirical knowledge of our own "reason" but have to assume it in order to get on with thinking and acting, how can we have any empirical knowledge of others' reasonableness? We must also take that as a given. The assumption that we are dealing with others who reason is a given—a gift we give each other. It cannot, then, be something "deserved" or required in punishment. It may even be considered as a "mercy" itself. So the fundamental idea of moral "desert" as what is *owed* is itself called into question. Responsibility is given, not deserved.

2. In retribution, we claim that in giving the offender back "his own deed," we are treating the offender as reasonable. But "his own deed" was to treat others precisely not as creatures of reason but as means to his ends, with complete disregard for their having ends of their own. By treating the offender with dignity and humanity, as an end in himself, we are not giving him "his own deed" as a universal law.[22] Retributivism's claim of proportionality in punishment is called into question. Instead, it seems that in respecting the offender's dignity and keeping the penalty "humane" and in line with what is due to a reasonable being, we are not giving out desert but mercy. The dignity limit on punishment is itself a mercy, a gift.

3. In defining punishment in retributive theory, we have a perspective problem. Whose perspective governs? From whose point of view do we define punishment? Whose intentions and beliefs matter? Retributive theories take several different perspectives. That of the subject, or the punisher, focuses on what the punisher intends or believes. That of the object, or the offender, focuses on what corrects the errant will of the offender. That of the indirect object, or the victim, focuses on what repairs the moral injury to the victim. That of the reader, or the community, focuses on what has the social meaning of "punishing." The grammatical categories hold us captive even while our speech about punishment defies them. None of these perspectives seems to capture what punishment is. For example, we can say that one can be punished even if one does not think one is ("he thought it was just bad luck, but it was really a punishment from God"), that one can intend harm to someone as punishment yet fail to punish ("she took her brother's Nintendo away as a punishment, but it was just another move in a continuing war of aggression"), and that one could be punished in private even if the record is sealed and no victim or community "reader" knows of it. Everyday language, of course, may be sloppy, and we *could* define punishment to exclude the validity of one of these statements. But it is not immediately apparent why we should privilege one of these points of view over another.

Hegel's account of punishment solves the problem of perspective because he can, in his own philosophical system, posit an objective, Archimedean standpoint of universal spirit. In Hegel, punishment is man's reconciliation with his own finitude by way of taking a perspective that allows him to see himself as an albeit imperfect manifestation of reason, spirit, or God. To truly understand punishment, according to Hegel, is to take a god's-eye view of it. But Hegel can take this perspective only from the standpoint of a philosopher's god, a perspective not possible for Kant (or for any secular account of punishment, as the previous chapters outlined), except, perhaps, as a convenient assumption.

4. True proportionality in sentencing requires perfect calibration—perfect knowledge of the offense; the relevant motives, beliefs, and intentions of the offender; and any mitigating or aggravating circumstances. Any sentence that is too heavy or too light is wrong from a retributive standpoint, and fails to treat the offender as fully rational. In other words, retributive justice requires judgments of perfect equity. Yet, within the Kantian framework, it is impossible to "know another" like this—as a noumenon, as he is "in himself." Such knowledge is godlike, not human. Only a philosopher's god or Hegelian world spirit could know these things.

5. Hegel and Kant fail to explain the significance of the harm done in crime. While our intuitions about "seriousness" of crimes are based primarily on assessments of criminal intent, the harm done still matters. Are we mistaken to think murder a worse crime than attempted murder? Are we mistaken to think that reckless driving that kills is a worse crime than reckless driving that does not? Why do we care about the harm done at all, if the victim is not, at the level of spirit (or reason), a victim at all (her or his "Kantian self" is untouched) and if all that is left to "fix" is the condition of the offender's will? Is the criminal law's concern with harm done just a legal historical accident that should not have survived the separation of crime from tort? Punishing purely for mens rea, however, seems to suggest we *should* punish for thoughts or mental states alone. Perhaps there is some connection between intentional wrong and harm done that retributive theory is missing.

6. Hegel fails to explain the significance of remorse, yet juries, judges, and victims take remorse into account instinctively. For Hegel, the wrong remains in the criminal's will, and its universal significance, severity and the proportionate sanction are all dependent on the maxim of action of the crime. So, what difference does or should later remorse make? This question will occupy us in chapter 4.

7. What do we do about offenders with children (dependents, debilitated parents or spouses, employees, etc.)? Do we ignore the others who will be harmed by the punishment, since they, too, are not "really" harmed? Is the loss of parental rights and responsibilities (and the family bond) just a side effect that is irrelevant to the sentencing calculation? What do we do about offenders who are heroes (who have risked their lives for others in the past) or who have done great works of community service? Do we ignore these? What do we do about offenders who grew up with poverty, with child abuse, or in other intolerable circumstances? All of these circumstances, often taken into account in sentencing, are irrelevant from the perspective of righting the errant will of the offender.

8. How could we ever afford (or aspire) to institutionalize a system of punishment that requires a sanction for *every* crime, on pain of disrespecting the humanity of both offenders and ourselves?

Many of these objections to Kant/Hegel-derived theories of punishment have been made by others. John Braithwaite and Philip Pettit, for example, argue for a more conciliatory, less retributive approach to punishment.[23] But though they make very telling points against many of the modern retributivists (especially insofar as these theorists tend toward casting punishment as a good *for* something else),[24] and though they argue convincingly that a strictly Hegelian form of punishment would be both infeasible and politically dangerous (as asserted already, we cannot, after all, punish every crime), they never make much headway against the fundamental kanticism that punishment is a moral requirement, essential to the dignity of an offender.[25] So, while they argue that mercy might be a better policy, they never really challenge its questionable philosophical underpinnings. A world in which mercy is the lady of the house might be kinder and gentler and more workable, but the charge that it would demean our humanity and nobility is not laid aside. The shadow of the Grand Inquisitor remains.

Other nonutilitarian theories have also recently been put forward to respond to some of these objections. Among them are victim-centered theories and communication theories. Because of their influence and the importance of what emerges from considering them, I will discuss them a bit here before turning to a theory of punishment that would better fit the turn away from kanticism that I suggested in the first two chapters.

II. VICTIM-CENTERED THEORIES

The victims' rights movement generated a backlash against retributive theories of justice, arguing that a focus on the wrongdoer alone was demeaning to the victim. Recent scholarship has, from many angles, argued that punishment should be victim-centered, not offender-centered; that it should acknowledge and even perhaps dignify emotions of righteous anger and even hatred; that it should recognize the right of victims to have a say in the accusation and sentencing of those who have wronged them. In the philosophical literature, Jean Hampton and Jeffrie Murphy's early book *Forgiveness and Mercy* first suggested that anger and hate could be righteous and that retributivism should be reformulated to recognize that the wrong to be righted was not a defect in the soul or character of the offender but the victim's shame and lost dignity.[26] Robert

Solomon rehabilitated vengeance as "a socially constructed emotion that can be cultivated to contain not only its own limits but a full appreciation of the general good and the law as well."[27] In legal academic circles, George Fletcher, among others, suggested that the purpose of the criminal trial "is neither to change society nor to rectify a metaphysical imbalance in the moral order" but to "stand by the victim,"[28] and he offered up procedural reforms to allow victims standing in the criminal process.

The movement has been extremely influential. Offices of victims' rights have sprung up in most jurisdictions. Victims are allowed to participate in sentencing offenders through victim impact statements and to watch executions,[29] and victims are consulted with regard to plea bargains.[30] A "victims' rights" amendment to the U.S. Constitution was proposed.[31] Victim-prosecuted claims for civil penalties and punitive damages have gained new support.[32]

At its core, the victims' rights movement challenges Kant's and Hegel's assumption that "there are no victims" because no one can be injured in their Kantian dignity. *Harm* can be compensated in tort law, says the Hegelian retributivist, but the *wrong* that concerns the criminal law leaves no mark on the victim's soul, only on the offender's.

Jean Hampton articulates a victim-centered alternative to retributive theory that tries to avoid a utilitarian position of "satisfying victims" or fixing the *harm* (which, again, might be done by parades, tort compensation, relocating victims to safer, gated communities, or allowing them to revenge themselves, rather than through anything we might call punishment). Her challenge is to articulate a theory of righting *wrong, not harm,* that includes righting something besides the unreasonable will of the offender. She argues that the seriousness of the crime is the extent to which a victim has suffered a moral injury to her or his dignity. Crime, she explains, involves an offender's disrespect of the victim and a claim of moral superiority. That claim must be denied through punishment, while the victim's status is restored. Hampton acknowledges that criminals do not always seek to make themselves superior to their victims (they may seek only equality, for example, as when a black South African attacks a wealthy white South African during apartheid),[33] but she argues that crime is nonetheless inherently victim-demeaning as a false statement about what the victim deserves *as a Kantian reasonable person.* The message of superiority, then, is not part of the defendant's mens rea but is read off the crime itself, as a violation of the respect due to reasonable persons.

However, Hampton switches to a different level of abstraction when she asks how this "false message" can be corrected through punishment. In several instances, Hampton acknowledges that it is not the victim's subjective sense of personal dignity nor the victim's reputation that must be restored, or we would have sentencing that varied according to the "value" of the victim, that is, according to either the victim's subjective self-respect or the community's moral evaluation of the victim's character. Victims with no sense of dignity could not claim to have suffered a wrong. At the same time, Hampton claims that punishment must heal the harm to the "realization and acknowledgment" of the victim's admittedly untouchable human dignity.[34] By the time she tries to specify what this amounts to, it is hard to separate her position from a view that punishment is compensation for real psychological harm and loss of reputation.[35] For example, she argues that "diminishment" violates the "victim's entitlements" given her or his inherent dignity.[36] Is this different from harm? Further, Hampton writes that crime "threatens to reinforce belief in the wrong theory of value by the community" and "can encourage the infliction of similar injuries by people who find appealing the apparent diminishment of the victim and the relative elevation effected by the wrongdoing."[37] This begins to sound like both deterrence and compensation for dignitary or reputation harm. In the end, it is hard to separate these dignitary harms from what would be compensable through traditional tort damages.

Moreover, it is not clear how punishment vindicates the victim's dignity. Hampton's answer is that suffering cancels the criminal's message of superiority by "lowering the wrongdoer, elevating the victim, and annulling the act of diminishment."[38] Although Hampton claims that the punishment must not be itself disrespectful to the offender, if punishment is thought of as righting the balance of domination/subjugation in some sort of moral seesaw, it would seem to require that the offender be humbled or shamed in order to bring him or her back down.[39] Yet, to demean and humble the offender is to disrespect him or her, breaching the relationship again rather than healing it. A cycle of revenge would seem to begin here, rather than end.

Despite these objections, there is something to be learned from our unease with the traditional view that there are no victims in a moral sense, and it has to do with the moral significance of consequences. Again, our kanticism tells us that consequences do not matter, morally speaking. We should not punish someone who does great harm accidentally, because there is no "bad will" to punish. Yet in many areas of our actual criminal law, consequences do matter and used to matter still more. Despite the reforms suggested by the Model Penal Code,[40] most jurisdictions still do punish completed crimes more severely than attempted crimes.[41] Likewise, offenses that result in great losses are generally punished more harshly than those that result in small losses,[42] mens rea being equal. The doctrine of public welfare offenses[43] and vicarious responsibility for some organizational leaders[44] lingers on, despite academic complaints.

From a kanticism standpoint, the result element of a crime appears as an unreasonable bit of "moral luck."[45] We cannot control the consequences of our actions; holding us responsible for them is to make sentencing turn on chance. Yet, as Michael Moore argues, the same kind of luck or chance may be inextricable from mens rea, conduct, and attendant circumstance elements of crimes as well.[46] He points out that causation is extremely difficult to separate from the "mens rea" of crime, because a momentary mental distraction can be just as significant in the causal chain leading from forming an intention to committing a crime as the wind's effect on the trajectory of a bullet.

The puzzling and uncertain place that harm has in criminal law boils down to a simple truth: our minds are not in control of the world (or even of themselves), and yet we are responsible for our actions. If we were perfect (disembodied) creatures of reason, we could not act in a world at all. But we are not creatures of reason; we are beings-in-a-world. As we shall see, as beings-in-a-world, we are obligated to respond to consequences that we neither consciously risked nor intended. The wrong and the harm are not as distinct as retributive theory would have us believe, and the victims' rights theorists have a point.

III. COMMUNICATION THEORIES

A set of contemporary punishment theories that purport to allow leniency or reconciliation to take a more important role, but that also aspire to retain the retributivist insistence on respect for the offender's personhood, are "communicative" theories of punishment.[47] R. A. Duff's theory is among the most comprehensive and closely reasoned, so I will treat it as representative, to some extent.

"Communication" theories of punishment try to explicate punishment as a form of communication or confrontation with the offender that "negates" the crime by denouncing it and inflicting what Duff calls "secular penance."[48] Like Kant and Hegel, Duff argues that punishment must respect the moral personhood of the offender. However, respecting moral personhood does not require bringing the offender under her or his own universal law. Instead, it requires that the denunciation or communication not "bypass" the moral reason of the offender but at least attempt to persuade the offender, to show the offender the nature and extent of her wrong and argue that she should repent of it. This argument may include an imposed (involuntary) penalty that serves to drive home the message about the nature and extent of the wrong as well as providing the offender an opportunity to focus and reflect over time on the nature of her crime, come to a "deep" remorse, and "make clear to the victim and to the community as a whole" that she "really does repent her crime" and "seeks to make apologetic reparation for it."[49] While reconciliation with the community is thought of as an "end" here, it is an end "internal to practice" and must be achieved through the workings of reason, so that the offender is "treated" not as an object of nature to be motivated by force but as a reasonable being to be engaged.

While I am much in sympathy with this line of argument, there are difficulties with the way communication is conceived. The "communication" of wrongdoing cannot really be the point of punishment (as a goal), or a lecture or well-researched ad campaign, for example, could be the more appropriate mode of proceeding, causing less suffering, more persuasion, and so on. Duff acknowledges this point but responds that we need "hard treatment" in order to make us (distractible, morally imperfect human beings that we are) *really attend* to the crime we have done and "seriously repent" (107). But are there not cases in which a television ad campaign would do more to awaken our contrition than a legal penalty? The power of art to move may be stronger than the power of the probation officer or prison warden. Why should an honestly and thoroughly repentant offender need to undertake a prison term, say, in order to publically demonstrate the sincerity of his remorse over a period of time? If sincerity is the only issue, then there may be better ways of "demonstrating sincerity"—a lie detector test or brain imaging, for example. Does imposition of a more painful undertaking really demonstrate more sincerity; that is, does more pain yield more honesty? Or does it merely make the offender more wary, bitter, and secretive?

Moreover, the "message" of punishment is not in addition to the punishment itself but must be inherent or implicit in it. Any explicit message attached to the practice itself is neither necessary nor sufficient to make something a punishment. For example, when I separate and isolate my children in a "timeout" after they have been trading insults, they do not need to be told that the deprivation I inflict is because of a wrong they have done, or that "this is a punishment" rather than a mere whim of mine. Conversely, my daughter will often impose a self-styled "punishment" on my son with all the express communication of her intent that theories of punishment as communication might seem to envision. As Duff recognizes, saying something is a punishment does not make it one (and my son certainly does not take it as such).

The key difficulty with the "communication" analysis that precipitates these kinds of objections is based on the "communication" idea itself. The theory seems to envision the process of punishment as society's trying to implant a meaning in the defendant's head. This stems from a prior understanding of language (and meaning itself) as the intention of the speaker, which then is transferred through language to the mind of the listener. The intention of the speaker determines meaning, just as, in Duff's theory, the intention of the punisher determines punishment. Language, or the pain imposed as a "communication," is a tool by means of which the speaker's "meaning" comes through to the listener or offender.

But as Lewis Carroll famously pointed out in Alice's encounter with Humpty Dumpty, language is not the slave of intention anymore than law is what we "merely posit."[50] As Heidegger teaches us, we *find* (and sometimes fumble for) words, themselves already imbued with a history of meaning, and they help us formulate and clarify our thoughts in the first place. Intention does not precede meaning; it follows it, is formed in and framed by a "prearticulation" of our world that is already there in practices and history. As Hubert Dreyfus explains, "A surgeon does not have words for all the ways he cuts, or a chess master for all the patterns he perceives"; yet the possibility for words is *already there* in the very discriminations of significance that both masters make.[51] Speaking is more like a pointing to something already "outside" of my mind than it is like a mind dump or download of my brain into another's.[52] Likewise, the meaning of punishment is not in the intentions of the punisher but is what appears from a place in which we see together that a wrong has occurred. Sometimes the offender already sees the wrong. Sometimes it is necessary for me to point it out. But what you see is not what I have in my mind and "communicate" to you but the wrong itself, the thing that my talk is about in the first place. What you experience or undergo when you see the wrong—not what or how I "communicate" to you—is what punishment is. This changes the perspective from which we look at punishment, from the "content" of a "communication" of my "intention" to what is to be seen. I do not impose pain on you in order to communicate a message about the seriousness of your wrong. Instead, I point to the wrong. Looking at the wrong, experiencing the wrong, undergoing the wrong as a wrong, *is itself* painful.[53]

Once punishment is no longer couched as "communication," the question whether some "other mode" of communication will better generate remorse simply does not arise. Pain unconnected with the wrong is just pain. Saying "See what you've done" and administering an electric shock at the same time would disconnect the pain from the wrong and associate it instead with the saying or the sayer. Yet "punishment as communication" theories seem to take the view that making the "message" painful will cause the defendant to associate the pain with the wrong. The point, however, is not to make the message painful in order to "get" the offender to associate pain with the wrong. This is mere behaviorism of the kind Duff abjures, and, indeed, he would object to this restatement. Yet this displacement of punishment's focus from the "wrong" to a "communication about the wrong" has this consequence. That is why a "painful" message is not always associated with remorse but is (perhaps more often) associated with resentment.[54] The point is to "point" to the wrong itself; that, not the message, is what the offender should attend to. Punishment is not my "intention" to "communicate" a message of condemnation about the crime from my consciousness to yours, in a painful way that will cause you to have a negative association with the crime, but the evocation of a memory of the crime itself, as I will explain in chapter 4.

Finally, there is a curious leap in the "punishment as communication" theory when it comes to the measure of punishment. Why is the penance or punishment to be measured by the wrong done, instead of by what is necessary to induce remorse, given, say, the likelihood of insincerity of remorse or the history of falsehood? Duff tells us that "a harsher sentence portrays the crime as more serious."[55] But to whom is the crime so portrayed? If the "whom" is the public, then this account becomes expressivist, not communicative, and threatens to turn into a Durkheimian or Feinbergian utilitarian theory about punishment as an occasion for reinforcement of community values and "expression" of condemnation.[56] If the "whom" is the offender, then why should it necessarily be the case that "a harsher sentence portrays the crime as more serious"? As I pointed out already, it is a common experience that a particular offender may become truly remorseful with only a word, while a harsher penalty may evoke resentment, not repentance. Duff's proportionality requirement (making the harshness of the sentence fit the crime) smuggles in features of traditional retribution that are not accounted for by the condemnation/remorse structure. It is the penalty that ought to fit the crime; not the "communication" of the penalty. While the proportionality of crime and penalty may make more sense in Duff's theory as *secular penance* or *expiation*, it does not make sense as "communication."

Duff's theory describes many things that seem key to a theory of punishment: moral suasion, remorse, and penance. The problem is that using "communication of condemnation" and "sincerity" of remorseful response as a way to describe or understand them seems not to fit with the retributive ground that Duff wishes to retain. What Duff's account brings importantly to the fore, however, is that the *personal confrontation with the wrong is critically important to what punishment is*. The next chapter expands on that insight.

CHAPTER 4

A New Approach: The Mercy of Punishment

As the last chapter sketched out, traditional accounts of punishment, whether utilitarian or retributivist, are not adequate. Yet they provide us with direction. We must articulate an understanding of punishment that sees it as (1) more than a *tool* for achieving something else, (2) somehow connected with both the wrongful intention and the harmful consequence of crime, and (3) giving central consideration to a personal confrontation with the wrong. Finally, to explain how this understanding of punishment can coexist with mercy, we must explain how mercy can be nondemeaning and not in contradiction with ideas of equality and responsibility.

If we take the turn to Heidegger and Levinas suggested in chapter 2, what is punishment from that new perspective? Taking a cue from Heidegger's "The Origin of the Work of Art," as suggested in the last chapter, we might look at punishment as a work,[1] rather than as a tool. As a work, punishment stands apart from the intentions of any user, viewer, maker, or person punished. Punishment becomes an event, a coming-to-presence of a truth, and not a mere act of violence of one person upon another to be justified. We must ask not what punishment is *for* but, instead, what truth punishment opens for us.

To parallel Hegel's account of retributive punishment, the truth of punishment from our new place of understanding must be deeply connected to restoring us to full humanity. But if we consider ourselves *Dasein,* as beings-with-others-in-a-world rather than as beings of reason, then all the answers change. Wrong is no longer to be understood as a failure of will and reason. Punishment can no longer be the restoration of an offender to his or her full humanity as reasonable/willful. Punishment, if it restores, would restore us instead to our full human condition as being-in and being-with.

As we have seen, being-in-and-with has a temporal dimension. We did not compose ourselves from nothing; rather, we live and think by taking on themes given to us by a past and improvising on them in light of an imagined future. So it is helpful, in understanding what punishment is, what truth it shows, to think of punishment in temporal terms. Punishment, like being-in-the-world generally, has always a past, present, and future aspect.

Heidegger describes these three moments of our being-in-the-world. He calls the past aspect of being-in-the-world *Befindlichkeit,* often translated as "thrownness" or "attunement" (though more literally, "where we find ourselves"). As we are human, we always come to our understanding of the world in medias res, from the middle of an ongoing cultural, familial, and historical story, and we understand ourselves and our world only on the basis of where we happen to begin from, where we happen to have been "thrown" into the plot. Likewise, our understanding is only from our embodiment, from the bodies, senses, and emotions we start with and from which we know and perceive our world. As explained in chapter 2, our emotional attunement channels and "tunes in" our thinking.

Heidegger calls the present aspect of being-in-the-world *Verstand,* "understanding." The present gathers our past and projects it into a future. It is how we understand and make sense of where we have been thrown, knitting past and future together in our thinking and our doing. Our understanding "owns up to" the limited future possibilities available to us from a past that we did not create. So, instead of seeing "choice" as a godlike moment of infinite freedom in accord with universal reason, as law's kanticism might, Heidegger sees our doings and thinkings as conditioned and channeled and made available by our past and by the possibilities open to us in a limited future.

Heidegger calls the future aspect of being-in-the-world *Rede,* or "speech." *Rede* is the coming to language of sense and meaning of the world and its people. It is the future aspect of being-in-the-world because language always points beyond itself, to other analogous things: for example, the simple word *chair* encompasses many chairs we have never even seen. Our words morph and embrace the unknown, launching us into the future through their capacity for analogy and metaphor. One might say, for example, "Oh, so this new contraption is a 'far-hearing'—a 'tele-phone.' I get it." Because words allow us to make sense of the new, they allow us to project from past experiences, to promise, to guide, to direct, to command, to go on in the same way.

The next sections try to use these three temporal aspects of being-in-the-world to explain what wrong and its punishment might be from our new, "grace before reason" being-in-and-with perspective. Because, as I will argue, one feature of the work of punishment is that we experience temporality in an unusual way, the discussion will be clearer if I begin with the present aspect of punishment (the self-understanding of punishment as "for a wrong"), return to the past aspect (the attunement from which we see the wrong), and then discuss the future aspect (the coming to language of the wrong).

I. THE *VERSTAND* OF PUNISHMENT: WRONG AS "OBDURATE INDIFFERENCE"

The first question in understanding punishment is, what does it mean, from our being-in-the-world perspective, to "own" a crime, to say that there was a wrong in the past and the wrong was *mine*? This is the problem of responsibility.

Our kanticism would say that responsibility depends on the maxim of our action—our purpose in our doing. The present aspect of responsibility, in the terms of our kanticism, is a "choosing." The question traditionally put is, knowing what we knew then, could we have done otherwise? Criminal law (and its modern distillation in the Model Penal Code) spells out responsibility into three criminal mental states of culpability: the familiar trilogy of purpose, knowledge, and recklessness (awareness of substantial and unjustifiable risk).[2] Without action-plus-at-least-awareness-of-risk, criminal responsibility is "disfavored," and negligence liability and strict liability are thought to be inappropriate as the basis of criminal liability. How could you have acted differently at the time if you were not aware of any risk? If you could not have acted any differently, how could you be said to have freely chosen to do wrong? Likewise, from the kanticism standpoint, responsibility for a nondoing seems suspect and exceptional: I should be responsible only for what I will and *choose* to do, not for all the infinite things (in that infinite and unconfined moment of choosing) that I did *not* choose to do.

So, what is the nature of responsibility from the new place that Heidegger and Levinas call us to? To spell this out would require a book of its own. But thanks to others who have approached this question before, I can say at least enough here to allay the objection that an approach grounded in being-in-the-world-with-others undermines responsibility or puts us completely at odds with our practices.

Desmond Manderson, in his book *Proximity, Levinas, and the Soul of Law,* thinks through the question of Levinasian responsibility with regard to tort law. The first important point is that, unlike in our kanticism, the default rule is not "no responsibility." The default position in Levinas is that I am responsible whenever I am able to respond.[3] My duty extends to all of those who are in proximity to me, and it is a duty to respond to their need of me, whether I am the cause of that need or not.[4] Whether I have breached my duty to respond, Manderson says, may depend on what other obligations to respond I had at the time, how unique my ability to respond was, and whether others were better able to respond. But the duty itself is based on being-with, or proximity, not, at least primarily, on fault or choice to do wrong. Hence, "duty to rescue" becomes the paradigm of responsibility in tort, and negligence or intentional tort liability is derivative.

As beings-in-a-world, we can be responsible for not-doing without that responsibility becoming infinite. We come from a past; we do not have unlimited choice in every moment but have, instead, a sculpted and channeled set of choices. Not doing what we are called by situation and proximity to do is a failure to respond, to be responsible.

In a similar fashion, criminal responsibility must now be grounded in being-with, marked off from tort law perhaps only by being a yet-more-serious failure to respond. So when do we breach our duty in such a way as to be criminal? This requires working out the second piece: if I am responsible insofar as I am able to respond to others in proximity, then when is my in/action wrong?

If we recur to Kant for a starting place, he tells us that a violation of the moral law treats rational nature as a means only, not as an end in itself. In other words, I am wrong when I fail to respect others as fully reasonable. Translating this after our turn to Heidegger requires changing this account a bit, because rational nature is no longer what "we" are. What "we are" is *Dasein*, those who are already in and already with, those who have a relation to Being and to each other. So, wrong is treating *Dasein* as a tool, which means *not* seeing the other, for the being of equipment always hides, and so the other disappears in one's own projects and goals. Not seeing the other is also to hide one's own nature as being-with from oneself, to seem to be other than *Dasein*. As in Kant's and Hegel's accounts, wrong estranges us from others and from ourselves. So when we use people, they become invisible to us. They are, for us, merely in the way or on the way to something else—money, satisfaction of desire, power, status, or merely finishing a project. I myself come to inhabit a world cut off from the others "that" disappear, a world of self-reference, so absorbed in my doings that I fail to see all the ways in which what I do or do not do depends on, connects with, and involves others. As I imagine myself less and less "with" others, I find myself more and more in a solipsistic world of fantasy, self-justification, secrets, lies, and self-deceptions. The perspectives of offender and victim diverge, creating a place where no language, no sense, no conversation is possible. As becomes apparent in the discussion that follows, the split in perspective (victim-centered vs. offender-centered vs. witness/community-centered) that has haunted theories of punishment is the rift created by the wrong itself and is part of what must be healed in the work of punishment.

So, wrong is a failure to attend to others. This may be both a harm as a mindless using or a failure to attend to another's urgent need of me.[5] In this disunion of wrong, we see ourselves no longer in the light of a world but as disconnected, estranged, unable to "be ourselves" with others, misunderstood, unique, lonely, different, or superior. A *Dasein* cut off from world is no longer *Dasein*. We need the history, culture, meaning, sense, place, and reliability of world in order to know or be ourselves at all. We are ourselves only with others.

By contrast, when we live with others "justly" and "graciously," they do not disappear as equipment, but their own "end-in-themselvesness," "purposiveness," or "on-the-wayness," shines through for us. We see our connection with others, our working together, as part of a pattern woven from all of our particular capabilities and interests and projections, past and present. The experience of working well with someone else means anticipating their needs, fitting into a rhythm of work with them, each improving the projects of the other. Good cowriters or cooks or surgical teams or orchestras or football teams or marriages or furniture makers or factory operations or conversations or classrooms all share this sense of rhythm, anticipation, mutual dependence, and mutual appreciation. Sometimes, when the work is flowing like this, it sings. This is the just as the fitting, the beautiful.

But there is also the element of sublimity. We cannot assume that we know everything about our partners-in-work. There is always a height, a hidden well of depth, an experience unshared. We tender ourselves humbly, not expecting full understanding, only reaching toward a better footing. Practices of discretion, dignity, manners, compromise, tact, space, silence, humility, respectful disagreement, reasoned non–ad hominem discussion, and forms and limits of polite address[6] enact the sublime element of the just in being-with.

How do we translate these ideas into the traditional doctrine of criminal law? Samuel Pillsbury takes us part of the way there by suggesting that traditional accounts of the minimal criminal mental state of recklessness as "awareness of risk" do not really capture the heart of what is "wrongful." His work on crimes of "indifference"[7] suggests that the basic criminal mental state is more like the "obdurate indifference"[8] of one who ignores others and is "indifferent" to their worth as human beings, rather than the positive knowledge of a risk to others in choosing to act.[9] Our paradigmatic criminal is not merely a Jack the Ripper but also an Ebenezer Scrooge, Judith Shklar's coldhearted and indifferent judge,[10] or even ourselves as legislators, when we enact three-strikes laws or harsh mandatory penalties with "obdurate indifference" to the concrete results in particular cases when those rules are applied.[11]

Traditional "recklessness" as *conscious awareness* of the risk, in fact, seems less wrongful than such indifference, because at least when we notice a risk to others, we are on the way to being aware of our connection with others.[12] What is *my* wrong, then, is a failure to see the other, an "obdurate indifference" as to how my doings and omissions affect and connect with others. In the following brief sections, I sketch the beginnings of the doctrinal shift that this perspective might allow, showing that many of the current "puzzles" of criminal law make more sense if we think of "obdurate indifference to others" as the basic criminal wrong.

Causation and Proximate Causation

First, our "effects" on others assume a new importance. The "crime" is located not just in my errant and disobedient will, in my mens rea, but in *my failure to care about and respond to* the "effects" of my actions/inactions on others.[13] Every class studying criminal law puzzles over why we punish murder or vehicular homicide more seriously than attempted murder or reckless driving, if the culpable mental state is the same. We puzzle over why we have a duty to rescue when we have caused harm only innocently. The drafters of the Model Penal Code attempted to change the law in this area to accord more with kanticism principles, equalizing the penalties for attempted and completed crimes. But their attempt was to no avail; states continue to impose much harsher sentences on crimes that cause harm.

From a being-in/with understanding, it is easier to explain why we take the proximate consequences of crime into account in grading the severity of crimes. I am a body, not just a mind. If I care about others—that is, if I am true to my being as being-with—then what happens to them matters to me. In causing, even innocently, a trauma of suffering, I am implicated in that pain. I share in it, *own* it, respond to it; it is *mine*. The more pain I cause, the more pain I will feel. If my causation is coupled with a selfish act or failure to respond, my sense

of ownership of that suffering will be even greater. As we will see later, this remorse *is* the pain of punishment, the way in which the punishment fits the
crime. The "agent regret" that commentators try to explain away as severable
from criminal culpability is, on this view, natural and just, not a somewhat irrational reaction to a tragedy "not my fault." As beings-in-a-world, we rightly
feel responsible for harm we cause. Our bodies are us. When they are involved,
we are involved. This means that sometimes we will be held responsible and be
punished out of proportion to or even without a "choice" to harm.

Though this idea seems heretical, it makes more sense of our actual criminal law: we are much harder on those who cause harm, mens rea being equal.
In our criminal law, we do allow forms of liability—vicarious liability, felony
murder liability, conspiracy liability, and strict liability—that are not strictly
tied to "bad choices" and that make us responsible for consequences we may
not have foreseen or even known of. In fact, we do this far more frequently than
we think we do.[14] Fathers must pay child support whether or not they intended
to have children; liquor stores must pay fines whether or not they intended to
sell to minors; those who nonnegligently cause an accident are held responsible
for seeking help for those injured; those who negligently or intentionally injure
are responsible for all injuries to their victim, no matter how out of proportion
to their fault; those who have sex with those too young are held responsible regardless of their lack of knowledge of their partner's age; those who conspire
with others may be responsible for their coconspirators' actions, no matter if
they knew or anticipated the act or even knew the coconspirator; those who
commit serious felonies may be responsible for deaths that occur in the course
of that felony, no matter how unlikely or unintentional; batterers may be guilty
of murder whether or not they intended to kill; drunk driving that accidentally
causes a death is sentenced far more harshly than drunk driving that does not;
and so forth. Intention still matters as an indication of how *much* we have repudiated our connection with others, but it is not always determinative of
wrong. Proximity and consequences also matter. Though Holmes may be right
that even dogs know the difference between being kicked and being tripped
over, tripping over the dog still calls for a response—at the least an apology and
a reassuring ear rub. My hope here is that if we openly acknowledge that criminal responsibility not only is for "bad choices" or "bad people" but is sometimes what "happens" to us, then we must also understand sentencing differently, as I explain later in this chapter.

We do not and should not, however, claim responsibility for a share of all
the suffering of everyone forever, for that would again be to see ourselves as

godlike, unconditioned by our "thrownness" in a world. We can only respond and be responsible, as we are in criminal law, for consequences proximate to our place, capacities, and movement in the world.[15] Proximate cause is not therefore an arbitrary cutoff of liability for reasons of efficiency or "policy," as it is sometimes understood, but an explicit legal recognition of our finitude and the way in which responsibility is local to a point in space and time. Causation that goes "too far" or lasts "too long" moves beyond the spatiotemporal limits in which I live and within which I respond and am responsible. The temporal limits are also limits of what I can be expected to enfold in my day-to-day care.

Grading of Offenses

Thinking through these ideas of "proximity and "indifference" may also give us more insight into the way in which we understand the grading of offenses. Betrayal or injury to those closest to and most in need of us is usually considered "worse"than injuries to those less in need of us. This would explain why child neglect, a crime of omission and negligence, seems "worse" than intentionally check kiting. What is culpable is not so much the intention to do wrong but the betrayal of connection and the indifference to another's vulnerability to and dependency on us. Likewise, crimes done from "passion" seem less serious than crimes done from a "calculating coldness," precisely because the latter crimes proceed from a *lack* of connectedness with others, while the former proceed from a strong, but distorted, connection with others—even though the purpose to injure in both cases may be the same.

On the same principle, the victim's behavior may matter, too. Being-with means that wrong is about relationships, not mental states. Early versions of the provocation doctrine emphasized that responsibility for harm may be shared: if the victim assaulted or seriously wronged the defendant, the defendant's penalty was mitigated, even though retributive theories struggle mightily with the rationale for such mitigation. If one examines only the culpable mental state, defendants who are provoked still intended to kill wrongfully. Why the actions of a victim should matter is not clear.

Further, juries and prosecutors are naturally more sympathetic to, for example, a father who attacks the nonnegligent driver who accidentally killed his child, even though a strictly retributive account of punishment could not take such an "innocent" provocation into account at all. Similarly, a strictly retributive account cannot understand euthanasia as anything less than intentional murder. A being-with account of wrong can explain our tendency to mitigate responsibility in these cases, despite kanticism, precisely because it can acknowledge the victim's provocation, causation, suffering, or consent as relevant to the nature of the wrong. Acknowledging that wrong is immersed in relationships may also explain the importance in our criminal procedure requirement of *confrontation*, as I argue later in this chapter.

Defenses

Traditional theories of duress did not allow a defendant to kill an innocent person to save oneself. Yet, from the frame of kanticism's standpoint of individual culpability, it is hard to see why I cannot prefer the saving of my own rational self to the saving of another person's rationality. Both are equal in the kanticism tradition. But in a being-in/with frame, the heroism that criminal law requires makes more sense. I cannot be I without the other. If Levinas is right, I have a duty to prefer the other over myself. The other, at a height, requires the sacrifice of self.

Being-with demands heroism in this situation, not selfishness. In accord with the traditional theories of criminal law, it only justifies killing in self-defense or defense of others when a wrongdoer immediately threatens life or serious injury. The self-defense allowed by the traditional rule of criminal law cannot, then, be premised on a right to choose self over other; it must instead be grounded in a right to resist wrong. Though the Model Penal Code has changed the duress rule to allow an excuse for killing an innocent when threatened with death, this doctrine does not jibe with traditional doctrines against using innocents as "shields" or with traditional rules refusing duress excuses to those who are told to kill or be killed. Like the Model Penal Code's proposed rules equalizing penalties for attempt and completed crimes, the code's new duress rule has not been followed in many states. That we have refused, for thirty years, to adjust criminal law in accord with kanticism in these areas suggests that our intuitions are deeply against such reforms. It seems that what we actually do may be more consonant with a view of ourselves as being-with and with an extensive responsibility for others not entirely limited by principles of culpability and mens rea.

The details of an entire criminal jurisprudence understood from a being-with perspective would need more working out, of course. The point of this section is merely to sketch out the place from which it must start and to show, I hope, that we would end up in a more familiar, rather than less familiar, place. Theory cannot determine practice but can, at best, illuminate it. The key point here is that understanding ourselves as, at core, beings-in/with, rather than beings of reason, may help explain many things about the criminal law that retributive theory cannot.

II. THE *BEFINDLICHKEIT* OF PUNISHMENT AS PAIN

From the context of our present, or moment of *Verstand,* we are coming to understand wrong as a failure in our response to others, an obdurate indifference to their reliance on us or vulnerability to us, or an intimate causal connection to their suffering, which is now in the past. What is the *Befindlichkeit* of punishment; that is, where do we find ourselves? What is the emotional mood or attunement associated with the experience of a past wrong as wrong?

This question opens up a helpful window, because one of the continuing puzzles about punishment is why we tend to think it must be painful. Why does community service not seem like punishment, we ask?[16] Why do nonpainful punishments, like fines for the rich, seem to be mere "taxes" that fail to convey opprobrium or come across as crime-trivializing "slaps on the wrist?" Why can we not be satisfied with just "communicating" the wrong to the offender through mediation or conversation?

Perhaps the answer is that pain is the *Befindlichkeit* of punishment. This is reinforced by the etymology of the word *punishment.* Philippe Nonet connects the Greek root to Ponus, the god of toil, sorrow, and pain, offspring of night and discord.[17] In French, *poena* means "pain," from which we have our English word. Nietzsche suggests that the etymological connection to pain and to Ponus, the issue of discord who works in pain, may point to something crucial.

Nietzsche tells us that "pain is the most powerful aid to mnemonics."[18] This is helpful already, because the wrong done is always in the past, and we know that righting the wrong (if this is what punishment does) must have something to do with the past. So, perhaps, the pain triggers a memory of the wrong, or vice versa. What is revealed or experienced in this memory?

As we have seen, some theories of punishment hold that in punishing, we are hurting the offender's false pride so as to vindicate the victim's worth. Is the worthiness of the victim or the ordinariness of the offender something that pain reveals? Not always or necessarily—not all victims are worthy, and not all offenders are ordinary. Other theories of punishment hold that in punishing, the law is vindicated or reinforced. But what kind of law would need vindication or reinforcement through pain? Only an uncertain law, perhaps one that we have trouble remembering. Even so, it does not seem that inflicting pain would make an uncertain or questionably just law more well-founded, as opposed to more memorable. Nor does it seem that frightening citizens with pain would make them more respectful rather than merely more wary. The law that is only remembered in pain is a law that would seem to command not respect or awe but only conformity—the law of a gunman.

So what is the memory of one's own wrong (as wrong)? At least in serious wrongs where the harm caused is profound,[19] a memory of the wrong is painful—indeed, traumatic. Psychological accounts of trauma point to several of its features that would seem to help us understand the *Befindlichkeit* of punishment. First, trauma is often an experience delayed—an experience that one was numb to at the time and later "first" experiences as a vividly painful, intrusive, "possessing," and repetitive memory or dream.[20] Second, "the history of a trauma, in its inherent belatedness, can only take place through the listening of another."[21] Third, what is traumatic is not just physical pain but senseless and meaningless pain, the loss of hope, the loss of love and loved ones, the loss of security and "common sense"—all resulting in the loss of self.[22] Fourth, the experience of trauma is connected with a loss of language—an alexithymia—again underscoring the shock of its "meaninglessness" and inability to capture the emotions in speech.[23] Fifth, victim trauma often involves "survivor guilt" and a transference with the enemy, perhaps as a way of making sense of the loss through self-blame.[24] Sixth, the experience of witnessing another's trauma, being the "addressee" of the delayed experience of trauma, may also involve "a transference of pain" and create trauma for the witness.[25] Seventh, the "capacity to witness and the act of bearing witness in themselves embody some remedial quality and belong already, in obscure ways, to the healing process."[26] Eighth, owning up to one's own failure and shame is particularly painful and may require the mediation of speech to work out the emotion.[27] Finally, trauma has the potential to split the ego, splintering the perspectives of offender and victim (as I noted earlier).

In this psychological literature, then, one begins to see certain parallels emerging. Neither the offender nor the victim may experience the wrong as wrong when it occurs. In fact, the more shocking or wrongful the wrong, the less likely is it that those involved will feel it or fully experience it at the time.[28] Hence, the *Befindlichkeit* of the wrong comes *after* understanding, rather than before, as a present experience of a past that was not experienced before.

To illustrate this phenomenon, Freud cites Tasso's epic hero Tancred, who "unwittingly kills his beloved Clorinda in a duel while she is disguised in the armour of an enemy knight." Freud explains, "After her burial he makes his way into a strange magic forest which strikes the Crusaders' army with terror. He slashes with his sword at a tall tree; but blood streams from the cut and the voice of Clorinda, whose soul is imprisoned in the tree, is heard complaining that he has wounded his beloved once again."[29] Trauma, concludes Cathy Caruth, interpreting Freud, "is not locatable in the simple violent or original event in an individual's past, but rather in the way that its very unassimilated nature—the way it was precisely *not known* in the first instance—returns to haunt the survivor later on."[30]

Not only may the traumatic experience of wrong be delayed, but it is chaotic, for wrong dissolves the bonds of mutual understanding that make understanding and even selfhood possible. Trauma, as the literature explains it, involves repetitive, obsessive dreams that prevent one from returning to a stable understanding of the world. The world has become chaotic, and one is forced to reexperience what one cannot assimilate, what does not make sense. In the *Befindlichkeit* of punishment, the split of perspectives caused by the wrong itself is patent: victim and offender are cut off from each other, each locked in a separate kind of trauma that cannot be brought to language and therefore cannot be shared. Hence, we must now talk about the pain of wrong from each perspective separately before we can bring them together again.

Fear

The victim's trauma is marked by an inability to articulate emotions, by a loss of language. The wrong was senseless, meaningless, an act one cannot understand, carried out by a human-appearing monster who does not share one's core sense of right and wrong. The trauma is caused, in part, by the "being hated in the act."[31] The victim's world is topsy-turvy. How could such a radical misunderstanding be possible, the victim asks? Was I at fault somehow to generate so much hate?[32] The senselessness and groundlessness of the violence is at the root of the victim's pain. Extreme fear and anxiety accompanies this loss of meaning. Nothing can be taken for granted. No one can be trusted. A "reasonable" universe would not let such things happen; therefore, the universe must no longer be reasonable.

From this standpoint, anger and accusation are a response to this senselessness, a response that insists the wrong be labeled as wrong, a response that needs desperately to give the violence a meaning and to leave the horror of senselessness behind. From anger and accusation comes the desire for vengeance, a desire to blot out and destroy the person who injects such radical uncertainty into the world, to slay the perpetrator as an "irrational" monster, a harbinger of unreason. Anger is a desperate desire to escape the senselessness of the wrong. But anger is only fear put into action.[33] The fear of senselessness is still operating, and that fear of senselessness recurs as the past violence is experienced over and over again in trauma, unable to be assimilated, unable to be comprehended, paralyzing and silencing the victim.

Remorse

The offender, too, experiences trauma, in a different, though parallel, way. Remorse, like guilt, requires that one believe one has done wrong. But remorse is more than a cool belief or recognition. The Latin roots of the word *remorse* mean "to bite again." Unpacking this metaphor reveals much about the essence of this emotion/cognition. First, biting is painful. Bites are jagged, tearing, unclean, animal-like, ignoble, inhuman, disgusting. One experiences revulsion at one's own deed, one's own crime.[34]

This bite is also a rebite, a return of a bite. Remorse is the return of one's own crime, again and again. In remorse, one becomes one's own victim. The victim is another I, a singular, concrete, vivid *face*, not a general category, type, group, or number[35]—hence the effectiveness of racism in avoiding remorse.[36] One feels the pain of the crime one has committed and the particular loss to an irreplaceable other that one has caused.[37] But the pain rebounds in a peculiar way: one is both the biter and the bitten. Not only does one suffer the pain one inflicted on one's victim, but one also suffers both the pain and the degradation of having inflicted it. The pain is re-flected. One is pained both by the pain and by one's own reflection as the one who inflicted the pain.

Remorse bites again in another way, too. It recurs; it lives inside one, and it continues to bite. There is no way out from oneself. In the deepest circle of his Hell, Dante imagines sinners are eaten over and over and over. The biting of remorse is remorseless and eternal. Nietzsche says that it would take a truly heroic being to will the eternal return of the same. To own and live with each of our actions through an eternity of lives would be the ultimate heroism and the ultimate horror. Yet that is the nature of remorse. We must own, hold to us, and keep with us each of our actions, though it bite and sting.

Hence, remorse is often accompanied by forms of self-inflicted pain. Oedipus blinds himself, monks whip themselves, teenagers cut themselves. Offenders seek out destructive relationships or onerous forms of service, like Briony in Ian McEwan's novel *Atonement*,[38] who volunteers as a nurse's assistant in the military hospital during World War II to punish herself for falsely accusing her sister's lover of rape. One way or another, the remorseful demand their own suffering. The physical pain seems to blunt the mental pain, to ease the biting conscience. Physical pain may seem less painful than remorse, may seem to re-place it and externalize it—literally, to expiate it. But unless the physical suffer-ings keep recurring, remorse, like the vengeful anger of the victim, only perpet-uates the violence, and something else must be done. Expiation alone does not destroy the self-hatred and self-disgust of the offender. Remorse rebites.

Remorse may also be accompanied by various attempts to escape oneself. The remorseful Judas commits suicide; the remorseful Rochester in *Jane Eyre* pursues dissipation and pleasure through all the capitals of Europe; "Lord" Jim in Joseph Conrad's novel by the same name flees his remorse from port to port. But short of suicide, the attempt to escape remorse, as with trauma generally, is usually unsuccessful. As McEwan's remorseful character Briony puts it: "The only conceivable solution would be for the past never to have happened . . . She longed to have someone else's past, to be someone else, like hearty Fiona with her unstained life stretching ahead, and her affectionate, sprawling family . . . All Fiona had to do was live her life, follow the road ahead and discover what was to happen. To Briony, it appeared that her life was going to be lived in one room, without a door."[39]

Remorse, then, both reconnects the offender with the victim in the sharing of the victim's pain and also results in a self-loathing that is a form of self-exile. This occurs as the offender sees her or his own failure to respond to or prevent the victim's suffering, which, as a suffering from senselessness, is due to the be-trayal and breach of trust of the offender. The self-isolation cannot be undone by the self but is in need of the other.

In these ways, remorse thus reflects retribution: like retribution, remorse is a boomerang of the crime back on the offender. The offender gets his own law thrust back on himself and experiences the pain of the crime, the world as it would be if the offender's act were a universal law. But unlike retribution, re-morse is not measured. The offender must live with his biting deed. He must own it. In the pain of remorse, we come to an understanding of the wrong as our own. For Heidegger, this returns us to the present, the moment of *Verstand*, in which we see ourselves most clearly and understand our own place "in the world."[40]

III. THE *REDE* OF PUNISHMENT AS SENTENCE

The senselessness of the wrong abandons the victim and wrongdoer who expe-rience it before an abyss: "Oh, my god, what have you done?" "Oh, my god, what have I done?" "How could you?" "How could I?" Victim and offender seek to re-signify the experience of the wrong. How can this senseless, hateful crime and suffering have meaning? The *Rede* of punishment is the coming to speech (and therefore to sense) of the wrong. From the point of view of the offender, the *Rede* of punishment is confession; from the point of view of the victim, it is testimony. But there is a need for these sayings to be heard, for these separate points of view to fuse. This happens when wrong comes to (a shared) language in a shared space. This sharing imagines a third perspective, that of a witness.

The *Befindlichkeit* of the witness is compassion—"suffering with" both parties. Indeed, compassion, "like the sympathetic spectatorship of the tragic audience," is often characterized as the appropriate emotional tenor for a judge.[41] Unlike anger, which sees only the wrong and its senselessness, compassion seeks understanding, puts the self in another's place. This experience of witnessing can also be traumatic, precisely because the violence is so senseless, so hard to assimilate, and therefore so fear-inspiring.[42] Yet, to have a witness to the *saying* of the wrong by both the offender and the victim as the wrong is first experienced as a wrong, *after* the event, requires that the wrong somehow throw off its senselessness and isolation and come to language in order to come to presence to the witness. In the third, future moment, the wrong comes to be articulable, comprehensible, human rather than monstrous, no longer debilitating, but allowing one to move into a future.

The *Rede* of the witness is "sentence"—a unification of confession and testimony into a narrative that makes "sense" of the wrong and allows it to move into a future. Ideally, in this future moment, the three points of view sundered by the wrong—victim, offender, and witness—finally come back together.

Confession

One of the key points made by the trauma literature discussed earlier is that only later, in memory, may an offender be able to experience the wrong as wrong, and this often must happen with the help of a "witness." Confession, then, may be the first experience of one's own wrong as wrong and is usually made to a witness who can allow the wrong to come into speech and allow the offender to "own" it.[43] This is nearly impossible, psychologists tell us, unless the witness is a "thou": "One has to feel love to be able to believe in its existence. Most of all, one has to feel love in order to be able to accept one's own self and one's own past."[44] To quote a former death-row inmate, "You relive your crime many times, or approach near to it in your thoughts and then back away from it in horror, appalled by it. You would turn backward. You would show your re-morse—as condemned men sometimes do, one to another—the remorse you hide with your fear in your heart and mind you would show to the one with the power and the given promise to understand and not condemn you, to the one you cannot find, unless perhaps you are a person who finds him in God."[45]

This insight may seem foreign to our current denunciatory understanding of punishment,[46] but it is not foreign to the experience of legal practice. Police interrogation manuals understand and exploit the need of the defendant to confess, and they counsel that the effective police interrogator must often mas-querade as a friend. It is textbook interrogation technique for the interrogator to feign a demonstration of compassion that, often enough, leads offenders to trust and stirs them to confession and even to expressions of remorse. The stan-dard interrogation manual advises,

> The solicitations of a sympathetic investigator may allow the suspect to believe that if the investigator can understand the reasons for his crime, others too may be more understanding. Much can be gained by the investigator's adoption of an emotional ("choked up") feeling about it all . . . This demonstrable attitude of sympathy and understanding may be rather easily assumed by placing one's self "in the other fellow's shoes" and pondering this question: "What might I have done under similar circumstances?"[47]

A skilled interrogator can tell when offenders are ready to "give it up." They sigh, crumple, "break," "spill their guts," and sometimes even cry. Interrogation manuals reveal the truth that offenders are anxious to find a friend, that con-fession to another is a need for the remorseful and allows the wrong to be ex-perienced as wrong.

Testimony

Likewise, the victim of a crisis may come to fully experience and assimilate a trauma only later, in telling about it. This also requires a loving witness, and it involves a "survivor" guilt that must be owned or expurgated through the testi-mony. Those who really hear the testimony undergo pain themselves in sharing the "senselessness" of the wrong.[48]

When the offender is the victim's witness and the victim is the offender's, as sometimes happens in a trial or victim-offender mediation, the transference may become complete, with the victim becoming offender and with the offender becoming victim, the two changing places like the boys in John Knowles's novel *A Separate Peace*.[49] The despair of remorse is echoed by the despair of the victim/witness, both (in that moment, at least) "without hope" that sense can be restored, for any hope (of leniency or of reform) would belie the sincerity of the remorse and the generosity of the witness's response.[50]

Here we might see a new reason for the drama of the trial, with its personal testimony and right to confrontation. Especially in the *dramatic* use of trials, the trial is portrayed often as a moment of personal confrontation between victim and offender and often as a moment of testimony and confession. The victim/offender relation is not then a seesaw of indignity, as Jean Hampton would portray it, but the coming face-to-face with the other, looking together at the wrong as wrong and experiencing the pain and shock of it together *for the first time*. Caruth reads the parable of Tancred and Clorinda in a similar way: "It is possible, of course, to understand that other voice, the voice of Clorinda, within the parable of the example, to represent the other within the self that retains the memory of the 'unwitting' traumatic events of one's past. But we can also read the address of the voice here, not as the story of the individual in relation to the events of his own past, but as the story of the way in which one's own trauma is tied up with the trauma of another, the way in which trauma may lead, therefore, to the encounter with another, through the very possibility and surprise of listening to another's wound."[51] The way in which trauma opens up the self allows the possibility of an encounter with the other, and the sharing of that trauma is part of the punishment that restores being-with. Through the pain of understanding the wrong as wrong and through the trauma of being opened up to the victim's pain, the offender is brought out of his or her selfishness and inattention to the other and reunited with his or her own being as being-with. The victim is likewise restored; in sharing the trauma and letting it come to language, sense and meaning are brought back, and the frightening image of the defendant as "sense-destroying monster" is itself obliterated through the defendant's own language of confession.

Sentence

Out of the *Befindlichkeit* of traumatic pain (fear, remorse) comes the *Rede* of testimony or confession, as the wrong is "witnessed" and perhaps first experienced as wrong. But because the wrong is experienced with another, it is also a healing. As each suffers with the other, the other becomes essential to seeing the significance of the wrong and therefore to giving meaning to the self. The ones confessing/testifying and the witness are changed and bound by what they have experienced together. The wrong calls out for significance, for meaning, that is only possible in the sharing of it through language.[52]

The remorse and confession of an offender heal the breach between offender and victim to some extent simply through their mutual acknowledgment that the suffering was indeed wrongful.[53] The hate is gone. The act now is clearly seen as "wrong," and there is a "we" now that sees this and articulates it as a wrong together. No one stands outside to laugh or revile or to claim that the suffering was "right" or "fun" or "insignificant" or a "cruel but inevitable fate."

But even after the wrong is seen together as a wrong, the remorseful offender, caught in a solipsism of self-hate, is still left to bear his own senselessness. How can he continue to live with this "senseless" crime as "his"? The confession transfers the pain of senselessness from the victim to the offender. But it remains there in all its painful biting, an open wound of trauma.

As we saw, the remorseful call for their own punishment, but someone must *accept* the sacrifice tendered by the offender. The next step Duff and others call for is "penance," which we may understand, from our different perspective, as a sacrifice tendered by the offender to restore "sense" to the suffering. As Levinas understands, when suffering is undertaken "for another," it is no longer senseless; it has meaning. Dying for one's country, working ceaselessly to put one's children through school or to feed the hungry or to fight for a truth— even when one's purposes fail, such sacrifice for others gives effort, deprivation, and suffering a "point," a meaning, ennobling it. The sacrifice is not, however, a "payment" or equivalent: the victim's loss is sublime, unique, and unmeasurable. The sacrifice can only be tendered as a gift and must be accepted before it can truly heal the remorse. To complete the renewal of a being-with, a mutuality is necessary, an acceptance of what cannot be full payment. This is the "sentence," the saying of a settlement, the saying of sense again in the world.

Who accepts this settlement? The settlement must be accepted by a witness, who occupies the place of hearing the confession/testimony and saying the sentence with a view to the future. If the victim can come to a mutual place of hearing and witnessing and no longer be apart from the offender, then the victim (no longer a victim, but now a witness) could potentially accept the settlement. In daily life, this happens all the time, as we reconcile with each other for small wrongs or inadvertent harms. But it is also possible for the witness who accepts the settlement to be a different person than the person wronged. The "sentence" looks to the future, not the past. It is a question of allowing the offender to let go of the re-bite of remorse and allow others (not just the victim) to rely on her again, to trust herself and to have others trust her. Any witness who has "gone through" the pain of the coming to language of the wrong as wrong—hearing, in this place of traumatic sharing, the extent of the breach of trust and having "felt" the pain of the wrong as it comes to presence in language—has standing to accept settlement. The witness does not have the lived experience of the past that the offender and victim do, but if the witness has been compassionate, then he or she has as much "understanding" of the wrong as can be had through language, and, as language is our way of understanding the wrong "as wrong," the witness has as good an understanding of the wrong as either the offender or the victim. Whatever cannot be expressed in the third moment of *Rede* remains silent for us, and no one can say it. Perhaps sometime it will appear in language, like the facts of a common-law case that are not considered "relevant" but remain in the background or like the "taken for granted" that does not come to consciousness until later. But settlement is the best we can do (at the time and in the place we are thrown), and no one who lived through the trauma could articulate the settlement any better just then. We go forward with humility, not certain that we have said "everything" about the wrong. There is risk in this. But the risk is not one that falls on the victim alone. The risk falls on all who are in mutual reliance with the offender in the future. The risk is a necessary one; it is part of our obligation to be with each other.

The Place of Mercy in Punishment: Compassion, Lenity, Humility, and Risk

What is the work of mercy in this "sentence," then? It is no longer separate from punishment but blended with it.

First, the mercy in punishment is to become *aware* of the underlying primal mercy or grace of our mutual dependance as beings-with-others-in-a-world; we come to experience compassion. The compassionate witness to wrong sees others—those we "suffer with," both victim and offender—in their being as suffering. The "suffering" here is understood not as mere physical pain but, more basically, as our being "thrown," as our having a past and being affected in a personal, unique way, being vulnerable and dependent on one another. In their "thrownness," each person is singular, each has a certain glance, a way of laughing, a curious twist of expression. Each loss caused by an offender is irreparable, irrevocable, irreplaceable—a lost possibility that will never be again. The offender in remorse moves from *not* thinking of the victim to being aware of the sublimity of the victim in all her precious and peculiar vulnerability and lost possibilities. The victim likewise suddenly feels her own vulnerability, her own "thrownness," as a deep sense of betrayal, a loss of reliability on a world that has a pattern and makes sense. Primal mercy or grace comes to appearance in punishment, then, in its more familiar guise as compassion, an awareness, experience, and articulation of our mutual reliance and vulnerability.

Second, we witness the victim and offender "in time," finite in their ability, in medias res, having come upon their world late and leaving it early. Mercy cuts off the infinite rebite of remorse and the infinite causal chain of responsibility or vengeance that would otherwise be ours and that would make any act, as a true beginning, impossible.[54] Mercy is in part, then, a kind of principle of proximate cause, confining responsibility to make responsibility possible as a true "response" to what was already there, beyond one's control. Mercy provides an "end" to the narrative of wrong, shaping the story and giving it a sense, a sentence. It allows a settlement as sacrifice to imbue the past with meaning "as wrong," and it allows the future to reach a conclusion. So mercy is present in punishment as lenity, a cutting off of responsibility, an ending of the reverberations of a wrong.

Third, to hear Levinas, we see the other as "higher." The limits of our own "thrownness" and our own "finitude" entail that we cannot take the "with," the *com*-in *compassion*, too seriously. We cannot assume we have plumbed the depths of the other. The other must appear to us as both revealing and hiding, as all that appears does. We cannot reduce him or her to a character, to a "criminal," to a "victim," or to a "sufferer."[55] We cannot appropriate; we cannot grasp; we cannot assume.[56] We cannot say truly what the offender may "deserve."[57] We cannot say truly what the victim experienced. Any settlement must be rendered and accepted in humility. Mercy, then, becomes not disrespect but, rather, a greater respect we give the other—not presuming to know what is "deserved." Mercy is present in punishment as humility.

Finally, punishment and mercy come together as a settlement and compromise that opens up a future, not as the "just deserts" of retributive theory. In this settlement, we commit to trust once again, to repose again upon the offender and allow him or her to bear his or her weight and shoulder his or her place in the web of mutual reliance. The sentence of settlement throws us back upon each other, where we are always "at each other's mercy," acknowledging our mutual frailty, mutual dependence, mutual trust. So mercy is present in punishment as risk.

IV. PUNISHMENT AND MERCY: SUMMARY

To summarize, from our new perspective, punishment is the shared *memory* of a wrong as wrong.[58] It is coming, in the witnessing of trauma (i.e., in confession and testimony), to see the wrong as wrong. To remember the wrong as wrong is for all parties to see the other in her or his being as other, instead of as something to be used. To see the other in her or his being as other, is to feel the pain of separation from the other, to feel the other as "at a height" and as calling for us. To see the other in her or his being as other is once again to belong with the other. It is to restore the part of the self that is itself only in relation to the other.

In this way, the pain of separation transforms into the pain of compassion, of suffering with—seeing our mutual "thrownnness" already into a world. This pain is not a harm to be minimized but a way of being that shows us a truth.[59] The memory of wrong, then, brings out of itself the reunion with the other and with the self, the recognition of one's own being as being-with. The reconnection or "at-one-ment" with the other comes not through reason but through the (painful) experience of letting others be present to you in compassion.

The answer to Duff, here, then, is that remorse is essential to the understanding of punishment. Yet punishment is not a communication plus penance that induces (through the offender's conscience) remorse; it simply is the memory of the wrong as wrong, seen from the *Befindlichkeit* of remorse on the offender's side, in the fear of senselessness from the victim's side, and, ultimately, in a unifying compassionate "sentence" of settlement from the witness's side.[60] Punishment's proportionality to the wrong is a feature of its pain in confronting the wrong—the remorse of the offender, fear of the victim, and compassion of the witness.

The confrontation with the wrong calls for another aspect of mercy as a settlement of sense—a sentence—from a witness who has undergone the experience of the wrong as wrong in language and who can undertake to settle the terms of a future relationship with the wrongdoer and victim. The coming to language in itself puts the wrong into a narrative between past and future, so the wrong no longer is a senseless extrusion incapable of being put into words but is a "sentence." The coming to language also allows for projecting the story into the future together, allowing for a future sacrifice or settlement to give sense and trajectory to the story of the wrong.

The compassionate witness who pronounces sentence need not be a third person but may be only a renewed being-with of the victim and offender through language. The "witness," in this sense, may be the union of victim and offender coming together to see the wrong as each other's witnesses, or it may be a mutual friend, judge, jury, or other community representative. The moment of coming to language is a moment that takes all the parties to a shared understanding of the wrong in a shared tongue, and it is this shared experience that can project sense into a future.

The settlement is not a deserved penalty. It is not a compensation to be paid to the victim (though it can be a gift to the victim). It is not a statement about the seriousness of the community's disapproval. It is not a disincentive to commit future crime. It is a settlement of one's remorse with all those one is "with," allowing one to assume one's place in the community of mutual reliance. It is a sacrifice that, through its tender, gives meaning to the wrong and puts it into a narrative that will allow a future to make sense of the past. The settlement varies by what is "acceptable" to find a place of mutual recognition, compassion, and reliance. This settlement may be only the pain of experiencing the wrong as wrong together, or it may be a further work of sacrifice as penance by the wrongdoer, accepted by the witness.

V. QUESTIONS AND OBJECTIONS

1. Should only the victim have legal standing to forgive? Or should the victim at least be first in line to be given that choice?[61]

Confession serves as an expression of remorse and an acknowledgment of the experience of wrong as wrong. As noted earlier, this acknowledgment of wrong, the standing together to see the wrong as wrong that can happen through language, heals the victim's sense of being "hated in the act" and helps cure the victim's sense of isolation. It can bring the victim into a place of conversation where the victim and offender stand together. In that place, however, each becomes also a witness, and as a witness, the victim ceases to be victim, torn away from sense and from his or her own security in being with others, just as the offender's isolation ends also.

Any further sacrifice or settlement is not then owed to the victim (qua victim). It is the witness who can move into a future that includes a willingness to risk future dealings with the offender, to take them back into the fold in some way.[62] Mercy of this kind—a willingness to take the risk of future dealings—can be extended by anyone who, having witnessed the "wrong as wrong" of the offender's crime, will accept the sacrifice offered and risk future dealings with the offender. The mercy may seem cheap or even wrong if the person extending it is not particularly at risk in the future, but it is not at all cheap if he is. From this standpoint, a particular victim could not necessarily "stand in" for the whole community to extend mercy for all, unless the victim is also a witness, sharing that compassionate and unified perspective on the wrong while still at risk from the offender. In being a witness at risk and in a relationship of community with the offender, the victim is in no better position to be merciful than other witnesses who are also at risk and in relationship with the offender. In other words, victims, as such, would have no special standing to be merciful, since as a particular victim, they cannot represent all future possible victims and cannot "speak" or pass "sentence" until they become witnesses and no longer victims.

It is true that we cannot really understand the future risk or experience the offender in the way the victim can, and so the victim has knowledge, testimony, that we do not. But our deference to the victim's experience, like our deference to the offender's confession, is not the same as saying that the victim has a special "right" to grant or refuse mercy or to pass sentence, for that "right" is a matter of the future, not the past. This fits with our current judicial practice: victims are generally allowed to testify about their experience but are usually not allowed to recommend a penalty or to veto a plea bargain. Victim-offender mediation may seem a counterexample, but it could also be understood as a way in which we delegate the community's right to settle the past for the future to a particular victim, who is also, through the mediation process, a witness. Community mediation or traditional forms of trial could be just as appropriate in reaching a sentence that settles the wrong.[63]

2. Are some crimes unforgivable?[64] Is the breach of being-with so great that we can never heal it?

Declaring a crime unforgivable is an absolute judgment that presumes certain knowledge of who an offender is and will be for the rest of his or her life, so that we can say we will *never* risk a relationship with him or her. Never is a long time. Even if we cannot "imagine" change significant enough to allow us to risk a relationship *ever*, our imagination, too, is limited by time and experience. Totalizing knowledge of an other is impossible for us finite, time-bound humans. It is part of treating each other with dignity that we—not as a matter of fact, but as an ethical duty—cannot presume to know each other now and forever. The sublime in the other is the Levinasian reinterpretation of Kantian dignity, a wall we cannot breach without being other than who we are, without presuming to a totalizing knowledge that is itself totalitarian and inhuman.

This response, however, may seem too abstract, too easy. Again, we cannot be sure of our understanding unless we try to judge from the concrete case. To gain further insight, I look more closely at the context of atrocity in chapter 6.

> 3. If remorse "calls for" settlement or mercy, then is mercy granted "for a reason" after all?

Jacques Derrida argues that it is only when we pardon *for no reason* that pardon or forgiveness is seen in its truth. Only the unforgivable can really be forgiven, he argues, for it is only when there is no reason to forgive, when one does not deserve to be forgiven, that true forgiveness, completely divorced from law and desert, is possible.[65] Forgiveness of the unforgivable, compassion without a ground, is the kind of forgiveness that gives forgiveness its very meaning as "undeserved," according to Derrida, and is therefore forgiveness at its purest.

First, remorse calls for mercy not in the way of justifying it but just in the way of *needing* it. Responding to a need is not the same thing as responding for a reason. Giving to those who need the gift does not make the gift less giftlike or more "deserved."

Second, the view that mercy must be completely "free and unconstrained" to be true mercy may be another rebound of our kanticism—our notion of "free" will, or a mercy given by a perfectly unconstrained god of philosophy. Mercy is unconstrained by "reason" and "rule" and "desert" but is not therefore completely "free," random, or arbitrary. Like all being-in-the-world, it is conditioned by a past.

> 4. Is mercy conditioned on repentance?

Making mercy a quid pro quo of repentance is to make both repentance and mercy impossible. Punishment is a work, not an intentional action on the part of the offender or the victim or the witness. Sometimes it happens; sometimes it does not. We may try to create institutions that allow it to happen, but we cannot *make* offenders see the wrong as wrong, any more than we can *make* our opponents in arguments see our point. I may intend to punish you, or I may intend to convince you, but my intending does not make something so. Likewise, you may look for a ship without seeing it, just as you may try to be remorseful (or compassionate) without being remorseful (or compassionate). If we make mercy contingent on remorse, then both the "apparent" repentance and the "apparent" mercy are shams.

If, however, punishment is a coming together to see the wrong as wrong, then remorse may happen, and so may mercy. In that work, it may even become hard to determine who is remorseful and who is merciful, as the perspectives of offender, victim, and witness come together. But this may not happen. The dispute over what "really happened" may continue. When we cannot see the wrong as wrong together, we settle in conditions of uncertainty. The settlement we come to in such cases is not a deserved punishment or even punishment at all but just a way of moving on (as if saying, "Sorry, we think you are guilty, even if you don't. Here are our terms for the future. We'll keep trying to come to some mutual understanding about what happened, but if we can't, then, if you undertake this sacrifice, we'll let it go and move on"). It is still possible that the putative offender will come to see the wrong as wrong and that remorse will come later, maybe even *because* of a witness's compassion, as for Raskolnikov in *Crime and Punishment.* Or perhaps we will find that the offender was not at fault to begin with—or perhaps not. The point is that we are not unilaterally determining the putative offender's moral desert once and for all.

Does this mean that there are some cases in which we are not "saying the law" and "vindicating the victim"? Yes, it does. It means being willing to live in some moral uncertainty in some—maybe even many—cases. We can still say that we believe the victim's version and not the offender's, and we can still support the victim. We can still assess a penalty or demand a sacrifice, but we have to remain humble about whether we are right to do so. Again, the conversation with the putative offender and our respectful engagement with her or him continues. Sometimes we find that an offender was right after all and that a post-sentence exoneration is the right thing to do.

A law that did not allow for any future appeal, claim of innocence, or revision of sentence would be arrogant in the extreme as well as possibly bootless. The conversation and effort to see the past together may continue, perhaps even after a "decision" is legally final. Our finitude means that even when we try to bring an end to the past, perhaps by ironically acknowledging that we cannot reach a perfect answer and therefore have to declare ourselves "done," we cannot necessarily control "the end" anymore than we can control the future (for the future is always about the past). The past may reach forward to prick us, even when we thought the case was long over.[66] Law, like history and language, remembers.

We should engage even when an offender completely repudiates our law and asserts propositions that we believe to be evil. We have a moral imperative to be with that person. Indeed, treating him as a nonperson is not possible. If Hitler really were nonhuman, then the problem of Nazism would be no problem, would not unsettle us or frighten us. We could write the whole episode out of history as an anomaly, an aberration, or we could externalize it as a visitation of the devil. The real problem is that Hitler was human. The evil of his perspective, the horror of what he (and those who followed him and those who did not stop him) were capable of is *our* problem, and we cannot simply judge him, dismiss him, and disengage. Instead, we must interrogate ourselves. What is it about that perspective that was so alluring that an entire nation was swept up in it? Why and how could he do such horrific things and not repent of them? How is it that so many turned their backs and demonstrated obdurate indifference to what was going on? Only insofar as we can see ourselves as with the offender can we respond to those horrors and be alert to their insidious dangers. We have to keep trying to come to a place of mutual understanding of the wrong as wrong, or we fail to fully appreciate its dimensions, its seductive powers, and the extent to which it continues to exist and implicate us. I address these questions further in chapter 6.

5. Is this theory completely unrealistic and without application to current penal institutions?

On the contrary, in some ways, this theory gives us a deeper understanding of our current penal institutions, even though it is aspirational. For example, from this new standpoint, the work of just punishment begins not with the sentence but with the trial.[67] We might be able to better understand the *drama* of the trial, which, as we know already,[68] is not necessary to the mere uncovering of the facts necessary to convict. Fact-finding could be done by an administrator or panel of investigators. Though truth-finding is of course a critical part of the trial, more is going on in our trials than determining whether an offender is guilty or innocent. The defendant is "on trial." He or she has a "right" to be there, to witness the witnesses and the victims, and to confront them (and, conversely, they may confront the defendant, whose presence and demeanor are interpreted even though he or she may choose not to speak). The trial is public. The defendant's fellow citizens sit in judgment, in "witness" to the wrong as wrong. The trial is the reenactment, through testimony and evidence, of the crime, the bringing forth of the memory of the wrong as wrong. The defendant, of course, may (and often does) deny that this memory is true, contesting the state's portrayal of the crime with his or her own dramatic narrative, but the prosecution's case is nonetheless a dramatic presentation of a version of the wrong, not only for the jury but for those defendants who have, up to that point, refused to acknowledge their responsibility. Like Hamlet's play for the regicidal Claudius, the trial attempts to evoke the wrong as wrong, personally, vividly, and painfully.

The jury gives a verdict, a truth-speaking. When jurors convict, they face the defendant. They say the wrong as wrong. If they are convinced by the prosecutor's presentation, they confront the defendant with his or her guilt for the wrong. All of this is the careful calling up of a painful memory. The defendant then has a right of allocution—to speak without mediation or legal consequence, to express remorse or to apologize. If the defendant indeed remembers and experiences the wrong as his or her wrong, he or she will be in pain, will experience remorse. The sentence, then, ideally, is a settlement of the crime, an "offering" on the part of the defendant, because only the acceptance of the community can bring the defendant back from self-exile.

The format of a typical sentencing hearing (in an indeterminate sentencing system) has precisely this character. The offender often apologizes, expresses remorse, and suggests a sentence. The prosecutor suggests a different sentence. The judge determines sentence. Or, even more frequently, the parties reach a plea and sentencing agreement.[69] The prosecutor's, jury's, and judge's perceptions of a defendant's remorse, studies tell us, play a large role.[70]

Determinate sentencing systems could also be interpreted as consonant with this new place of understanding. If we are determining a "settlement," then perhaps it is better if we do not try to judge the extent of an offender's remorse—not because we do not believe in it,[71] but out of respect for the sublimity of the offender (we cannot know him that completely). A sentencing system in the old sense of penalty can be a way to handle crime and reunion without requiring the soul-searching intrusiveness[72] of judging remorse or desert. Moreover, such a system alleviates the fear and uncertainty of defendants who are thrust into an alien system with only a stranger/lawyer, who they may not completely trust, as their guide. It also alleviates the sense of indignity some defendants experience when they feel they must grovel for favor before an authority figure who may not be a compassionate judge. Yet if we rely on a determinate sentencing system, we must understand these penalties as "merely" settlements—not as "deserved" and accurate accountings of moral culpability. If we sentenced with more humility, we would sentence with less indignity.

Mandatory sentences are not ruled out, in principle, either. It is possible to be so afraid of judging that we try to avoid it completely, letting the settlement stand "given" as a mandatory penalty tied to a definition of a kind of crime. However, our current system of mandatory sentences is so punitive that it is used mostly as a tool for inducing cooperation or pleas. It does not eliminate or "humble" judgment but, instead, serves to label offenders as *beyond* settlement and atonement, as well as hiding the fact that prosecutors still exercise charging discretion in these cases (the very individualized judgment that mandatory sentencing schemes supposedly forswear). Far from recognizing the tragic and sublime unknowable in offenders,[73] mandatory sentencing, as we practice it, degrades and denigrates them.[74]

Mandatory sentencing (like unarticulated plea bargaining where an offender is simply given a "number" to accept or reject, and either the offender is not privy to the discussion involved in the plea's negotiation, or there simply is no discussion) also tends to cut off the discussion of the wrong, which is so necessary to the settlement of it, and the renewal of being-with and mutual trust that follows from a common place of understanding. The formal statutory elements of crimes are, by nature, general, each form of crime covering a multitude of sins. Burglary, for example, can cover the well-oiled work of a professional art thief, the bloodthirsty housebreaking of a psychopath, or the use of a former lover's key to retrieve disputed possessions. Without some discussion of the nature of *this* wrong and the consequences to *this* victim, the settlement seems itself senseless, exacerbating, rather than healing, the parties' sense of isolation from each other and reinforcing their sense that the world is meaningless. A more satisfying settlement may be reached when one understands one's wrong in connection with others. A common law of sentencing, such as is developing under the federal sentencing guidelines, at least has the virtue of enabling discussion of the wrong, its consequences, and its relative seriousness or significance compared to others. No event is exactly the same; no victim is exactly the same; no offender is exactly the same. But to make sense of the wrong requires allowing it to come into language, allowing it its place in the set of analogies that guide conduct and allow for judgment. Having a language in which to discuss the seriousness of the crime helps bring out features of the wrong that might otherwise remain silenced. Having some flexibility to tell a different story, to invoke a distinction with a difference, also contributes to the richness of our mutual experience for the future.

By saying all of this, I do not mean that a traditional trial and sentencing is necessary to punishment, only that the trial and sentencing structure as we know it allows for the possibility of a work of punishment. Other institutional-ized forms of truth-telling confrontation may be appropriate or even better ways of trying to make space for such a confrontation.[75] Of course, the con-frontation with wrong and work of punishment may take place outside of any institution. My goal here is not to set forth an institutional blueprint for a more merciful approach to punishment and sentencing, for that has already been ably done by others,[76] but merely to provide the philosophical underpinnings that might support a reconciliatory, rather than retributive, understanding of punishment and to combat the view that mercy is demeaning.

6. Does this theory create inequality?

As in Anselm's agonized questions to God quoted in the introduction to this book, giving "less" than a person deserves is often understood as creating in-equalities and thereby injustices. While such inequalities may be acceptable in personal relationships, goes the argument, the government must treat its citi-zens equally under law. Sentencing as settlement would seem, from this per-spective, to undermine the rule of law.

The first part of a response is, of course, that equality does not tell us what must be equalized. Each case is unique. Which factors do we equalize, and which do we ignore? Whenever we create a general category of crime or sen-tencing and then apply only those factors to a set of cases, we lop off some of the nuances of each situation. Could we ever construct a perfect sentencing sys-tem that took into account all and only the relevant factors? Of course we can-not. Not only are the categories we can create themselves finite, but we are both finite and temporal. We learn and change.[77] Under the federal sentencing guidelines, for example, the U.S. Sentencing Commission leaves room for dis-trict courts to discover new "differences" in a case that place the case outside the norm of the usual crime of that type. When a judge finds such a difference and "departs" from the guidelines, is the judge treating the offender unfairly or more fairly by treating the offender differently?

This common scenario also points out something else about judging. In al-lowing for departures from the "heartland" or "normal" case, *we assume that the particular judgment "on the facts" will be more sensitive and accurate than the judgment according to the preestablished rules.* Following the rules is sometimes not the right thing to do, because our particular judgments can be better. Rules are based on experience; experience is not determined by rules. This recalls Heidegger's point that our practical knowledge of "how" in a context is more fundamental than our theoretical knowledge. Rules of judgment, then, are best approached as rules of thumb, because particular judgments can be more reliable than the rules. If we do not allow for divergence from the "rule," then we will not be treating like cases alike but will be treating different cases alike, and treating different cases alike is just as unequal as treating like cases differently. The common-law approach of analogy rather than deduction allows for judgment to be informed by past cases without being determined by them.

Another important feature of judgment and language comes to the fore here as well. As pointed out in chapter 2, the categories of language and, by extension, law are not "containers" of things all alike but a network of more loosely connected ideas. Ludwig Wittgenstein famously pointed out that the terms of our language denote things according to their "family resemblances";[78] terms are not categories describable by necessary and sufficient definitions. George Lakoff, in investigating the way in which other languages divide up the world differently, also argues that some of the items that fit in a linguistic category seem more "central" than others.[79] This maps directly onto our experience of judgment in law as consisting of "easy" and "hard" cases in applying rules, "heartland" cases and outliers, paradigm cases and "gray zones."[80] The rules themselves do not say what the central cases of application are; we intuit them through judgment and our background knowledge of how our language is to be understood. So the very determination of which cases are "like" overflows the categories of law and language. As Kant recognized, there are no rules for the application of rules.

But beyond the formal point about the impossibility of true equality under a rule of law, part of what is at stake in this objection is really not at all about equality in terms of logic or rule application. We object to unequal treatment because it often signals disrespect, a lack of concern, or an exclusion. As any parent knows, children always complain about differential treatment of siblings, even if there is good reason for the difference. These complaints are nearly always a plea for reassurance, for a sign that one is loved "as much," valued "as much," needed "as much." Usually a loving gesture is of more use in curing the "inequality" than an explanation of the reasons for the different treatment or even than giving the "same" to the different. When my daughter complains that I have "unfairly" bought my son a Nerf gun, it is not because she wants one herself.

Sentencing in our system may create many of the same dynamics. Because our kanticism requires that punishment be understood as what is "deserved," receiving a more severe punishment than someone else is often taken as a sign of disrespect: "What? I'm getting the full ten years and he's only getting five? You mean I'm a worse person because I got a college education and had a job than that guy over there who was addicted to drugs and never did an honest day's work? How completely unfair! I'm being punished for being more responsible!" Moreover, because both too little and too much punishment are equally wrong, there will never be a sense of peace about any sentence. How can a sentence perfectly accord with desert? It is humanly impossible. As a result, all sentences subject to any discretion are felt by both offenders and victims as unfair in one direction or the other. The move to mandatory sentences may be a result of this frustration: at least under mandatory sentencing, there is an *appearance* of evenhandedness, even if meaningfully different cases are treated alike. The differences are still there, but they are hidden, less able to be pointed out and to serve as a source of complaint and overt "disrespect." If I give both the boyfriend-burglar and the psychopath-burglar the same sentence, no one may know that the facts of the crimes differed greatly, and so even the two burglars may not be aware of any "disrespect" from the system.

Moreover, when punishment is understood as desert, discretion in sentencing creates a hierarchical relationship between judge and offender. The judge presumes to make this judgment of "desert" (which is, after all, humanly impossible); the offender is on the defensive, trying to "justify" himself or herself, trying to prove worthy of less punishment. The offender must grovel before the authority, his or her very worth determined by an almost stranger. The "unfairness" felt in such circumstances is often the inequality in the situation, not the sentence.

Thinking of sentencing as settlement, however, puts the matter in a different place. A sentence should no longer be thought of as an evaluation of an offender's worthiness or deservingness. Nor should it be the case that the "less" the sentence is, the worthier or less evil the offender is perceived to be. If we truly think of the sentence as a sacrifice tendered as a gift by the offender, there should be room for thinking of a more onerous sentence as a more generous gift. Though this seems entirely counterintuitive from our retributivist perspective, it is *possible* to think about comparisons between cases as we might look at charitable giving: "What? He gave ten days of community service and I only gave five? Wow, maybe I should do more."

In the same vein, a refusal by the community to accept a settlement need not be inevitably conceived as the offender's "fault" but may be a weakness of the community—as when, in personal relationships, we sometimes come to say, "I'm sorry, I know you are doing your best. I'm still feeling too fragile and I just can't get myself to trust you yet." Or a community may generously decline the offered settlement out of compassion for the offender's prior suffering, out of gratitude for the offender's prior acts of heroism or selflessness, or perhaps out of a profound sense of the community's complicity in the crime. (For examples, see chapters 5 and 6.)

In a settlement understanding, sentencing is less hierarchical and more about mutual understanding. It is future-looking, trying to find a way to trust (oneself, the other) again. No longer need it be painful or shameful: the pain comes already in experiencing the wrong as wrong. Prison time, as such, would not necessarily be the metric of such a settlement: we would not need to inflict further pain or shame, as other opportunities for sacrifice and service might be more appropriate to restoring being-with. There is already a vast literature on alternative sentencing and restorative justice; this discussion is only meant to show how we might move conceptually from retributivism to a new ground that would allow for such expanded sentencing choices. Retributivism, unfortunately, with its requirement that the *sentence* be painful, makes prison time the coin of the realm. Desert gets cashed out in lost and empty years of isolation rather than efforts at reunion. A settlement understanding, which sees that the pain of punishment is in seeing the wrong, not in serving the sentence, would make alternative sentencing choices more conceptually available.

Sentencing as settlement also acknowledges that the relevant considerations may change in the event of settlement itself. As settlement participants come to understand each other more completely, a bond may form among those engaged in the discussion. Mutual care and concern, a moment of revealed being-with, may enable trust without sacrifice. This possibility is part of the insight that judgment is always particular, embedded in a situation, informed by the coming to truth of being-in and being-with. The judgment of the case may change in the very moment of being judged.

Given the individual nature of settlement, do we need rules at all? Is all need for equality banished? The better way to ask the question would be, should we still try to bring settlement to language? I still believe that we should, but in the way of common-law reasoning, not in the way of rules. The point of a "common law of sentencing" in a model of sentencing as settlement would be helpful in much the way that knowing how much others are giving to charity is helpful: it gives us a lodestar or place to start from, eases the debilitating uncertainty and fear of authority that can be created in both victims and offenders by a lack of opportunity for participation and discussion before decision, and makes sure we are talking about important features of the case. My sense that we still need room for discussion and argument in sentencing is put into practice in chapters 5 and 6, in which I try to bring these abstract ideas into more concrete situations, drawing on our existing experience, reasoning case to case, by analogy, about our sense of what considerations are appropriate in settling criminal cases. Punishment as "settlement" or "mercy" may not hew to rule or reason, but it is not arbitrary whim either. Settlement is an art of judgment.

Does this individual settlement approach sound like an unworkable, overoptimistic ideal? On the contrary, plea bargaining currently resolves more than 95 percent of our criminal cases[81] and is just this: a settlement based largely on the likelihood that the prosecution's account of the crime is true and complete, but also often based on defense counsel's descriptions to the prosecutor of the defendant's remorse, family situation, and needs, as well as what other defendants are offering. Instead of being an "embarrassment" to our punishment theory, plea bargaining, done well, can be justified as "settlement," though it would be even better if at least some of these cases could be brought to language through, perhaps, a brief, joint statement of the case that could be available in future settlements.[82] The frustration that prosecutors often feel when a defendant turns down an offer may not always just be annoyance that the prosecutor has to go through the hassle and expense of a trial but, if the settlement seems fair, a genuine sense that the defendant is still in denial and *not* seeing the wrong as wrong. The trial becomes a necessary and painful effort, for the unremorseful defendant, to recall the wrong as wrong, as well, as it is more traditionally understood, as an effort to decide the question of whether there was a wrong in the first place. However, any real settlement should arise from a discussion involving the offender (and perhaps the victim), not a "take it or leave it" number scrawled on a piece of paper and presented perfunctorily to the accused. Of course, dramatic increases in sentencing after trial, which seem designed to punish offenders for going to trial, are extremely destructive of future trust and the possibility of true remorse and punishment. There are better and worse ways of practicing plea bargaining.

7. Is it unrealistic to expect "remorse" from hardened criminals?

Are the vast majority of offenders heartless monsters, cunning and manipulative, inveterate "fakers" of remorse, cold and calculating, enjoying the suffering of their victims and working "the system," rather than compassionate people who feel remorseful and ask to be punished? Of course, both visions of our "offenders" are equally distorted. Offenders are neither all-remorseful nor all-manipulative. Many are jaded, depressed, abused substance abusers, who ex-pect as little of others as they do of themselves. Some are remorseful; many are in denial; some are defiant and angry; some are beyond caring either way.[83] Most crimes are not planned; most offenses are connected with substance abuse, past physical/sexual abuse, or mental illness; most offenders feel help-less, not powerful. As I took my students to visit one prison, a guard asked, "Do you know the difference between the folks in here and you all on the outside?" After a few students attempted to respond, he shook his head. "Nothing," he an-swered sternly. "Nothing."

Many offenders do experience remorse. As mentioned earlier, one of the most successful techniques of police interrogation is to urge the suspect, in an understanding, friend-to-friend way, to "get it off your chest." So there is no special reason to think that "most" offenders are so different from "us" as to be remorseless or successfully manipulative.

The question, in the end, is what we should aim for or aspire to. I agree with Duff and others that we should aim for a system of punishment that honors the offender as a human being, capable of compassion and remorse. We should not assume that offenders are less human than we are.

VI. CONCLUSION

The distance we have traveled in seeing punishment this way is now clear. Pun-ishment is the shared memory of a wrong in its wrongness. It is a work that is-sues out of pain through the trauma of the offender's remorse and the victim's fear. I see (perhaps for the first time) the suffering of the other that I should have responded to before. The memory of wrong as wrong itself leads us on the way to reunion with others, through confession and testimony, and is settled in a sentence by a compassionate witness. Punishment is not, then, a giving of our own act of universal law to ourselves in order to respect ourselves but is funda-mentally a reunion, or "at-one-ment," with others, an experience of being-with. Mercy is integral to punishment as the compassion in witnessing the wrong as wrong in the confession of the offender, the lenity expressed in cutting off the consequences of the crime, the humility and reticence of considering sentence as settlement and not deserved penalty, and the acceptance of a risk of reunion.

I do not advocate any particular sentencing system here, for any sentencing system understood as "settlement" could fit this new place of understanding. Community mediation, victim-offender mediation, sentences determined by plea bargaining, and indeterminate or even determinate sentencing, properly understood and properly tendered, could all allow for the work of punishment. It still remains, of course, to work out, in context and practice, what mercy "looks like." Can we still say that, sometimes, mercy is appropriate or inappropriate, once we have taken the view that mercy is a gift, following no rule? Should we not face, concretely and in specific cases, the question of whether there are unforgivable crimes?

Heidegger would be the first to point out that abstract discussions cannot specify practices. If I am to argue that mercy is appropriate, I must do so on the ground. This is a tall order for a mere book, and no writing can ever hope to substitute for history and experience. However, the chapters in part 2 try to go some way toward putting these abstract ideas in some kind of context. Chapter 5 questions whether and when mercy in criminal cases is sometimes appropriate, by looking at some examples from the pardon context. Chapter 6 investigates the next question: are there unforgivable crimes? The conclusion includes meditations on two novels. The first meditation addresses the limits of both retributive punishment and victims' rights approaches in the context of *The Count of Monte Cristo* by Alexandre Dumas. It is a companion to the foregoing critique of retribution in chapter 3 from the ground of its own principles. The second meditation, on J. M. Coetzee's novel *Disgrace*,[84] addresses how, from our being-in/with perspective, punishment can be a painful shared memory of wrong, settled by grace in a new union with others—even outside the context of any penal institution.

Readers will see that missing here is any political theory that would justify or explain if and/or when the state has the right as a witness to punish or be merciful, as well as any concrete proposal for sentencing reform. The examples from institutional contexts that follow are not meant to justify our current institutions but are reflections on our practices, from which I seek to draw out analogies, common-law fashion, that may help us see mercy on the ground and in context. I think it is important to look to these contexts in order to flesh out the ideas in the preceding chapters—just as I would want to read through the case law pertaining to, for example, the application of the "innkeeper liability" rules I examined earlier. I am looking, in other words, to see how mercy is already at work in our institutions; to find patterns already there, though perhaps not usually noticed; to find examples and situations I may not have considered from the vantage point of my armchair; and, finally, to try to convey an *experience* of mercy with emotional cues, context, and content rather than just an abstract argument.

The fact that I am not going to address broader questions of political theory here, however, is not because there is nothing to say but because there is much more to say than I can say in this book. I will say only this: if we take up a humbler and more merciful approach to punishment that is more appropriate to human finitude, we cannot expect the state to create a perfectly retributive system, and therefore the absence of adherence to articulable universal rules of reason cannot be in itself an objection. Though this may seem anathema to many well-intentioned critiques of our very harsh and racially discriminatory penal system, I believe the all-or-nothing requirement of an expectation that the state can be some kind of philosopher's god[85] leaves us unable to separate our criticism of, for example, sadistic prison torture from our criticism of prosecutorial discretion. From the perspective of kanticism, both are abuses of power, just as is *any* un-rule-bound moment in the criminal justice system. Yet I believe we must distinguish the two, not just in degree, but in kind. Sadistic torture is more than a failure to follow rules; it is an intolerable breach of being-with that demonstrates a stony indifference to the suffering and dignity of others. Prosecutorial discretion, by contrast, is essential to the limits of human endeavor in redressing wrong, and, used well, it may demonstrate both good judgment and compassion, even if it is not bound by rules. If we think that the legitimacy of state power must rest on the state's realization of perfectly predictable, rational, rule-based practices, we are condemning our politics to failure and our public penal system to cynicism. We have to recognize that good judgment is, in Karl Llewellyn's phrase, *reckonable,* but not predictable, and that the fact that institutional actors do not "merely follow rules" (as if following rules were something mechanical) is not itself the kind of criticism we should be making.

Instead, there may be room for a politics that recognizes that government legitimacy may rest not on the extent to which a government follows rules but on the extent to which a government inspires long-term loyalty. Though patriotism and love of country can often coincide with xenophobia or warmongering, it is my sense that long-term love of country is only inspired by leaders who offer more than fear and by a penal system that offers not "equal misery" but compassion and hope for a renewed being-with. When the citizen knows that a government official cares, when a welfare officer or immigration official goes the extra distance to try to help someone cut through the red tape, when a state employer takes a risk and hires an ex-con, when a probation officer has and takes the time to listen, when a prosecutor spends time with the victim and clearly explains the court procedures and helps with restitution and counseling, when a police officer takes the time to get to know the people on his beat, when the district attorney helps a defendant find drug treatment or child care, when prisoners are treated as people who are more than their crime, then there is a different kind of possibility for legitimacy. The love of country—or perhaps more important, the love of one's compatriots—that these actions inspire is not a love that holds one's country to "either the duties or rights of a superior being," as C. S. Lewis puts it, but a love that makes one's country one's home. Understood in this more limited way, patriotism avoids both the arrogance of imperialism (even imperialism in the name of reason) and the disillusionment engendered by our inevitable failure to achieve a rational "kingdom of ends." We should love our country, as Lewis says, because it is "a poor thing, but mine own."[86]

As to future sentencing reforms, I will say only this: in thinking about sentencing in the public domain, we should be, at the very least, chastened by the philosophical insights we have gained. If we despair of making our public penal system more merciful, then, at the least, the moral pretensions of the criminal law must be humbled. If we should be wary of asserting that an offender is really remorseful, we should also be equally wary of asserting that an offender who did not receive a long prison sentence really "got off lightly." We should not presume to judge moral desert; instead, we should take steps to settle, as we can, for the future.

My "humble" opinion is that the political sentencing problem we face in the United States at this moment in time, as others have pointed out, is that we as a polity tend to assume that a sentence is morally correct only when it is harsh.[87] This assumption seems to issue from a place of anger, stirred by our incomplete knowledge of, fear of, and horror at violent crime, which fear has been reinforced and perhaps even exploited by those seeking power.[88] Ironically and tellingly, defense lawyers, who have perhaps the closest and broadest "view" of their clients, rarely react with the revulsion for and terror of their clients that the rest of us seem too often to do. We might think about that.

PART TWO

CHAPTER 5

The Ethics of Mercy: The Pardon Cases

In part 1, I suggested a rethinking of the relation between punishment and mercy from an understanding of humanity, at core, as a being-in/with rather than as a capacity for following universal rules of reason. After we have cleared away the philosophical objections to mercy that flow from the idea that universal rules are necessary to being human—that is, that mercy is irrational and therefore undignified and demeaning to creatures of reason—we still have to ask whether or not mercy is ethically appropriate for us. As finite beings who have always to understand from a past already given and whose best understanding is always concrete and situational, we must *find* mercy at work already in our existing culture and institutions. If it were not there already, somewhere, we would not have an idea of it.

This part of the book begins with an unusual sort of methodology, then, because instead of establishing "principles" or definitions or rules for mercy, I am digging through some of our cultural texts in order to *find* patterns of mercy. This is the lawyer's method: sifting through the case law to find analogies that will help guide us and eventually starting to see a pattern, often a spectrum, of easy and hard cases within which to fit the problem we seek to solve. These patterns are, as in any common-law reasoning process, temporally bound and therefore temporary, subject to change as new situations arise that add to our store of experience.

This chapter, using the context of pardons, tries to say something about appropriate and inappropriate mercy using a common-law method—looking for a "clear" case and then turning to the more complex and murky ones, reasoning by analogy, categorizing only provisionally and tentatively. Once the patterns of pardoning have emerged, we see how "easy cases" of pardoning practices bring out and underscore the key philosophical insights we have already unpacked: that we are finite, that we are already in a world and with others, that emotional attunement is part of how we think, and that our most reliable knowledge is concrete. Many of the "easy" cases of pardon that even retributivists would allow—for example, pardon for innocence—are based not on reason as rules but on features of being in/with. From there, I suggest that we should not balk at some of the harder cases of pardoning on the ground that they are "irrational" or "arbitrary," for they, too, stem from our finitude, being-with, emotional attunement, and situational ways of knowing.

Sorting out which pardons may be appropriate and which are not is not a matter of setting forth categories of acceptable pardons, as we shall see, because even within the categories we can discern, there are easier and harder cases. But within the limits given by analogical reasoning, there is still much to be said about the practice of mercy in the pardoning context.

I. A PARDON BESTIARY

I begin with a provisional taxonomy of pardons, trying to identify some "central cases" where our intuitions about the appropriate use of the pardon are clearer, then moving to harder cases. The categories are far from original: Professors Digeser,[1] Kobil,[2] Rappaport,[3] Sarat,[4] and many others have divided pardons into similar kinds. The first four categories reflect considerations internal to the case—equity, peacemaking, allegiance/remorse, and compassion. The fifth category consists of pardons that reflect considerations external to the case, for in my view, these pardons represent cases in which an executive is faced with a role conflict: the demands of the executive's adjudicative role in pardoning conflict with his or her role as enforcer of policy or head of state or leader of the legislature. Finally, I end with an example of a "hard case" of pardon.

I do not limit my examples here to pardons by the chief executive (governor or president) but include examples of "pardons" by anyone who waives or mitigates lawful or deserved punishment, including prosecutors, juries, judges, police, and victims, because the normative concerns at play in many cases are not unique to chief executives.

Pardons as Equity

In October 2004, Peter J. Rose was exonerated by DNA evidence of the rape of a thirteen-year-old girl. At his sentencing in 1996, he had sobbed, "This crime is sick; it's not me!" Through the Innocence Project and the efforts of students of Golden Gate University's School of Law, clothing worn by the victim was tracked down in the evidence repositories of California and retested twice. Both tests proved that Rose could not have been the rapist. He had served ten years of a twenty-seven-year sentence. Rose was the 157th convicted defendant in the United States exonerated by DNA evidence.[5]

Kevin Byrd was convicted of rape in 1985 and served twelve years before he was exonerated by DNA evidence in 1997 and pardoned by then-governor George Bush. The evidence used to exonerate him was slated for destruction in 1994 but, owing to record-keeping snafus, had been preserved anyway. Just after his exoneration, DNA evidence preserved in other cases was destroyed.

These cases are central, easy cases for pardon[6] —better justice for old cases that may be procedurally barred by courts.[7] These equity pardons involve individual cases of innocence, where new evidence of innocence is available.

But innocence is not always obvious. Consider Aleck Carpitcher, convicted of child molestation through the testimony of an eleven-year-old girl. Shortly after his trial, she recanted her testimony, saying she had made the allegation because she did not like his living with her mother and wanted to get him out of the house. The Virginia courts would not hear her recantation, because of a rule that barred new evidence twenty-one days after the conviction. But then the Virginia legislature changed the rule, allowing new evidence ninety days after conviction. While Carpitcher's case was pending before the state appellate court, new hearsay evidence turned up that the victim may have recanted her recantation, and evidence not introduced at Carpitcher's original trial suggested that he may have been involved in molesting young girls in the past.[8] Carpitcher's appeal was denied through the Virginia Supreme Court, on the ground that the victim's inconsistent testimony made it difficult to determine whether her recantation was true or the product of duress (as the state argued). (In proceedings to overturn his conviction, the burden was now on Carpitcher to prove his innocence by clear and convincing evidence.)[9] In October 2009, Governor Kaine denied without comment Carpitcher's request for a pardon, as Carpitcher began the eleventh year of his thirty-eight-year sentence.[10]

As every good lawyer (and every good mystery writer) knows, at one point in time, the question of guilt or innocence seems absolutely clear, but that certainty may not be determinate for all time, for the possibility of new evidence placing old evidence in a new light is always lurking. Justice is ineluctably temporal.

Beyond the individual case of innocence, equity may also account for pardons of classes of cases in which legal rules or procedures have lagged behind our sense of justice.[11] Governor Celeste pardoned battered women who could not make out self-defense claims under traditional rules;[12] and pardons have been extended in compassionate euthanasia cases[13] where the law required verdicts of premeditated murder. Governor Ryan justified his blanket pardon of death-row inmates in Illinois in part by the claim that the death penalty was not administered fairly or reliably and that the legislature had repeatedly failed to act to make the law more just.[14]

Still more controversial are equity pardons based on post-conviction "reform." The death penalty case of "Tookie" Williams in California is a prime example of a case in which an offender had reformed his life since his crime: a gang leader became a leader in the fight against gangs. Calls for Governor Schwarzenegger to pardon him emphasized that he was no longer the cold-blooded killer who had murdered the four victims and that his commutation would recognize his "good works." But, reciting the gruesome details of the murders, the strong evidence of Williams's guilt, and Williams's refusal to acknowledge guilt, Schwarzenegger declined to pardon him, and he was executed.[15]

Finally, pardons may commute sentences where service of the original sentence becomes more onerous than "average" because of old age, illness, susceptibility to rape in prison, loss of custody of minor children, or other circumstances. Kathleen Dean Moore considers this pardon a kind of after-trial equity that equalizes the "pain" of the sentence so that one does the same pain, if not the same time, for the same crime.[16] Professors Markel and Digeser argue that this sort of pardon is based on compassion, not equity. If justice required post-conviction readjustment, they argue, then the only sentencing option is the indeterminate sentence and the concomitant and dangerous problem of giving disparate sentences for disparate "sensibilities."[17]

Pardon as equity is thought to be an easy case, for it is merely better justice. But even this easy case conceals a troubling paradox. Surely innocence (the easiest case for equity pardons) is a good reason for a pardon? The difficulty is that any statement of reasons (or specification of the degree of certainty of innocence that is required to pardon) ossifies into rules and procedures that will be applied "consistently" and therefore, in some case or other, unjustly (resulting in the punishment of the innocent). We will then need a superpardon as equity to correct the injustice of the rule-based pardon as equity. The only way to achieve pardon as equity is to keep it ruleless and thereby lawless—making justice itself depend on the absence of legal rules.[18]

This illustrates why reason, in the sense of a set of logically consistent (and equally applied) rules, cannot be foundational for humans. We cannot achieve justice through such rules, as they are static and general and incomplete, while we (the finite creatures who articulate them) are learning, growing, innovating, extemporizing, improvising, changing, and getting new glimpses of the world and each other all the time. Our ability to get these glimpses, our attunement, our attentiveness, our immersion in the world and in relationships with others, is deeper and more foundational than reason. Pardon as equity brings this truth to light. Rules are heuristics; they are sometimes necessary ones, but they necessarily do injustices.

From this perspective, the kinds of equity most often done in pardoning reflect our finitude and the temporality of law. Equity to redress the injustice of procedural bar rules (as well as the procedural bar rules themselves) reflects the finitude and contradiction of human process: we cannot keep relitigating infinitely, and, at the same time, we never have perfect and complete information. Equity to acknowledge unique mitigating factors reflects the fact that law itself is finite and that its general terms, formulated in the past, cannot encompass all the changing possibilities in the world, especially when those mitigating factors may present themselves after sentencing is complete. Equity to acknowledge broader, nonlegal mitigating factors, such as domestic violence or mental illness, reflect the fact that enacted law cannot always keep up with our sense of justice as it shows itself to us in individual cases. Equity to acknowledge post-conviction amendment reflects the fact that a conviction and sentence take an accounting at a single point in time and cannot predict or assess the future or what the offender may become. The demands of equity can never be satisfied once and for all, for life, law, and knowledge of the world are always moving targets.

Pardon as equity reflects the necessary disjunct between law and justice, though it has little to do with leniency. It is relatively uncontroversial only because familiar concerns of innocence and extent of guilt are brought to bear on the particular case. But were we to understand this form of pardon as simply judgment itself, it might be deeply unsettling, for it reveals the pervasive indeterminacy and temporality of justice. Judgment is an art, and the individual determinations of equity and (beautiful) fit that it requires of us stem from our already being-in/with, from our emotional and perceptual attunement to the world to which we are already given over. Pardon as equity also demonstrates that true retributive justice is not possible through reason and that justice, insofar as we can approach it, relies not on reason but on being in/with, on the *gift to the guilty* we do not deserve. Equity pardons should lead us to think of punishment from a humbler and more human place—not as an accurate accounting of desert, but as a tentative settlement to renew being-with.

Pardons as Peace

Post–Civil War pardons by Presidents Lincoln and Johnson were classic examples of executive pardons as peace.

> Whereas it is now desired by some persons heretofore engaged in said rebellion to resume their allegiance to the United States, and to reinaugurate loyal State governments within and for their respective States; therefore, I, Abraham Lincoln, President of the United States, do proclaim, declare, and make known to all persons who have, directly or by implication, participated in the existing rebellion, except as hereinafter excepted, that a full pardon is hereby granted to them and each of them, with restoration of all rights of property, except as to slaves, and in property cases where rights of third parties shall have intervened, and upon the condition that every such person shall take and subscribe an oath, and thenceforward keep and maintain said oath inviolate.[19]

Such pardons were not unique. Presidents Washington, Adams, and Jefferson all used the pardon power to settle instances of rebellion and to reform the national community.[20] In our own time, the South African Truth and Reconciliation Commission provided a contemporary example of pardon as an attempt to negotiate a peace and to establish and renew community after racial violence.[21] Rwanda's efforts at a similar kind of mediation have met with mixed success.[22]

The peace pardon is usually general, not personal, extended to all those "at war" with the pardoning community (usually extending to acts that would have been criminal had they not had their genesis in war or political disagreements or to criminal acts only made criminal under color of later-discredited law or illegitimate authority). Lincoln was faced repeatedly with the difficulties of the distinction between war and crime: in 1862, he commuted the death sentences of hundreds of Indians involved in hostilities in Minnesota, allowing the execution of only those who "proved guilty of violating females [two]" and those "who were proven to have participated in massacres [forty], as distinguished from participation in battles." His hope, repeated in the Civil War amnesties, was "to not act with so much clemency as to encourage another outbreak on the one hand, nor with so much severity as to be real cruelty on the other."[23]

In the U.S. Constitution, the pardon power is granted in the same sentence as the war power. As Alexander Hamilton explained in Federalist No. 74, this is no coincidence.

> But the principal argument for reposing the power of pardoning in [the case of treason] in the Chief Magistrate is this: in seasons of insurrection or rebellion, there are often critical moments when a well-timed offer of pardon to the insurgents or rebels may restore the tranquillity of the commonwealth; and which, if suffered to pass unimproved, it may never be possible afterwards to recall.[24]

The power to wage war must have as its necessary analog the power to make peace. Except in the case of unconditional surrender, peace requires compromise, as the law of one side cannot be imposed on the other, and the laws of war no longer apply. The peacemaking, then, must stand outside the law, and pardon provides that extralegal immunity. The pardon's role here creates a new polity, includes outlaws as "inlaws," and expands the borders of legal jurisdiction through legal immunity.

Pardon as peacemaking thus allows us to glimpse a difficulty in the Kantian view of reason as the foundation of community. Derrida and Condorcet point out the now-familiar paradox that before a polity can be self-governing, the polity that will be voting must be specified in advance, on a nondemocratic basis. This aspect of the pardon power recalls us to the foundational fact that the being-with must precede Kantian notions of "autonomy," for no self-government is possible without first constituting a "self." The "individual" subject of liberalism is constituted by a particular cultural context and history, already embedded in a set of relations and practices that the "individual" has not "chosen."[25] Likewise, for peoples, conquest, chance, immigration, geographic proximity, and sheer accident will bring people to live with each other and, over time, constitute a people (or set of warring peoples) that govern themselves. But the people cannot choose the people. To this extent, the executive pardon's lawless character in the realm of creating or re-creating a polity through the peacemaking power can be no objection, for there is no legal or "reasonable" alternative.

But stopping here we remain with a sovereign power ungoverned by any ethics, a new god-on-earth of totalitarianism, unless there is a possibility for right action outside of law. Only through an account of a more primary being-with can such a nonlaw be found that could unify the warring positive laws of the treating states. If, however, we are already responsible to others and already with others, then our ethical and legal obligations are always and already there. The possibility of a community depends on there being already a being-with— which we have as a gift given to us who are already responsible to each other, before law. Pardon for peace, then, is merely a recognition of this already-there human community.

Pardons as Allegiance

President Lincoln wrote to Edwin M. Stanton, secretary of war, on February 5, 1864,

> On principle I dislike an oath which requires a man to swear he has not done wrong. It rejects the Christian principle of forgiveness on terms of repentance. I think it is enough if the man does no wrong hereafter.[26]

In 2004, an American soldier in Iraq refused to obey a direct order to "chamber a round" in his weapon before leaving the base perimeter. The commander could have convened a court-martial. But he did not. He knew this soldier well; he was a good soldier and had served well for nearly his entire tour of duty. But the soldier had had enough of killing. The commander decided to avoid a court-martial by assigning this soldier to duties within the perimeter for the short remainder of his tour. The commander acknowledged that he could not have done this at the beginning of the soldier's service; other members of the company would have taken it as favoritism, weakness, and it would have destroyed discipline. However, after having served together for some time, many of the company were sympathetic with this soldier, and all understood the commander's act of mercy, for no one wanted someone who had served so well to end his service by court-martial. They understood that the soldier had been responsible to the commander, and now the commander was being responsible for the soldier.[27]

Another officer at a military training camp confronted a young soldier who had gone AWOL to visit his girlfriend to try to convince her not to break up with him. The soldier acknowledged fault and expressed remorse. The officer knew him as a good soldier and did not want to ruin his career; the military was this soldier's best chance to rise above a tough childhood. So the commander gave him a minor punishment that would not be reflected in his future personnel records and did not kick him out of the training program. The soldier was extremely grateful, for he knew that the officer was putting his own reputation on the line. The soldier felt responsible to the officer; the officer was at future risk himself from the soldier's future bad conduct.

Victim-offender mediation also emphasizes what I call here "pardon as allegiance," though the allegiance in such mediation is forged between victims and offenders. Mark Umbreit tells the story of David and Maria Sanchez, owners of a local grocery store that was vandalized by Federico Angeles and his friends. The store owners remembered Angeles as a frequent customer. Angeles acknowledged the connection: "Everybody knows the 'J.' We get snacks there and meet people there . . . The parking lot behind the store is a good place to mess around with girls. Usually you don't get hassled there."[28] In their discussion, the Sanchezes expressed anger but also connection: Mrs. Sanchez said, "You look like a young man who wants to have fun, but you don't look like a bad man. It was important for me to see you. Now I remember you from before. You have been in our store many times. Why don't you help us?"[29] Angeles's cocky grin dissolved upon seeing Mrs. Sanchez in tears over the wreckage of her store (and her future). After understanding the extent of the damage he helped cause and its effect on the people before him, Angeles responded with remorse and agreed to work in the Sanchezes' store to help repair the damage, instead of going to jail.

Personal connection, presence, and remorse play a central role here. "It was important for me to see you" is the theme that echoes through many of these mediation stories—both for the victims and for the offenders. The victims needed to see the offenders out of the context of the crime, to counteract their own fear, to express their anger, and to try to understand why the crime occurred. The humanizing experience helps the crime seem less "senseless," less "random." The offenders needed to see the victims face-to-face in order to remember the wrong as wrong, seeing and hearing that wrong for themselves, perhaps for the first time, to confront the effects of their actions and to have the opportunity to apologize.

The pardon out of allegiance stems from an authority (or victim as authority) who can, after a personal confrontation or "witnessing" of the kind described in chapter 4, resettle a preexisting relationship for the future (even if the preexisting relationship is one created only by the crime itself). Executive pardons used to be conceived, at least in part, as "most personal"[30] in this way.

Blackstone states, "In monarchies the king acts in a superior sphere . . . Whenever the nation sees him personally engaged, it is only in works of legislature, magnificence, or compassion . . . These repeated acts of goodness, coming immediately from his own hand, endear the sovereign to his subjects, and contribute more than any thing to root in their hearts that filial affection, and personal loyalty, which are the sure establishment of a prince."[31] Likewise, Justice Marshall said in *United States v. Wilson*, "A pardon is an act of grace, proceeding from the power entrusted with the execution of the laws, which exempts the individual, on whom it is bestowed, from the punishment the law inflicts for a crime he has committed. It is the *private*, though official act of the executive magistrate" (emphasis added).[32]

However, by 1926, Justice Holmes would deny the "personal" nature of executive pardons, saying in *Biddle v. Perovich*, "A pardon in our days is not a private act of grace from an individual happening to possess power. It is a part of the Constitutional scheme. When granted it is the determination of the ultimate authority that the public welfare will be better served by inflicting less than what the judgment fixed."[33]

Pardon as personal allegiance is a much harder case to make within the mainstream liberal traditions. We do not like the hierarchy it presumes, the mutual obligation it entails, or the personal loyalty it presupposes. It is indeed a kind of understanding of the pardon that has faded away in most contemporary analysis of the institution of pardoning, at least outside the context of the military. The executive (as governor of a state or as president of the United States) seems too distant a figure to have a personal relationship of trust and future risk with and from the forgiven citizen.

But the allegiance pardon may make more sense at the more intimate levels of institutional discretion. The military has a practice of clemency that operates between commanding officer and soldier, where trust, loyalty, and mutual risk are critical and are put to the keenest tests. Outside the military, many contemporary reforms have aimed to reestablish personal loyalty to authorities in various areas of law enforcement: community policing, drug court, community or victim-offender mediation, intensive probation, or trial by (very) local juries. In all of these innovative approaches to law enforcement and practice, the emphasis is on trying to make personal connections between the police, judges, juries, and offenders, so that the offender is responsible to the authority and vice versa. David Tait has suggested that the pardon power itself should be decentralized, residing in local decision making (as it already does, unofficially at least).[34]

In these contexts, mercy is personal—part of the allegiance owed to and the protection given by an authority. But the authority is not immune from the wrong; on the contrary, the authority's power is lessened by the past wrong, and the authority is, both personally and in position, at risk from the future conduct of the wrongdoer. Mercy here is a gift, generates gratitude, reinforces the relationship of allegiance, and takes on the risk of future dealings with the offender. Remorse on the part of the wrongdoer is in part the grief of disloyalty to the authority and demonstrates the desire to retain the bonds of allegiance. Future wrong is not only a violation of a law but, more saliently, a personal breach of trust.[35]

Do allegiance pardons run contrary to our practices of holding each other responsible for our actions? On the contrary, we might see a place for clemency as creating or reinforcing bonds of loyalty and trust, responsibility *to* and responsibility *for* others.[36] Moreover, such person-to-person bonds are more tangible and less abstract than respect for law or laws can be. They make the obligations real to those who have them, and they place them in a context in which we humans are able to understand them best: the concrete and particular. They create the real, historical selves that can "be responsible" at all.[37] When the alternative is housing offenders for a period of years in large, impersonal institutions as an abstract "equivalent" to their crime and without any necessary contact with the victim or any other person to whom duties are owed, clemency of this kind does not seem out of balance with concern for instilling or reinforcing bonds of personal responsibility.

Consider the following thank-you letter from an offender whose death sentence was commuted.

> This is my first opportunity for personally expressing appreciation for your act of commutation of the sentence of death given to me. Actually, I feel this expression will continue the rest of my life, as I continue to feel an obligation to show justification of your act of clemency . . . For my part, I will want the rest of my life to at least be some proof of an amount of truth in these thoughts. It will be my hope that I will not only continue to justify your act of commutation, sir, but also give by my example some proof of the value of even a human life which was condemned.[38]

Clemency as allegiance allows remorse to play a key role, for the remorseful offender is one who understands himself or herself as having these concrete obligations and feels concrete pain at failing to honor them. To allow the remorseful offender to pledge his or her future allegiance and right action to another real person who can offer clemency is to reestablish the bonds of obligation that the crime broke.

Do allegiance pardons treat like cases differently? If one rapist gets ten years in prison and the next is pardoned, is not the first excluded and treated wrongly? We may presume so, if that is all we know about the cases. But what if we also know that the first rapist is unremorseful, boasts of his deed, and taunts his victim, while the second is tearful and remorseful and voluntarily puts himself into the hands of a community-based mediation panel of former rape victims and their families? What if, after long, agonizing personal mediation, the second rapist's victim accepts his word and accepts (along with other local community members, themselves potential victims) the risk that he will, despite his assurances, reoffend?

The problem with the argument from equality is that the interaction that results in clemency may itself make the case "unequal." If our practical knowledge is irreducibly particular, personal confrontation yields knowledge and forges relationships that cannot be completely reduced to factors or rules. New responsibilities to and for another may be forged even in the process of settlement.

It may also be argued here that not all offenders have the "personality" or legal representation to establish rapport with authority figures and that clemency rewards those who are charming, charismatic, articulate, likable, white, well educated, or well represented. (This may be especially troubling considering that "glibness and superficial charm" may be traits of the worst-feared psychopaths.)[39] But if such inequalities are objectionable, they are objectionable not just at the highest levels of clemency but at every level of the criminal process, from initial interactions with neighbors (who may or may not call police), to the police (who may or may not arrest), to the prosecutor (who may or may not prosecute), to judges (who may or may not grant bail or accept a plea), to the jury (who may or may not find one credible). We cannot escape the limits of our own humanity. Face-to-face confrontation is the basis not only for our judgments of each other but, even more important, for establishing relationships with one another. Even if statistical factors could enable us to better predict recidivism,[40] we have an *ethical* duty not to assume that we can know everything about someone. The sentencing process, then, is not an exercise in prediction but an ethical encounter in which both parties can be changed by what they experience there, whether trust is extended (by saying, e.g., "I'm counting on you to fulfill your commitments today") or humanity is denied (by saying, e.g., "The defendant is a piece of trash, clearly unable and unwilling to control his actions").[41]

The only remedy for discrimination and manipulation in the criminal or pardon context rests first on trying to find wise and experienced decision makers, aware of their potential prejudices and alert to racism, sexism, and bias. There is no technological or institutional replacement for the ethical relation. Of course, a good pardoning process should also include some provision for information about defendants from others who know them well, should allow the possibility for friends or advocates to speak on behalf of the inarticulate and tell "their side" of their story, and should have a process for checking the facts.[42]

Pardons as Compassion

All of the following expressions of compassion and lack of compassion come from President Lincoln's letters.

To Edwin M. Stanton, Hon. Sec. of War—
March 1, 1864

A poor widow, by the name of Baird, has a son in the Army, that for some offence has been sentenced to serve a long time without pay, or at most, with very little pay. I do not like this punishment of withholding pay—it falls so very hard upon poor families. After he has been serving in this way for several months, at the tearful appeal of the poor Mother, I made a direction that he be allowed to enlist for a new term, on the same conditions as others. She now comes, and says she can not get it acted upon. Please do it. Yours truly, A Lincoln.[43]

To George G. Meade
Aug. 21, 1863

At this moment I am appealed to in behalf of William Thompson of Co.K.3rd. Maryland Volunteers, in 12th Army Corps said to be at Kelly's Ford, under sentence to be shot to-day as a deserter. He is represented to me to be very young, with symptoms of insanity. Please postpone the execution till further order.[44]

To George G. Meade
October 8 & 12, 1863

I am appealed to in behalf of John Murphy, to be shot to-morrow. His Mother says he is but seventeen . . . I therefore, on account of his tender age, have concluded to pardon him, and to leave it to yourself whether to discharge him, or continue in the service.

To Stephen A. Hurlbut
December 17, 1863
    I understand you have, under sentence of death, a tall old man, by the name of Henry F. Luckett. I personally knew him, and did not think him a bad man. Please do not let him be executed, unless upon further order from me, and, in the mean time, send me a transcript of the record.[45]

To George G. Meade
August 27, 1863
    Walter, Rainese, Faline, Lae & Kuhne appeal to me for mercy without giving any ground for it whatever. I understand these are very flagrant cases, and that you deem their punishment as being indispensable to the service. If I am not mistaken in this, please let them know at once that their appeal is denied.[46]

Clemency for the old, the young, the sick, those with extraordinary family burdens, those subject to child abuse or domestic violence, war veterans, the disabled, and other sympathetic cases is also apparent in earlier presidencies[47] and is reflected currently in the reduction of sentences by downward departure under the Federal Sentencing Guidelines and in clemency actions in the military context.[48] The pardons from compassion often come after an emotional plea by a parent or respected authority or by the offender. Like remorse pardons, they are often founded on the empathy present in a person-to-person exchange. The most common grounds for compassion are those that most of us would find make either the crime more tempting or the punishment more onerous or are a response to other hardships the person has endured in life.[49] Compassion may also arise spontaneously, based on a sense of common ground that cannot be articulated in these categories—"I personally knew him, and did not think him a bad man"—and here it is most controversial. Compassion pardons may be unconnected with remorse.

    Compassion pardons are hardest for retributivists to accept. Standard jury instructions, for example, direct jurors to set aside sympathy or compassion.[50] However, contemporary discussion on the place of emotion in thought bears out the insight that our emotional tenor does indeed play a critical role in making certain aspects of our situation salient or even apparent; in calming, focusing, or directing our thinking; and thus in helping us make sense of what we experience.

Many of our actual legal practices (as opposed to our jury instructions) incorporate emotional attunement. We insist on live testimony by witnesses (in our confrontation clause) and on the drama of an emotionally charged "trial," and we stress the importance of "demeanor," "eye contact," "body language," and "presence" in evaluating evidence.[51] We defer to the trial court and the jury because "they heard the testimony." We allow capital defendants the right to address the jury in person at the sentencing hearing, without being subject to cross-examination. We do so because these kinds of person-to-person interactions cannot necessarily be completely narrated in written "facts" or "reasons" yet yield knowledge that is much more familiar and easier for us to interpret than abstruse statutes, complex case law, or philosophical moral discussions. Again, our primary, foundational experience of the world derives meaning from the concrete and personal: effortlessly and without even noticing it, we distinguish the sigh of despair from the sigh of impatience and from the sigh of relief. No one who has seen a trial and then read the appellate report of it could argue that the two experiences give identical kinds of knowledge, even if all the "relevant" facts have been included. The personal and emotionally charged meeting between judge and offender may yield "reasons that reason cannot tell."

As I outlined in chapter 4, the emotion of compassion may be particularly appropriate for gaining insight into the crime or character of one who is to be judged.[52] It is an emotion that disposes one to see similarities where they may not be obvious, potentially overcoming, rather than reinforcing, prejudices and prejudgments. It is an emotion that concentrates one on the particular and individual, calling one's attention to detail, making the ordinary salient in its little uniquenesses. It is an emotion that humbles, closing the gap in status that may exist between judge and defendant and moving the judge away from a tendency to be inattentive, dismissive, intolerant, skeptical, lazy, or impatient (all of which are occupational hazards).[53] Compassion is an equalizer, combating the hierarchy that may exist between offenders, between victim and offender, and between judge and offender.

So it is at least possible that an interaction between a defendant and a clemency giver can and should be affected by compassion. Compassion may be triggered by and may in turn reveal aspects of a defendant's crime or situation that matter yet cannot be fully expressed by an abstractly stated principle or reason and, indeed, may sound inadequate when so stated (e.g., "because he is old" or "because he is ill"). The result may be a judgment that rests not necessarily on "bias" or "caprice" but on a better understanding of the crime or defendant, one that cannot be articulated in rule form.

Compassion does not necessarily destroy or compromise responsibility.[54] Compassion by a judge or decision maker may convince an offender that the "system" is not "out to get" him or her and that officials are not impersonal and unreachable but human and even humane. Compassion may show the offender that the judge does sympathize with his or her plight and still sees the offender as a member of the human circle, rather than a monster, outlaw, scumbag, or jerk, defined entirely by his or her crime. Compassion may stir an answering emotion in the offender, making tangible to him or her again the bond with others that the offender may have rebelled against, ultimately leading the offender to take responsibility for his or her actions rather than to deny them.

In our era of mutual suspicion and national and international culture wars, it seems very ill timed for me to be arguing that "local knowledge" as a basis of ethical action will yield compassion rather than more xenophobic mistrust and violence. Yet the way in which we can and have swept international "law" away as well suggests that recourse to general principles and law will not curb violence either. For example, it is at least arguable that the more vivid and particular photos of abuses at Abu Ghraib were more effective in changing interrogation and detention policies (and perhaps even in swaying the decisions of the Supreme Court) than arguments about the Geneva Conventions.[55] The concrete effects of our fears and policies brought "in our face" can still bring us to see justice in a particular case where it is otherwise hidden in general "principles." Compassion is still possible, and compassion can even bring the outsider "inside."[56]

But what if the authority pardons out of love or friendship? Is it not a conflict of interest to pardon someone one loves—a spouse, child, sibling, friend? To extend the thought, can one pardon oneself? There is something of personal love in all compassion pardons, reflecting the underlying bond of being-with that compassion brings to the fore. But even though the authority is personally affected by the case and feels compassion, the authority (whether president or victim) must pardon on behalf of others who cannot be there to experience and judge for themselves. The claim must be that others *could* have experienced this case with compassion, based on the person and the record.

Because compassion is based in a personal interaction, however, the experience cannot be easily shared or communicated to the polity, making it difficult for a pardoner to explain. How does a decision maker allow us to "judge-with"—to share the experience, to feel the compassion, to be convinced that the offender is remorseful? Despite "reality TV," we cannot get that close. In fact, art may bring us closer than C-SPAN or Court TV can. The novelist or playwright or movie producer can sometimes make characters real for us, make us feel compassion for them, even "convince" us of remorse.[57] However, the recourse to narrative also presents the danger that a "real" case will seem less "real" than a novelized one, that we will expect the wrong cues and fail to be moved by a reality that seems thinner or more conflicted than fiction.[58] This is the challenge for the legal advocate, and whether and how judges, governors, or other pardoners can communicate the experience of compassion to a democratic constituency is an open and difficult question.[59]

Extrinsic-Good Pardons

As he himself reports, California governor Pat Brown refused to pardon criminal Richard Lindsey not because of factors intrinsic to Lindsey's case (the crime, his circumstances and character, his community standing, the harm done, the need to repair the relationships breached, etc.) but because of concerns that had nothing to do with the case or its merits.

> Inside the quiet Governor's Mansion late that November night, I became in a very real sense a scale of justice. The case against Lindsey was loaded with horrible details of the savage brutality that can lie hidden inside a human being until something makes it erupt. It was the kind of crime which seemed to cry out for vengeance, for ritual punishment as swift and terrible as the act itself.
>
> Weighed against this were the doubts raised by his mother's letter about Lindsey's mental history, an issue that I felt had never really been carefully explored during his trial. Then, too, if the death penalty was designed to be a deterrent against future crimes, I couldn't for the life of me see how killing Lindsey would keep another madman from attacking another little girl somewhere down the road.
>
> I had been governor for almost three years, and in spite of some setbacks I had managed to get a lot done. I was fighting a conservative legislature to spend more money on a growing state, to improve its schools and its mental health facilities and its working conditions. Should I risk, did I even have the *right* to risk, destroying any of that because of one demented criminal?
>
> Rose Marie Riddle was dead, and nothing I could do would bring her back. By letting Richard Lindsey go to the gas chamber, I was giving her parents and people like them a chance at a living wage. The scales tipped. I picked up my pen and on the first page of the clemency file wrote these words: "I will take no action." I dated it November 10, 1961, and signed my name. Four days later, Lindsey was dead. That same week, the farm labor bill passed through committee and a few months later was signed into law.
>
> Why then, has the Lindsey case troubled me all these years[?][60]

On the merits, Brown would have pardoned Lindsey because of his long-term mental state that suggested organic brain damage and insanity. Even were one to accept the possibility that pardons can be based on nonretributive justice factors like repentance or compassion or peacemaking, Brown's nonpardon falls into another category of utilitarian or, perhaps more accurately, extrinsic-good pardons. Other examples of extrinsic-good pardons include the pardons used to pacify the public into acquiescing in harsh laws,[61] nonpardons used in an election year to convince the public one is "tough on crime," pardons to those who will agree to pioneer in new communities or serve in the armed forces, pretrial clemency to a soldier because the commanding officer cannot spare personnel to serve on the court-martial,[62] pardons to those supported by others who will reciprocate in political or personal favors, pardons (or immunity) used to secure testimony against others,[63] or straightforward pardons for purchase.

Some cases (like bribery) are clear abuses of the pardon power, but other cases are not so clear. Is it wrong not to pardon, for example, in order to gain support for legislation that will help many others; in order to be reelected (or, to put it more neutrally, because one's constituency would not approve); to convince a legislature to pass a moratorium on the death penalty; or to avoid insurrection, riot, or mutiny? Is it wrong to pardon in order to gain volunteers for dangerous missions, to avoid tying up key personnel for a trial who are needed in combat, or in order to save administrative resources for other cases?[64]

Unlike courts, which have the obligation to decide cases on their merits, executive officials have multiple roles, and the adjudicative role is only one of them. As they balance these roles and their priorities, pardon decisions may become instrumental to duties and considerations required by the executive's other roles. The ethical problems expand: when considering a pardon application, should the executive's adjudicative role always trump the executive's other roles?

The Hard Case of Darrell Mease

In January 1999, Governor Carnahan pardoned triple murderer Darrell Mease. A Missouri hillbilly who grew up in the Pentecostal Church and was drafted into the Vietnam War after high school (just after his seventeen-year-old wife bore his first child), Mease left the United States a good old boy who did not drink or swear and who wanted to be a preacher someday; he returned addicted to alcohol and suffering nightmares. After Mease's two failed marriages and a long run of job instability, Ozark drug lord Lloyd Lawrence recruited him for his operation manufacturing methamphetamine.

One night, after Lloyd got Darrell to try some crystal meth, Darrell's drug-induced paranoia (and Lloyd's reputation as a rapist) made him believe Lloyd was going to try to molest his girlfriend, Mary, to whom he was devoted. Darrell decided to leave right away, stashing the drugs they had made where Lloyd would not be able to find them. After several months of traveling and hiding all over the South and the Southwest with Mary, Darrell discovered that Lloyd had put out a contract to kill him for stealing his drugs. Believing that his only option was to strike first, Darrell staked out Lloyd's vacation cabin, lay in wait for three days, and killed Lloyd, Lloyd's wife, and Lloyd's paraplegic grandson, by firing a powerful shotgun into their heads at close range as they drove out into the woods on four-wheelers.

After he and Mary were apprehended, Darrell underwent an intense and tearful jailhouse conversion (which even cynical observers tended to credit) and proclaimed to the press that "God was his Lawyer." His faith that he would not be executed was unshaken, even when his conviction and death sentence were affirmed throughout the appellate and habeas process and the execution date was set. Then, in a public relations gaffe, Darrell's execution was originally scheduled for the same day that Pope John Paul II, a staunch opponent of capital punishment, was to visit St. Louis.

Though the Missouri Supreme Court tried quietly to reschedule the execution for a later date, the press caught on and pilloried the state for its hypocrisy. Governor Carnahan was told that the pope would ask for Darrell's pardon. The circumstances of the request, made at an interfaith prayer service near the end of the pope's visit, have been reconstructed by investigative journalist Michael Cuneo.

> The pope read his homily with a shaking hand and a quavering voice, closing with a ringing entreaty to all Americans: "If you want peace, work for justice. If you want justice, defend life. If you want life, embrace the truth —the truth revealed by God." There was no explicit reference in the homily to capital punishment. It was a stirring event—the comparative intimacy of the cathedral, with its byzantine mosaic-clad interior, the sumptuous music that both preceded and followed the homily, the passage from Isaiah expertly rendered by a prominent local rabbi. Everything was in perfect pitch, graceful and harmonious, with not a single note off-key. Then, a little before six, after the last canticle had been chanted and the last prayer recited, the pope struggled to his feet, gingerly

negotiated the steps in front of the altar, and slowly made his way over to the front left pew where he chatted briefly with the Gores before moving on to Governor Carnahan.

The two men exchanged greetings, and then the pope, his face a scant six inches from Carnahan's, said: "Governor, will you please have mercy on Mr. Mease?"

And that was it. Will you please have mercy on Mr. Mease? The most direct request imaginable. The most specific request imaginable. It wasn't about the death penalty in general. It wasn't about sparing anyone else on death row. Just Darrell—nobody but Darrell.

The governor nodded, almost imperceptibly, and the pope moved on, working his way laboriously to the rear of the cathedral with his entourage in tow.[65]

The governor explained his subsequent commutation order as coming "after careful consideration of the extraordinary circumstance of the Pontiff's direct and personal appeal for mercy and because of the deep and abiding respect I have for him and all that he represents."[66] This pardon was the result of a personal and immediate appeal.

The political fallout was complex. Even opponents of the death penalty thought there were far worthier candidates for pardon than Darrell, yet Carnahan had used up all his pardon-related political capital on a clearly guilty triple murderer. After Mease, the Missouri executions proceeded apace, one every month, as Carnahan fought off election-year allegations that he was soft on the death penalty. Pope John Paul later wrote on behalf of another Missouri death-row inmate (Roy Roberts) who had a more-than-plausible claim of innocence, but "safely back in Rome now," the Pope "was much easier to ignore."[67] A year later, Carnahan was tragically killed in a plane crash and posthumously elected to the U.S. Senate over opponent John Ashcroft.

Carnahan's pardon for Darrell cannot be grounded in equity, peace, remorse, or the usual grounds of compassion, for none of these are prominent in Mease's case. This pardon came to a man of unshakable faith (who already felt forgiven, not remorseful) whose guilt was unquestioned, without extraordinary circumstances of sympathy to recommend him. It happened because of a fluke of timing and the extraordinary personal intervention of the pope. This pardon looks like grace at its most alarming, its most unpredictable, its most arbitrary, a true instance of forgiving the unforgivable. Was it divine intervention or luck? Even if it was the former, what place can divine intervention have in secular government? Yet, as Cuneo points out, the crime itself can be understood as a confluence of extraordinary events: the absence of any one of several factors would have changed Darrell's decision to flee and kill. Had events unfolded differently, Darrell, an inherently likable and straightforward good old boy, might have become a preacher and not a murderer. The specter of moral luck pervades this story and makes it the most difficult case of all.

II. GOOD PARDONS, BAD PARDONS

Assuming one could agree that some equity, allegiance, or compassion pardons are appropriate, have we justified all pardons? Have we cut away all ethical grounds for criticizing any exercise of the pardon power? Is the executive's pardoning decision one to which we must meekly submit, no matter how corrupt?

Even if there is little legal recourse, moral discourse is still open. But without Kantian rules of reason, the kind of moral discourse we have must be concrete and on the ground. Moral critique of pardons must proceed case by case.

Corruption

The pardon must be a personal act of grace exercised by a person who undertakes the risk of future relations with the offender on behalf of all of the community of potential victims. When an executive (or victim) is acting for personal gain,[68] he or she is not speaking for all. The easiest case of this kind is selling pardons, and as the 1923 impeachment of Oklahoma governor J. C. Walton demonstrates, there is legal as well as moral recourse here.

But there are other kinds of personal gain. Pardoning friends or relatives seems an inappropriate personal gain, but what about *not* pardoning personal rivals or enemies? Moreover, how personal must it be? If an African American president were to refuse to pardon a former Ku Klux Klan member, would that be inappropriate? What about pardoning (or not pardoning) for political advantage? What about pardoning (or not) for personal emotional satisfaction?

Again, we cannot take the easy route of arguing that no personal considerations should ever affect a pardon. Yes, a pardon can proceed out of personal weakness and inability to make hard decisions. But a pardon that is grounded in a personal contact with an offender and generates compassion may also be morally acceptable as a genuine experience of connection and renewal that generates responsibility to and for. There will be hard cases as well as easy cases, and all must be judged by analogy, on the ground.

Dehumanizing Hate

Pardoning or failing to pardon out of dehumanizing hate[69] violates the foundation of being-with because it is a rejection of the bond of humanity with another. The executive dehumanizing either victim or offender (e.g., by pardoning the white lyncher because his victim was "only" a "Negro" or by refusing to pardon the rapist because he is a "monster") denies to both victim and offender inclusion in the human world. But spelling out what counts as "dehumanizing" hate is not simple.

Justice Stevens, dissenting in *Ohio Adult Parole Authority v. Woodard,*[70] argued that "no one would contend that a governor could ignore the commands of the Equal Protection Clause and use race, religion, or political affiliation as a standard for granting or denying clemency." But Stevens's attempt to articulate what is at stake here cannot be read as requiring simple equal treatment. If one takes the view that the equal protection clause requires the government to treat us "equally," then denying all petitions or flipping a coin to determine clemency would be sufficient. This does not, played out, accord with the grounding thought that government ought to respect its people and treat them with dignity.[71] In our traditions and practices, treating someone with dignity is not a simple rule but depends on context and nuance. On the one hand, it seems that a governor could decide not to pardon someone in part because the offender holds fast to, for example, anti-Semitic views, despite the fact that these views may be characterized as "political." On the other hand, it seems that a governor could take into account the (sincere and abiding) religious conversion of an offender in deciding to pardon, despite the fact that the pardon depended on the defendant's "religious" views.[72]

Moral Luck

Justice O'Connor suggests, in *Ohio Adult Parole Authority v. Woodard,* that a governor could not just flip a coin to pardon or arbitrarily deny prisoners access to the pardon process.[73] Such "arbitrariness," she believes, would violate due process.[74] Darrell Mease was pardoned just because he happened to be scheduled for execution on the same day the pope came to town. Is pardoning him like flipping a coin? Kevin Byrd was pardoned only because evidence in his case happened not to have been destroyed as it was supposed to have been. Is that like flipping a coin? Offenders who committed murders the day before their state legislature reinstated the death penalty will not be executed; those who committed their crimes the day after may be. Is that like flipping a coin? Offenders who commit murder in Houston instead of Austin or on one side of the Mississippi River instead of the other may be executed, while the others will not be. Is that like flipping a coin? Moral luck pervades the system; it is part of being finite and in time. When do we account it "arbitrary," and when do we not? Again, the question is not tidy or subject to neat conceptual resolution.

Why does "flipping a coin" strike us in the first place as an inappropriate basis for a pardon? I would argue that it is not because it is arbitrary or random but because it is disrespectful. To make a decision with that kind of impact on an offender in such a way, using a form of decision making usually reserved for the trivial or for "games," signals (in the context of our culture) that the offender's case does not matter. (One could, however, imagine a different cultural meaning for "flipping a coin" that would change that meaning—if we, for example, believed that a divine power would intervene in the coin flip to tell us what justice required.)

I would argue that a similar inference of disrespect could be drawn from an executive's refusal to look at or consider any pardon applications. Even if an executive must, for extrinsic reasons (that we agree are appropriate), deny a pardon, the executive should face the case, should give the offender the dignity of a personal response. For example, when Lincoln heard of the 303 death verdicts in the case of the Indian uprising in Minnesota, he called for the transcripts and records, because he took seriously his pardon power and the personal responsibility it gave him for the fate of each citizen.[75] Governor Pat Brown likewise reported that his initial inclination upon taking office was not to look at the file of his first death penalty case, after being assured by aides there was nothing in it, but that decision troubled him. The next day, he called for the file and, after reviewing it, ended up commuting the death sentence.

We respect leaders who face up to and take personal responsibility for these wrenching and tragic choices. This is the "personal" element again that I stress is so important to the conception and exercise of the pardon power—the responsibility for and to others, even when one refuses to pardon. A refusal to reach the merits at all is disrespectful.

Jon Elster tells of an Athenian law, enacted by Solon, that disfranchised a citizen who refused to take a side during a time of political faction. According to this law, the citizen is expected to "'espouse promptly the better and more righteous cause, share its perils and give it his aid, instead of waiting in safety to see which cause prevails.'"[76] From our new standpoint in which responsibility means the ability to respond, we have an obligation to others not to be disengaged and in a state of "obdurate indifference." This Athenian law reminds us of our duty *to judge even under uncertainty* and *to risk injury from and with others* because we are, at root, being-in and being-with.

By contrast with flipping a coin or never looking at the files, the pardon in Byrd's case does not seem "arbitrary," even if it was only by chance that evidence could be recovered exonerating him and even if there were other innocent inmates whose evidence was destroyed and who therefore cannot obtain the same advantage. We know that what stands between guilt/innocence and conviction is often luck (whether any fingerprint or DNA is recoverable, whether the crack investigator is on vacation, whether the neighbor happened to be looking out the window, whether memories are accurate, whether the suspect happened to be at the wrong place at the wrong time). But this sort of moral luck (good or bad) is not considered "arbitrary" or a denial of due process; it is simply a result of the finitude of human knowledge—a finitude we have to live with. Pardons partaking of this same "luck" do not seem wrong, any more than the contingencies that are part of any investigation yielding necessarily incomplete knowledge make judgments wrong. Solon's law does not require us to choose the right side, only to judge as best we can and take the risk of being wrong.

Likewise, pardoning Mease at the pope's request does not have the same meaning of disrespect or disregard for either Mease or the other prisoners on death row that not judging or "flipping a coin" would have. Quite the opposite, it was out of respect that Carnahan pardoned him—respect for a moral authority other than the state.[77] Whether Carnahan should have pardoned him is still an open question, but the pardon was not "arbitrary" or "random" in the sense of treating either Mease or others as though they did not matter.

Governor Carnahan's pardon of Darrell Mease is a hard case not because it is random but because it raises the question whether a state can ever recognize a higher authority. Perhaps the legal system would be better if such pardons were never allowed. We certainly could not allow the pope to determine sentence in *every* case. Nor was there any reason to think that the pope chose Mease's case for any intrinsic reason (the pope never met Mease), so there is no argument here that there was a face-to-face interaction that changed the nature of the case. Yet Carnahan's pardon is symbolic of a moment that opens the possibility of some authority beyond the authority of the state and law. Can the state recognize the possibility of grace or miracle? Or is that possibility categorically foreclosed, so that grace must necessarily be understood as luck? The Mease pardon is, in my view, a hard case for these reasons. One could certainly say that such a pardon is wrong. But I have a hard time condemning Carnahan for being swayed. Would I think him a better governor if he refused when the pope looked him in the eye and asked him to be merciful? Religious or not, I can admire the gesture of respect here and the possibility that a governor could be personally moved by such an appeal of moral authority. I might prefer the moved, human (though perhaps imperfect) Carnahan to a *Biddle*-like "absolute authority" who is unmoved.

What about the "luck" involved in getting access to a governor or authority figure? Is this luck also to be eliminated from the system? Many of the key events in our lives are a matter of happenstance: who we marry, what job we get, who our friends are. When is such luck an ethical problem?

Again, the answer is much more complicated than is often suggested. There will never be absolutely "equal" access to the pardon process. Even if everyone is entitled to have a clemency application prepared by counsel and reviewed by an authority,[78] those who have the "luck" to have drawn a sympathetic trial judge or compassionate prosecutor or good public defender or merciful victim and who can garner their support will be more likely to succeed, and few would claim that such a pardon process was wrong or unfair. But when the president's brother is paid to "get access" to the pardon process, we rightly bristle. Mease's case was brought to the governor's attention by the pope. Weeping mothers seemed to move President Lincoln to careful examination of several cases. Are these, too, cases of unequal access? In my view, this is the level at which we need to have an ethical discussion, finding cases in which a pardon was clearly inappropriate and then wrestling with the cases that are closer and less clear, not eliminating mercy completely nor setting out abstract rules to tame it.

When We Are Wrong

Governor Brown painfully recalls the case of Eddie Wein, whom he pardoned and later allowed to be paroled. Once out of prison, Wein continued in the same pattern of sexual abuse and murder that he had begun twenty years before. For many, cases like this are reason enough never to permit pardons. They believe we cannot take the risk.

We already take the risk, of course, with those released without pardon, many of whom (because of the necessary imperfection of law) are not meaningfully different from those left in prison. And we must also remember that only the released who reoffend will ever be known to us. Those who die in prison or remain incarcerated who would not reoffend if released do not make the news. The waste and torment of their lives is never disclosed; the good they might have done if released is never revealed. We may choose to eliminate all mercy and therefore all risk,[79] but that would condemn us all to a merciless state.

III. THE MERCILESS STATE

Grant Gilmore observes, "In hell there will be nothing but law, and due process will be meticulously observed."[80] Imagine a world in which all public officials operate by the book, with no compassion, no quarter.[81] Tom Wolfe gives us such a glimpse in the novel *A Man in Full*,[82] as he puts his proletarian everyman, Conrad, through an excruciating nightmare of lawfulness.

After saving the life of a coworker, Conrad, "the best worker in this whole fucking place," is laid off from his job at a frozen food facility. His wife and two children were hoping to move out of a cramped apartment and into a condo, but now that is impossible. His mother-in-law is convinced Conrad is a failure. Conrad now must drive into San Francisco for a job interview at the unemployment office. According to the rules, he must take a typing test, which he fails because his hands have become so clumsy from the grueling physical labor at the refrigeration plant. When, defeated, he returns to his car, he finds that another driver has pushed his Hyundai into a red zone and up onto the sidewalk and that a tow truck is about to tow it. His wife, kids, and mother-in-law are waiting for him; he has the only available car. But his pleas are ignored: "I told you it's too late. Once the summons is made out and the dispatcher's notified and the tow's hooked up, then it's a tow, and ain't nothing nobody can do about it once it's a tow."[83]

So Conrad must call his wife with the bad news. But he has no change for the phone, and the store has a sign that reads "No change without purchase." He buys a candy bar to get change. Then Conrad walks across town to pay the fine. After waiting in a long line to pay his fine, he finds out that the fine is twice as much as he thought, because there is a separate fine for parking on the sidewalk and for parking in the red zone. Now he needs more cash. Once again, he has to find change and call his wife. She must take a taxi to a Western Union office and wire the money. Now Conrad has to find a Western Union office. He walks across town again. He gets the $77 to redeem his car and discovers he must go all the way to the slums of East Oakland to retrieve it. He waits for a bus, but it is the wrong one. He walks six more blocks, then he waits for another bus. It is the right bus, but he does not have the right change. Asked if he will take a five-dollar bill, the driver says, "No can do." So Conrad again tries to find someone who will give him change. Then he must wait for another bus.

By the time Conrad reaches the towing lot, seven hours have elapsed since he was towed, it is getting dark and dangerous on the streets, and it is only fifteen minutes before the office of the tow lot is to close. Sweating with anxiety and exhausted, he waits in line and comes to the front just as the office is closing. He is then told that he needs another $77, because the towing is $77 per hour or any part thereof, and his tow took one hour and ten minutes. Conrad exclaims, "This is—not right!" But the man at the counter "gave Conrad a look of glorious indifference and motioned his head toward the sign. 'There's a line here,' he said, 'There's people waiting.'"

This is the merciless state.

CHAPTER 6

Miscarriages of Mercy?

When the problem of mercy arises, the conversation-ending question is often, would you forgive the Nazis? Such a question is usually meant rhetorically, as the reductio ad absurdum that ends debate. How could one forgive the Nazis? Yet, if we take the question seriously, there are three different problems to unpack here. First is the question addressed in the last chapter: are there any pardons that are wrong, and how can we reason about them if we have rejected kanticism? My answer in chapter 5 was to point to a "common-law" approach to ethical argument that allows for decision making with only provisional rules and that allows for the possibility of acting on the basis of face-to-face judgments that cannot always be immediately articulated. Second is the question of standing: how can anyone have standing to give mercy when the victim is dead and unable or unwilling to forgive? I addressed this problem in chapter 4 by pointing out that because mercy (and punishment) are now about moving from a place of seeing the wrong as wrong to a settlement and future being-with, the past victim has no special standing. Instead, standing must be granted to all witnesses to the wrong who can be "potential victims" in community with the offender. Third is the question I propose to address here: aren't some crimes so horrendous as to be categorically unforgivable?

Simon Wiesenthal, in his famous book *The Sunflower*, describes his own dilemma of conscience when a dying SS soldier named Karl calls Simon to his bedside to confess his part in an atrocity. Simon is then a young Jewish man, just out of college before the Germans take over Poland. He has been incarcerated by the Germans because of his Jewishness and, every day and every minute, experiences the degradation, starvation, death, sickness, humiliation, and dehumanization of a Nazi work/death camp. Simon fully expects to die soon at the hands of Karl's fellow SS officers. He expects his body soon to be shoved disdainfully into a mass grave and forgotten. Yet Simon listens to Karl's agonized confession, holds Karl's hand, retrieves his mother's letter from the floor when it falls, brushes away a fly, and helps Karl get a drink of water.

Karl tells how he joined the Hitler Youth and later became an SS trooper against his parents' wishes. He participated in herding hundreds of Jewish families into a house and then shot those who tried to escape after the building had been set afire. He is haunted by the face of a child he shot, as his parents jumped with him from the second story. Like Freud's account of the voice of Clorinda, the traumatic image of this child came to Karl later, on the battlefield, and he froze, unable to fire. He was hit, then, half his face blown away. But even dying, Karl is tortured by his deed and seeks the solace of confession.

Simon believes that Karl is sincere in his repentance. He even feels compassion for Karl's suffering. But when Karl says he cannot die in peace without a response from Simon, Simon finds nothing to say. He leaves the room in silence. Later that evening, throughout the war, and in the time following, Simon is in turn haunted by his traumatic encounter with Karl. Was he right not to offer forgiveness?

The day after Karl's confession, when Simon is marched back to his degrading work at the hospital, Karl is dead but has "bequeathed" Simon his possessions, on the top of which is Karl's mother's name and address. Simon refuses the possessions but remembers the name and address. After the war, he visits Karl's mother. He does not tell her that her son crammed hundreds of Jewish people into a house and then set it on fire. He does not tell her that her son watched and shot as a mother and father, holding their young son and shielding his eyes, jumped to their deaths from an upper story. He allows the soldier's mother to remember him as "a good boy" who was the priest's favorite, who was pious and helpful, and who joined the Hitler youth against their wishes. Was Simon right not to tell her?

In the extensive commentary that accompanies the newest edition of Wiesenthal's moving story, the debate continues. Some argue that murder can never be forgiven, because only the victim of a wrong has standing to forgive, while others argue that forgiveness is always right, no matter the crime, if an offender is remorseful. Others argue that the crime itself was unforgivable, because not only were its victims innocent but they were treated as nonhuman. Still others argue that the criminal was unforgivable, because he knew better, as his remorse proved. Yet there is another possibility. It seems to me that Simon *did* forgive the man. He did not offer verbal forgiveness in response to the man's request for absolution. Indeed, as many point out, the SS soldier had no right to ask for absolution: forgiveness is a gift, not a right, and the expectation of it belies true remorse. But the story continues.

Perhaps the soldier recognized the unfairness of putting Simon, a prisoner and a Jew, on the spot. How could Simon respond at all truthfully without risking his life in such a situation? Was Karl not showing great selfishness in asking Simon to listen at all? Yet who else among those Karl could confess to at that Nazi hospital would not be too ready to forgive him? Certainly anyone else at the hospital, any priest or nurse of the Nazi regime, would have given him "easy grace."[1] None were potential victims of the anti-Semitic hate Karl wished to repent. So Karl's last act is to put himself into Simon's power. The one thing that could still hurt Karl, on the verge of death, was, as he told Simon himself, for his mother to know of his crimes. By any retributive account of desert, Karl certainly *deserved* for his mother to know his crimes; he *deserved* disgrace. He did not *deserve* a sunflower on his grave; he did not *deserve* to be remembered well or, indeed, at all. So Karl gave Simon the power to tell his mother what he "really was" and provided Simon with his possessions to serve as "evidence" of Simon's truth.

Simon had the power to punish Karl. He had a tool of vengeance and truth. But Simon refused it. He *was* merciful. He *did* see Karl as a "distinct individual," an entire human being, not merely as a "Nazi beast."[2] He allowed him to remain, in his mother's memory and in Simon's own memory, as, at least for part of his time on earth, a "good boy." Simon gave Karl his sunflower, even though Karl had denied that sunflower to so many, including all of Simon's family and friends. The question, then, is not whether Simon was right to deny Karl forgiveness but whether he was right to be lenient?

Cynthia Ozick argues that Karl's moral misgivings and good background only condemn him further. Unlike the "brutes" who followed Hitler without knowing better, Karl should have seen Hitler and his anti-Semitism for the evils they were. Karl's "fine conscience" that enables his remorse should have kept him from becoming a Nazi in the first place. Any forgiveness of Karl is more deeply wrong, not less so, *because of* his remorse.[3] Vengeance, Ozick argues, is "justice that enlightens the world as to the nature of evil" and shows true compassion for the victim.[4] It is forgiveness that she finds "relentless" and "stony to the slaughtered."[5] Both the crime and the criminal, she concludes, are unforgivable.

I would like to address Ozick's argument by looking closely at U.S. war crimes and our own military justice system. I look to our own crimes because, in many ways, they are analogous; they share important features of Karl's crime. They are also atrocities, perpetrated in part because of an atmosphere of racism by soldiers in a context of war, and they are also crimes done not by the mentally ill, the abused, the loners, but by the "good boys," often the very best boys, many of whom join the armed services from the most noble of motives: to sacrifice their safety for their country. But most important, I look at our own war crimes because, from the standpoint of being-with, we are called always to see the offender as "insider," not "outsider." With the uncanny courage of one like Wiesenthal, we have to meet the Nazi's mother. As I pointed out in chapter 2, the Kantian injunction to "universalize" is reinterpreted from the standpoint of being-with as an injunction to be with the other. So, instead of asking whether the Nazis are unforgivable, let us ask first whether "our" crimes are unforgivable. Is mercy already at work in these cases somehow? What patterns do we see when we look closely at these situations? What meaning does leniency have? Have *we* been guilty of miscarriages of mercy?

In 2003, Iraqi general Mowhoush died in American custody after chief warrant officer Lewis Welshofer stuffed him headfirst into a sleeping bag and sat on his chest. There were also allegations that Welshofer used beating and waterboarding as interrogation techniques. Welshofer was convicted by court-martial of negligent homicide, reprimanded, restricted to base for two months, and fined six thousand dollars. Welshofer's commanding officer, Major Jessica Voss, received a reprimand for the death.[6]

Lieutenant Ilario Pantano was accused of shooting two suspected insurgents, already in custody, sixty times in the back as they searched a car for bombs at the direction of U.S. troops, then hanging a sign with the Marine motto "No Better Friend, No Worse Enemy" over their dead bodies. Charges were dropped after an Article 32 investigation and hearing, and Pantano was offered another command in Iraq. Pantano then resigned his commission and wrote his memoirs, *Warlord: No Better Friend, No Worse Enemy.*[7]

Zaidoun Hassoun and his cousin were out after curfew in Baghdad. An American patrol stopped them and told them to jump in the Tigris. Hassoun drowned. One soldier (Private Perkins) was tried for involuntary manslaughter and assault and acquitted of the involuntary manslaughter charges. He received a sentence of six months and a reduction in rank. First Lieutenant Saville pled guilty and received a sentence of forty-five days and forfeiture of two-thirds pay for six months. Neither was discharged from the army.[8]

In 2003, Sergeant Gary Pittman was accused of kicking and beating de-tainees, including fifty-two-year-old Nageb Sadoon Hatab, who died after he was beaten and left for hours in the sun with diarrhea. Pittman was convicted in 2004, received a sentence of ninety days, and was demoted to private.[9] Major Clarke Paulus was court-martialed for ordering Pittman to drag Hatab by the neck and was dismissed from the service (the equivalent of a dishonorable dis-charge for officers—he lost all his retirement benefits).[10]

Two prisoners, one of whom was an innocent taxi driver swept into custody along with his customers, died in an American prison in Bagram, Afghanistan, after they were repeatedly beaten and kicked in the common peroneal nerve over several days and chained to the ceiling. Court-martials resulted in sen-tences of two months, three months, and seventy-five days for three of the sol-diers and in reprimands for two of the sergeants involved.[11]

At the now-infamous prison in Abu Ghraib, guards, CIA operatives, and military intelligence officers beat to death, stripped, stepped on, used dogs on, threatened with death and electrocution, sexually assaulted, and humiliated prisoners and then took jeering photos of them. After courts-martial, Special-ist Charles Graner received a ten-year sentence and a dishonorable discharge; Staff Sergeant Ivan Frederick, eight years and a dishonorable discharge; Spe-cialist Lynndie England, three years and a dishonorable discharge; Jeremy Sivits, one year and a bad-conduct discharge; Roman Krol, ten months and a bad-conduct discharge; Armin Cruz, eight months and a bad-conduct dis-charge; Sabrina Harman, six months and a bad-conduct discharge; Michael Smith, six months; Javal Davis, six months and a bad-conduct discharge; San-tos Cardona, ninety days and a reduction in rank; and Megan Ambuhl, pay for-feiture and a less-than-honorable discharge. Lieutenant Colonels Steve Jordan and Jerry Phillabaum were reprimanded and relieved of command. Captain Donald J. Reese was reprimanded and relieved of command. Colonel Thomas Pappas received a nonjudicial punishment and an eight-thousand-dollar fine. Brigadier General Janis Karpinski had her rank reduced to colonel.[12]

Three marines convicted of electrocuting prisoners to punish them for throwing trash were sentenced to between eight and fifteen months.[13] Eight marines in Haditha were initially charged with killing fourteen unarmed civil-ian men, four women, and six children, but charges against seven of the eight were dropped.[14] Four soldiers were charged with raping a fourteen-year-old girl and killing her family in Mahmoudiya.[15] Three received 90 to 110 years in prison (with parole eligibility in ten to twenty years), and the fourth received twenty-seven months for obstructing justice. The other participant, tried in federal civilian court rather than by military court, received a life sentence without parole, when a hung jury could not agree on whether or not to sentence him to death.[16]

Journalists and human rights groups have raised concerns that courts-martial are not tough enough in responding to these crimes.[17] Human Rights Watch and the Center for Human Rights and Global Justice issued a detailed report charging that abuses by service members in Iraq and Afghanistan are far more widespread than Abu Ghraib and that "promises of transparency, investigation, and appropriate punishment for those responsible remain unfulfilled."[18]

We have seen similar cases and similar leniency in the Vietnam era. Lieutenant Rusty Calley was sentenced to life in prison for the roundup and slaughter of hundreds of women, children, and old men at My Lai. Witnesses told of toddlers gunned down as they tried to crawl away from the pile of bodies and of mothers shot trying to retrieve their children. Yet Calley was pardoned by President Nixon after serving only four months in prison and today manages a jewelry store in his hometown of Columbus, Georgia.[19] Private Michael Schwartz, sentenced to life at hard labor for shooting sixteen Vietnamese women and children as they stood in front of their homes, served only nine months before his sentence was reduced by a military superior.[20] A squad of American soldiers gang-raped and murdered two young Vietnamese girls, aged seventeen and fourteen, who were suspected to be enemy nurses. Both were brutally raped more than twenty times and forced to engage in oral sex at gunpoint, then, days later, shot. The soldiers tried to cover up the crime by forcing another prisoner to shoot the girls. Two members of the squad were found not guilty; none of the rest were prosecuted.[21]

During the more than ten years the United States was at war in Vietnam, at court-martials convened in the field, the U.S. Army convicted ninety-five soldiers of murder or manslaughter; the U.S. Marines, twenty-seven.[22] But many of these sentences were later commuted, and many more crimes were never prosecuted at all. Officers and soldiers testifying at the Dellums hearings[23] in 1971 related widespread uninvestigated and unprosecuted beatings of prisoners, old men, old women, and children (sometimes to death);[24] use of dogs (and pythons) to intimidate prisoners;[25] cutting off the ears and other body parts of dead enemy soldiers as proof of body count or as trophies;[26] burning the skin of prisoners,[27] waterboarding;[28] shooting unarmed civilians;[29] routine electrical torture of prisoners;[30] shooting wounded prisoners;[31] shooting groups of women and children;[32] burning occupied dwellings;[33] throwing blindfolded and hooded prisoners into sewage ponds;[34] throwing prisoners out of helicopters to encourage others to cooperate;[35] throwing old men, women, and children into wells with grenades,[36] starving prisoners to death;[37] putting prisoners into coffin-size cages in the hot sun;[38] refusing medical treatment to Vietnamese wounded;[39] forcing prisoners to dig their own graves;[40] and so on. New evidence in recently declassified Pentagon files reveals even more instances of unprosecuted war-related crimes against civilians in Vietnam, including unprovoked shootings of women and children, torture, and sexual abuse.[41]

These are brutal crimes that treat their victims as less than human. They are done by "good boys" who have no apparent excuse in an underprivileged background, mental illness, or defect. They are crimes done by those who are supposed to know better. How can we understand leniency—giving less punishment than is "deserved" or "due"—in the context of military courts-martial? Are we turning our backs on the victims? Are we forgiving the unforgivable?

As I have emphasized throughout this book, it is only when we understand the role that leniency plays *in context* that we can begin to say when it may be wrong. So I turn to a detailed discussion of these cases of crimes committed in war. Using a common-law method, I try to tease out patterns from these cases and make sense of them. How does leniency come to be exercised here, and what might it mean? Because military courts still operate in a discretionary sentencing paradigm, a look at military courts-martial can show us both the nature of cases in which mercy seems to be granted and how that mercy is institutionalized, allowing us to look at both the substance and process of these decisions.

In order to begin to understand the apparent military leniency we see in these cases, we must first understand the context of military life. As we will see, much of the mercy in military cases reflects a situation appropriate to an allegiance pardon, because the relationships between commander and soldier, judge and defendant, are relations of mutual risk, mutual responsibility, and mutual trust. The first two sections that follow explain how the military culture is reflected in the military procedure, which allows so many avenues for commander-to-soldier mercy. Then, after providing this context, I examine the hard cases of mercy previously described—cases of atrocities committed against enemy civilians and soldiers. An examination of these cases brings to light something new: we *do* seem to be more forgiving to the "good boys," as Wiesenthal perhaps was and as Ozick refuses to be. Perhaps we do so because we feel implicated in the very destruction of their "goodness" that the conditions of war seem to cause. This is another aspect of the allegiance pardon: to pardon out of allegiance is to acknowledge complicity, to take being with the defendant so seriously as to make oneself a co-wrongdoer, unable to condemn. Far from turning away from the victims, such pardons ought to broaden and deepen our sense of responsibility and make more urgent the need for reparation and sacrifice, not just from the offender, but from all of us.

I. THE MILITARY CULTURE

"The essence of the Marine Corps is family."[42] Family is a metaphor often used in the military to describe the bonds of its personnel.[43] One Marine sergeant puts it this way: "The Marine Corps is like a family, and we teach family values."[44] New recruits write their unit number on their hands and learn first of all to work together. One description of a military training exercise makes the point.

> As the platoon enters its temporary barracks in the receiving building, most of its members remove their "utility hats"—the enlisted Marines' everyday headgear. Several say, "Good afternoon, sir," to a passing civilian . . . They march to the mess hall for an early dinner, than back to the barracks, where Sergeant Lewis gives them twenty seconds to remove and hang up all their gear—hats, canteens, canteen web belts. The more astute members realize that the only way to do it within that limit is to aid one another. When Daniel Armstrong, a gangling, stork-like road construction worker from Florida, gets tangled trying to remove his canteen belt, Christopher Anderson, a smart, short black recruit who plans to study criminology at the University of Maryland, leans over and helps him. Sergeant Lewis watches in silent approval: They are getting the message.[45]

Marine lore prescribes, "Share everything, even the pound cake and cookies."[46] It warns, "Remember, if everyone does not come home, none of us can ever fully come home."[47]

This interdependence, teamwork, and loyalty is so important to military organizations that, in 1999, a forces-wide "military culture" survey by the Center for Strategic and International Studies was prompted by "concern . . . about morale, readiness, and cultural values."[48] The survey team said there is "a direct link . . . between military culture and effectiveness. The underlying culture of U.S. military forces is the foundation from which arise standards of behavior such as discipline, teamwork, loyalty, and selfless duty."[49] The study recognized that "modern military discipline emanates from unit cohesion and the example set by inspiring leaders."[50] It added, "Studies by academics and military experts have usually shown that high cohesion—mutual trust and shared commitment to unit goals—markedly enhances unit performance under stress."[51]

The combination of dedication to a common goal, pride in the organization, and the necessity for trust and teamwork in accomplishing that goal create strong bonds that are enhanced over time by common experiences, especially overseas[52] and in combat.[53] War memoirs are powerful evidence that comrades in arms "come to feel an intense love for one another."[54] In *Goodbye, Darkness,* noted biographer William Manchester recounts,

> I understand, at last, why I jumped hospital that Sunday thirty-five years ago and, in violation of orders, returned to the front and almost certain death. It was an act of love. Those men on the line were my family, my home. They were closer to me than I can say, closer than any friends had been or ever would be. They had never let me down, and I couldn't do it to them. I had to be with them, rather than let them die and me live with the knowledge that I might have saved them. Men, I now know, do not fight for flag or country, for the Marine Corps or glory or any other abstraction. They fight for one another.[55]

Trust of one's comrades and trust of one's leaders is interconnected. The hierarchy of military organizations means that responsibility is always *for someone* and *to someone.* Marine lore puts it this way: "I will never forget that I am responsible to my Commanding Officer for the morale, discipline, and efficiency of my men. Their performance will reflect an image of me." If one's subordinates get into trouble, that will be noted and reflected in the commanding officer's performance review. Officers are expected to "take care of their people."[56] As one officer put it, "My soldiers, by and large, were willing to charge a machine gun nest for me. My duty to them is *tenfold.*"[57] On the flip side, the subordinate must always have the support of his entire chain of command in order to get permission for leave, vehicle use, various recreational activities, and so forth. To reenlist, the soldier, sailor, or marine must be recommended by his or her superior officers. A reenlistment ceremony is a solemn occasion. The reenlisting service member is in full dress uniform, with family and commanding officer present, and the reenlisting member's senior officer speaks for him or her. Those up for reenlistment are the first to meet VIPs and are given places of special honor. When your superiors have supported you in all these ways, "you can't let these people down."[58]

Military culture at its best promotes and depends on relationships of teamwork and mutual responsibility. Both are in turn supported by the gratitude and trust created in allowing room for mercy. Mercy in such circumstances actually promotes, rather than destroys, responsibility for others. Mercy enables the defendants to make a fresh start, reflects the community's gratitude for prior service, and recognizes communal and command responsibility for crime. The mercy givers are themselves potential future victims, and they accept the risk of the defendant's future conduct. Mercy is not cheap and easy but reflects the mercy giver's willingness to take risks on the strength of the relationship with the defendant. Defendants are already in close relationship with their victims and their commanding officers, responsible to and for them in the future,[59] and bonds of gratitude, trust, and mutual commitment are formed and strengthened by the mercy giving. Lengthy or harsh punishment in such a community setting may generate resentment and leave "nothing owing," leading to defendants' sense of separation, disaffection, and lack of a sense of responsibility or commitment to others.

II. LENITY IN THE MILITARY TRIAL PROCESS

Fitting the close interdependence and trust relationships in military organizations, the military justice system, unlike the federal civilian system, allows for the operation of mercy at every stage of the criminal process. The military process reflects the tightness and hierarchical nature of the community ties.[60] First, "corrective training" may be imposed by a service member's immediate superior, which avoids any official record of wrongdoing and, like community policing at its best, can provide early correction of wrongful conduct and modeling of good conduct. At this point, technical crimes can be put in context: breaking into a fellow marine's room to watch television need not be treated as burglary; punching a superior in the course of a semifriendly drinking spree can be overlooked; failing to pay one's bills on time can be corrected by sitting down weekly with the commanding officer and writing the necessary checks.[61] Second, a whole range of nonjudicial punishments are available to commanders that avoid the need for formal trial and allow service members to avoid discharge.[62] Nonjudicial punishments are used frequently and at an increasing rate. In 2005, for example, the army imposed nonjudicial punishments in 45,299 cases, compared to 825 general courts-martial, 700 special courts-martial and 1,252 summary courts-martial.[63]

As one officer put it, "I would nonjudicially punish or correctively train a service member instead of something else more severe. It did build a bond between commander and subordinate. Many well-known leaders, Tommy

Franks, Colin Powell, tell stories of officers sparing their careers at an early age."[64] In this respect, at least, the system of military justice loosely resembles John Braithwaite's regulatory pyramid of restorative justice.[65] Where the emphasis is on restoring the community and teamwork that is so essential to developing a "tight unit" able to trust each other under the intense conditions of combat, discretion and mercy help build relationships of gratitude and trust.

Discretion remains in the formal processes. Like prosecutors in civilian cases, the "convening authority" of a court-martial[66] has untrammeled discretion to prosecute or not, as well as to determine the charges, regardless of the outcome of pretrial investigation. Additionally, the convening authority also has discretion as to which type of court-martial to convene: a summary court-martial, a special court-martial, or a general court-martial. Summary and special courts-martial have abbreviated processes but also cannot impose the most serious penalties, again allowing discretion to play a role in setting a "ceiling" on sentencing.

Before trial, military defendants, like their civilian counterparts, may reach a plea agreement that can specify a maximum sentence. Such an agreement can be accepted by the convening authority at any time. However, unlike a civilian defendant, the military defendant still has the opportunity to seek a lower sentence from the sentencing authority. Because the military sentences are indeterminate and set by the court-martial panel (or by a military judge, if the defendant agrees), the military offender will receive the lower of the two sentences, with the pretrial agreement setting the ceiling but not the floor.[67]

During trial and in sentencing, great importance is placed on the "military character" of the defendant, allowing the full account of a defendant's service to be presented to the panel, regardless of its relevance to the specifics of the crime charged.[68] This evidence may be the basis for compassion or allegiance-like gratitude for prior service by the court-martial panel that provokes an acquittal or reduces a sentence. Again, the practice is very different in our federal civilian courts; military service, at least until very recently, was rarely an important factor in sentencing.[69]

Another difference during trial is the extent to which evidence of a breakdown in command can serve to exonerate or mitigate a sentence. In a military hierarchy, responsibility cuts (at least) two ways. One is personally responsible for one's actions, but one is also responsible for one's comrades and subordinates. An officer is responsible for his or her soldiers. In the words of one former military lawyer, "You take care of your people on-duty and off-duty."[70] The "breakdown in command" argument lays partial blame for the offense at the door of the commanding officer, who is supposed to know his people so intimately that crimes do not have a chance to occur. The service member's behavior is not separate from the community in which he lives and works, and the community must shoulder some of the blame.[71] A court-martial made up primarily of officers may be especially critical of an officer who did not prevent a subordinate from getting out of line or who did not recognize a problem and deal with it at an earlier stage.[72]

Like the military character defense, the "breakdown in command" argument can be abused. But it, too, recognizes an important feature of military culture: its interconnectedness and the mutual responsibility it entails. As in the battlefield, the commander cannot leave his or her soldiers behind but has an obligation to back them up and take responsibility for them and for their actions. This kind of mutual responsibility is not always recognized in criminal law (except, perhaps ironically, in the law of conspiracy), and when responsibility does not go up the chain of command, the convening authority may be reluctant to punish those on the "front line."

In a case in which the penalty is mandatory or severe, the court-martial or military judge may append to its sentence a nonbinding recommendation of clemency by the convening authority.[73] This recommendation must be forwarded to and considered by the convening authority before final approval of the sentence.[74] Individual members of the court-martial also may make more informal recommendations of clemency to the convening authority.

After trial, the defendant has another opportunity for clemency and may file a brief asking the convening authority for a sentence reduction or dismissal of the charges.[75] The defendant has the right to assistance of counsel in filing this brief, and the sentence must be reconsidered by the convening authority if counsel was ineffective.[76] An experienced military lawyer, a staff judge advocate, advises the convening authority as to the lawfulness of the trial, the legal appropriateness of the sentence, and the clemency application.[77] These two functions—legal advice and clemency advice—may be contradictory.[78] A sentence may be appropriate to the law and culpability of an offender but be commuted nonetheless. The convening authority "may remit, mitigate or commute a sentence as a matter of grace alone. He need not be seized of a reason, nor be required to state one."[79] This opportunity for clemency is not a mere formality, but "the convening authority is an accused's last best hope for clemency."[80] The importance of the clemency decision is underscored by the fact that a defense counsel will be considered "ineffective" if she or he fails to advise a client of the opportunity for clemency and aid the client in preparing the application.[81] One military lawyer estimates that reductions in sentence are granted about 10 percent of the time,[82] and deferral or waiver of pay forfeiture for family circumstances may be more frequent, perhaps occurring in 25 percent of the cases.[83]

The Court of Military Appeals for each service (Army, Air Force, Coast Guard, and Navy/Marines), formerly known as service boards of review, have discretion to review the sentence as well as the legal aspects of the case de novo and may reduce, though not increase, a sentence.[84] Sentence review at this stage, however, is for "sentence appropriateness," defined as "the judicial function of assuring that justice is done and that the accused gets the punishment he deserves."[85] By contrast, the convening authority's clemency power "involves bestowing mercy—treating an accused with less rigor than he deserves."[86]

Although sentence review is not available at higher appellate levels, review for legal errors, including procedural errors in reviewing clemency applications,[87] may be sought before the Court of Appeals for the Armed Forces (CAAF, formerly the Court of Military Appeals), a court composed of civilian judges. Review of a CAAF decision may be sought by writ of certiorari from the U.S. Supreme Court.[88] After serving a specified portion of a sentence of confinement, a defendant may also seek a reduction in sentence from the service branch's parole board and appeal a denial of that decision to the secretary of defense.[89] Counsel is not required at this stage, but a defendant may receive aid from his military lawyer anyway.[90] Even if sentenced to confinement, a prisoner may be eligible for a "return-to-duty program" run by his or her service.[91]

Discretion to be lenient, then, is a procedural option that may be accessed at all levels of the military trial process—by the commanding officer and convening authority at the charging stage; by the convening authority during and after trial; by the court-martial itself in sentencing; by clemency brief; by appeal; and by seeking parole, pardon, or return to duty. The model allows the services to hold service members responsible for their actions but then to reintegrate and "forgive" them if they are repentant and committed. The discretion built into the system, especially at the posttrial clemency stage, reflects the ideal of mutual trust and obligation built into a hierarchical, interdependent military culture. For soldier-on-soldier crimes, the availability of mercy reflects the ongoing trust relationship and mutual risk inherent in the military organization.

III. WHEN THE VICTIM IS AN OUTSIDER

The harder cases of mercy or leniency in the military context are the sentences for war-related crimes[92] committed by American soldiers against "outsiders" or the "enemy," with which this chapter began. How should we think about military mercy when the victim is not an "insider" to the military community but an outsider or, even more problematically, an "enemy"? In that case, the mercy giver is not a potential future victim—making mercy seem cheap, "risk-free," and all too easy. Lenity may even reflect the opposite of a connection with others: the mercy giver's own lack of sympathy for or even animosity toward the enemy-victim. For these reasons, mercy extended to soldiers guilty of crimes against "outsiders" to the military community seems especially problematic and more likely to be "inappropriate" mercy.

A preliminary question, of course, must be, is this mercy at all? The apparent lenity in these cases (if it indeed exists) may be explicable in legal terms. Due to lack of witnesses and evidence, crimes are much harder to prosecute under conditions of war, resulting often in lesser charges or acquittals.[93] In a war zone without a "front," bodies cannot be found; evidence cannot be collected or preserved properly; witnesses flee or hide or simply move away. There are also more ambiguities about the use of violence in combat situations that require instantaneous choices. For example, did Ilario Pantano shoot two prisoners because they turned and made a sudden move toward him, as he claims, or did he shoot them, as his sergeant testified, because he thought they had been mortaring his men and because he believed intelligence units would only release them again? Finally, there are ambiguities of law: what exactly were the rules of engagement in effect for intelligence units at Abu Ghraib and Bagram, and how much force is too much force? How closely should the Geneva Convention's prohibition on torture be parsed? Is it torture to repeatedly kick a prisoner under interrogation in the tender nerve areas of the thigh, or is it only "torture-lite"? There are also ambiguities in orders—sometimes intentional sorts of ambiguities that give unofficial "permission" for atrocities, as in My Lai or Son Thang and perhaps Abu Ghraib. Finally, there is the question, when must a soldier disobey an order of a superior officer? When is such an order "patently illegal"?

The very possibility of the last question, of course, goes to the heart of the nature of law. If law is only "how the President parses the Geneva Convention," then there is no "patently illegal" order, for, ultimately, the superior's order is law by virtue of being the superior's order. Positive law is law. Taking this view, as we know, would exonerate Adolf Eichmann and Rusty Calley, both of whom defended themselves on the ground that they were "lawful" in this way.[94] But the fact that we did convict these men suggests that we cannot take this position. Law is not just following the rules laid down; it is judgment from a position of being-in and being-with. Just because either no one has ever thought to write a rule covering the situation or someone wrote a bad rule does not mean that we are not responsible for knowing how to respond, based on *all* our background knowledge of our world and on the basic and ineradicable imperative to see the other as our responsibility. What "we demand" in trials of this kind is that, as Hannah Arendt puts it, "human beings be capable of telling right from wrong even when all they have to guide them is their own judgment, which moreover, happens to be completely at odds with what they must regard as the unanimous opinion of all those around them."[95] In these cases of extreme cruelty, a willingness to exploit legal ambiguities in the Geneva Conventions, rules of engagement, or orders of superiors seems to deny the possibility of any law but positive law. Such a position may eliminate convictions of "our" soldiers, but it also destroys the conception of military (or any other) honor. Those who heroically succeed in controlling their fear and rage and who resist orders to butcher and torture are, under positive law ideals, criminals.

Of course, our willingness to exploit legal ambiguities in these cases may not evince a commitment to positive law but may instead be generated by sympathy or mercy. Even if we do not legally excuse our soldiers on the ground of following orders, we can yet show mercy, which is not the same as saying they acted rightly. This separation between liability and clemency accords with the structure of court-martial procedure in general: the court-martial convening authority can choose both to convene the trial and to pardon afterward, to exercise both justice and mercy. But even if both are possible, our original question remains: is mercy proper?

If we do have mercy operating in these sentences, are the sentences we are seeing in Iraq and Afghanistan to be compared with the trials of Nazi war criminals by German courts, where defendants whose crimes would have provoked the death penalty if tried in the civilian courts of the victim nation received only a few years from German courts? If so, should we take leniency in our cases, as Arendt does in the German cases, as a lack of seriousness about the crimes—the light sentence merely a token gesture to "obstinate" foreign opinion?[96] Is lenity in these cases only another example of a "thin blue line" where soldiers join ranks to protect their own? Are only the internationally notorious cases prosecuted, and are only the notorious defendants given stiffer sentences?

This is, of course, one possible explanation for the lenity in these cases—a mercy not generated by an experience of mutual recognition between mercy giver and mercy receiver but based on considerations of personal gain external to the case. This is inappropriate mercy. But if this were the "thin blue line" in operation, why are some of the less spectacular cases being prosecuted? Convening authorities could be using their discretion to avoid prosecution altogether. The very use of a court-martial makes the abuses public and damages the perception of the armed forces. Yet we are holding courts-martial, even in cases where there has been little publicity. In some cases where commanders have tried to hide abuses and avoid court-martialing soldiers, they have done so at the expense of their own military careers.[97]

It seems more likely that the motivations for lenity are mixed here. Given the honor-culture of the military and the sense that dishonorable conduct reflects on the whole community, it is unlikely that leniency would be motivated in every case by a desire to "protect our own." Certainly, many service members expressed revulsion and anger at their colleagues at Abu Ghraib, who tainted the honor of the military, overshadowed the heroic and compassionate acts of others, and compromised the mission.[98] Assuming (and it is a big assumption) that sentences in these cases cannot be completely explained by problems of proof or by strategic efforts to whitewash offenses and exculpate offenders—assuming, in short, that we are really seeing lenity or mercy that is a response to the facts or nature of the particular case or offender—what sense could we make of it?

Recurring Themes: Revenge and Mistrust

Nearly every serious war crime reported in Iraq and in Vietnam involved many of the following distinctive factors: (1) defendants stationed in an extremely dangerous, long, and harsh post in which hostile civilians were routinely involved in tricking, bombing, or booby-trapping soldiers;[99] (2) a recent loss of a trusted leader or beloved comrade to guerrilla attacks or explosive devices;[100] (3) a disrupted command structure in which a renegade, unbalanced, or first-time unit leader took charge;[101] (4) vaguely worded aggressive orders conveyed along with an atmosphere of anger, desire for revenge, and hatred toward a dehumanized enemy and with little or no attention given to articulating and reinforcing the limits imposed by the rules of engagement.[102] All of these factors played a role in the crimes committed at My Lai, Son Thang, Abu Ghraib, and Mahmoudiya, as well as in other horrendous murders and rapes of civilians in the Vietnam era.[103] Paradigmatic is the case of Mahmoudiya, where service members went on a killing spree after an Iraqi civilian who came up, smiling and friendly, to an American patrol shook hands with the soldiers and then shot two of them.

The crimes here are horrendous—gang rapes of young girls; repetitive tortures of innocent civilians; close-range shootings of crying children; obliteration of harmless and helpless toddlers, mothers, blind women, and old men. But over and over again, we also see the fear, hurt, and anger of young men who have lost their closest friends without being able to retaliate in a "fair fight" and who explode in random and sickening violence.[104] At some point, retributive justice and punishment may seem only to reinforce and reiterate the revenge instincts that create these tragedies in the first place, yet lack of punishment can also promote revenge.[105]

In the final section of this chapter, I suggest that lenity seems to be extended to service members under two conditions: (1) when their moral judgment is perverted by the military's own demand that soldiers suppress their compassion and humane feelings and treat enemies as less than human and (2) when soldiers act out of rage and revenge and grief. Lenity may not be as readily extended to service members who are shown to be less than honorable outside the conditions created in a war zone. In this way, mercy recognizes the mercy giver's own responsibility for the crime and avoids scapegoating those who lose their honor for the sake of their country. Insofar as this form of mercy deeply implicates the mercy giver in the crime, it is not easy mercy, caused by a lack of concern for the victim. Instead, mercy here should cause us all to share the shame, for it is the dictates of military necessity that demand that some of our most self-sacrificing citizens cross the lines of humanity and destroy their own nobility on our behalf.

War and the Perversion of Moral Judgment

Role Morality

Soldiers are taught to be "tough" and to follow orders without question. Moreover, they live in a "total institution," where the power of communal living, uniforms, and teamwork strip the individual of the usual idiosyncratic modes of self-presentation that make him or her different, creating a situation in which it is very hard to stand up, stand out, or question the way things are done.[106] Like judging, lawyering, and other institutions where participants are urged to leave the ultimate moral decision making to others (to the legislature, to the client, to the "process"), service members rely on authorities to set the "rules of engagement." Their job is to follow, not to make, policy. Comments by service members reflect their need to distance themselves from normal moral responses in order to perform their duties.

After Rusty Calley was prosecuted for murdering more than one hundred civilians at My Lai, other Vietnam veterans clamored for the ear of Congress. They wanted congressional hearings where they could tell the country that Calley's crime was not isolated, that he was not a "bad apple" but the product of the war itself. Congress would not hold official hearings. However, Representative Ron Dellums organized an "informal" hearing attended by some of the antiwar members of the House. Service member after service member told his story (without much apparent concern regarding self-incrimination), to demonstrate the severity and pervasiveness of war crimes in Vietnam.

All who testified felt that Calley was being scapegoated for crimes that were inextricable from the war itself, for the line between war and crime was deceptively thin. Calley's guilt was "every soldier's" guilt. Captain Fred Laughlin testified, "I didn't flinch when people talked about cutting off ears. I didn't flinch at the battle of Prec Loc when people said there were 197 [enemy killed] and not 13. So I have to be less quick to judge everybody."[107] Military intelligence agent Kenneth Osborn, who witnessed the murder of a civilian, argued, "I don't feel as if military justice . . . is effective in clearing up any moral points, but rather only tends to exonerate the Army."[108] Captain Robert Johnson testified, "At the time of the torture and the murder of the prisoner[s] . . . my moral frame of reference wasn't, it is wrong to kill prisoners, it is right not to. My frame of reference was, we are in a combat zone, this is real war, and we have got to get information from prisoners."[109]

Military culture extols "ruthless toughness" and prides itself on being able to set aside emotional reactions so as to follow orders dispassionately and accomplish the mission. Even the Nazis weeded out those who "enjoyed" killing or killed sadistically. They wanted dispassionate, professional killers. In bureaucratic killer Adolf Eichmann's case, Hannah Arendt points out that Eichmann turned his vice into virtue: in a perversion of Kantian ethics, he considered that his ability to "overcome" his natural, human aversion to killing was a duty and a virtue.[110] He was "tough" and able to kill (from afar, at least) dispassionately. He even refused to stop sending Jews to their deaths near the end of the war when Himmler ordered him to, on the ground that Himmler's order was based on selfishness and greed (hoping to curry favor with the likely victors), not duty. Eichmann's defense throughout his trial was that he bore no malice or ill will toward the Jews, that he was a normal, kind person who was doing his duty (facilitating the killing in the most humane way he could). The odious nature of his duty only made his obedience seem to him more noble.

The testimony of Lance Corporal Kenneth Campbell before the Dellums committee is chillingly similar to Eichmann's self-justification. Campbell admitted that he called for artillery strikes on an inhabited village from which he had received no enemy fire. When asked whether he ever thought he was doing wrong, Campbell replied, "It went through my mind, what am I doing? And it shook me for a while and my radioman, who I had become very close to, never said anything, but he just stared at me and the look on his face, you know, the idea that he conveyed to me was the same question I had, what are you doing, you know. And this rattled me, but going back to the old Marine Corps idea of being hard, I just pushed it to the back of my mind. I knew I could not think about it too long or else I would not be hard anymore, I would not be one of the elite killers anymore if I started having feelings. Besides this I rationalized it, I mean, this is what they had told me, nobody questioned it, it was the thing to do . . . I just had to put it in the back of my mind, because I would have been a weakling."[111] Army medical officer Dr. Livingston put it this way: "Even an individual who finds what is happening to be morally repugnant in some way is led to question his own values. This is true of anybody in a pathological association environment. The question always raises, am I crazy or is what is going on here crazy? When it is so large and so well organized as it is in Vietnam, it is very hard for an individual to assert himself."[112] Lieutenant Rusty Calley himself remains the classic example of someone who bought into the limited responsibility of his "role morality." In his memoir, he made the outrageously exculpatory comment "Personally, I didn't kill any Vietnamese that day: I mean personally. I represented the United States of America. My country."[113]

Over time, the intentional dulling of emotional reaction and humanitarian responses results in a zombielike numbness toward violence and death. Often, when war crimes are described, it is not the "old timers" but the "new guys"— still full of high ideals, chivalry, good intentions, and patriotism[114]—who feel the horror and shame of killing women and children and defenseless old men. For example, after witnessing the slaughter of ten Vietnamese women and children in retaliation for a soldier's death, a soldier related, "I was like in a state of shock and these guys did this so systematically like it was something done so many times before, it was easy. It didn't bother them, any of them, at least it didn't appear to bother any of them. Now these guys were old-timers, they had been there for a long time, you know? It was just cut and dried like it was understood that this was going to happen."[115]

In another incident, a first lieutenant described feeling "shocked" when he saw another military intelligence agent put a .38 revolver to a prisoner's head. He testified, "Not understanding what military intelligence policy was, being my first patrol, I stopped the man from doing that . . . But the thing I want to stress is not that I was more moral than the other people involved, but that no other man—and there must have been thirty men around—no other man—all of them seasoned soldiers—moved to prevent that man from being murdered on the spot."[116] One soldier tried to explain this phenomenon: "After your initiation to the realities of war . . . you just become numb to these things. You are—well, your emotions can't take it. You don't shock any more so you are tempted to just numb yourself and it gets to the point that it doesn't bother you until your buddy gets killed. But Vietnamese getting killed doesn't seem to bother you. You become so dehumanized, you become a stone."[117] Not feeling, in other words, occludes moral judgment rather than clarifying it.

For many Vietnam vets, the emotional impact of killing innocent people did not hit until much later. As with trauma generally, the wrong was experienced as wrong only in memory.[118] A soldier who witnessed an old woman and man thrown into a well said, "It seemed funny at the time—I don't know why, but just it was an unreal realization of what was really happening there. What they felt down there. The terror in their minds. What was felt with us was absolutely—I myself—was absolutely nothing. Later when I thought of it, it was really something else."[119]

Racism toward the Enemy

In the rhetoric of war, there is pervasive verbal derogation of the enemy, which creates, feeds, and expands racist categories. From the beginning of military training, recruits are taught (sometimes "officially,"[120] but always "unofficially" by the prevailing language used by others) to call the enemy by slurs and slangs, such as "krauts," "Japs," "gooks" (a slur originally used to refer to Nicaraguans in 1912),[121] "slopes," "slants," "dinks," and now "Ali Baba," "Johnny Jihad," "goat fuckers," "muhammads," "hajjis," "cunts."[122] As one soldier who testified during the Dellums hearings said about his experience in Vietnam, "There was always the attitude—it developed in boot camp . . . it developed in staging battalion before we went over and it developed all of the way through the time we were in Vietnam—we hated these people, we were taught to hate these people, they were gooks, slants, dinks, they were Orientals, inferior to us, they chewed betel nuts, they were ugly, you know, they ate lice out of each other's hair, they were not as good as us. And you could not trust them."[123]

American commercialism, with its tendency to judge people by their possessions and standard of living, contributes to this racism. As a captain in Viet-nam put it, "With me, I couldn't help but somehow view these Vietnamese as a little less than human when we went in and destroyed their homes. They weren't really homes, they were just hooches. I wouldn't have had the same zeal if we were destroying red brick homes or split level homes in suburbia."[124] The same judgments seem to hold today in Iraq: "I don't like to say it, but after a while, when you have the rifle, and you see how the Iraqis look at you and how they live, . . . then some of our guys feel superior—like the people in Haditha or Fallujah aren't quite human like us. You don't think of them the same way. That's not right, but it does happen."[125]

But beyond whatever racism a soldier already brings with him to the bat-tlefield, the "racism" of war is insidious; even service members who have re-spectful attitudes toward the culture or race of those they are fighting at the be-ginning of a war succumb to it. For example, in Ilario Pantano's memoir, he starts his tour in Iraq armed with polite Arabic phrases, many copies of *Islam for Dummies* that he passes out to his men, and a determination not to use terms like "man dress" (referring to the traditional dishdasha robe worn by Iraqi men) that he finds "belittling."[126] By the middle of the battle narrative, however, he is referring routinely to "an Iraqi in a man dress" and using terms like "cunts" (268) and "goat fuckers"(223) to describe the enemy and "Sheik Butt-Fuck" (199) to describe untrustworthy civilian leaders. Three months after the polite greetings and handshakes he exchanged with civilians he met on his arrival, he is threatening uncooperative civilians with Abu Ghraib in order to get information.[127] John Crawford writes of an encounter after spending a year in Iraq, "I went to the gas station yesterday to buy some cigarettes. An Arabic man was working behind the counter. He turned when he heard the door chime and gave me a broad smile. I walked out. I never wanted to hate anyone; it just sort of happens that way in a war."[128] Again there are echoes of Vietnam. Captain Bartek emphasized "the brutalizing [effect] . . . the war has on Ameri-cans . . . the subtleties that have creeped into our own minds and into our own emotions when we look at a Vietnamese. There is a certain repulsion there. Cer-tainly we are intellectually committed to erasing it, but it is a difficult thing to do. That was again the effect of the policies in Vietnam."[129]

Rage and Revenge

In addition to the role-based norm of intentionally silencing one's feelings of humanity and a pervasive war-generated racism, war narratives demonstrate that human responses to enemy civilians as fellow human beings disintegrate after a long period of guerilla combat, especially in conditions, like Vietnam and Iraq, where civilians hide or help enemy soldiers or simply refuse to warn American soldiers of known dangers. Soldiers' mounting frustration, humiliation, and anger at civilians, in both Vietnam and Iraq, spilled into racism, rage, and violence when their military "family members" were killed by land mines or bombs or ambushes that civilians knew about but failed to warn of.[130] This rage and revenge, in turn, reinforces racist categories and generates violent retaliation. As one soldier put it during the Dellums hearings, "My attitude and feelings were, to the people over there, were exactly—I couldn't care less what happened to any of them because I had buddies and friends shot and killed, wounded, too."[131] Soldiers in Vietnam who began their tour by handing out candy to children and playing ball with them ended by abusing them, kicking them, beating them with rifle butts, and making trophies of their hair:[132] "They slugged every little kid they came across."[133]

The devaluation of victims that pervades these war crimes, especially in wars in which the enemy melts into the civilian population, may not even be at core about race but precipitates out of grief and revenge. Race is then used as a ready vehicle and label for this anger, enabling service members to stifle their feelings of humanity and kill on command. Hence, the "role morality," racism, and revenge in these stories feed and reinforce each other, enabling service members to become "killing machines." The hate, anger, and mistrust of all civilian members of the enemy state is part of a radical breakdown of public trust. Soldiers in Vietnam and perhaps in Iraq report feeling that they operate in a "war of all against all"— a Hobbesian state of nature, in which many of them assert an absence of all law, all justice. Service members articulate lenity sometimes in this way—as an inapplicability of principles of individual responsibility in such a context: "If one can say 'waste dinks,' there no longer is a moral frame of reference, there is no longer a moral judgment."[134] At least part of the ugly specter here, then, is the possibility that lenity is exercised on racist grounds, propagated and internalized by methods of war itself, that the lives of the enemy victims are not "worth" as much as the career or honor of an American service member. In Vietnam, this racism even had its own acronym: MGR—the "mere gook rule."[135]

IV. CONVICT AND FORGIVE

It is possible that lenity in war-related crimes is based on racist attitudes generated by the rage of war. Looking at the anecdotal evidence from courts-martial, however, this hypothesis does not seem adequate to explain all the sentences. It seems that some defendants are still treated more harshly than others for the same kinds of war-related crimes against the same enemy victims. A different hypothesis, more consistent with military culture, is that courts-martial are lenient toward soldiers whose moral judgment was perverted by the conditions of war, while they are harsh toward soldiers whose dishonorable conduct appears to "spill over"—either predating or postdating the combat or war.

The great emphasis in military trials on character evidence and the offender's prior service record, while often mystifying to civilian commentators, may be the framework for a possible noncynical account of appropriate mercy in sentencing war-related crimes. When a soldier has committed a crime, his or her military record says a lot about who the soldier was "before." If the defendant was honorable and self-sacrificing going in and yet has become hard, cruel, and full of hate, his or her very character is a tragic casualty of war[136]— of what we required the soldier to do and become in order to accomplish the mission.[137]

Mercy in the context of military justice may also serve to counterbalance what could easily become a culture of cruelty. If overcoming one's natural aversion to killing (which is required for being a successful soldier) requires a perverse self-discipline of "toughness" and emotional distance that can be mistaken for virtue, this seems more reason to acknowledge the important place of sympathy and humanity and mercy in moral judgment, rather than to require the same toughness and emotional distance in those who do justice.[138] If the conditions of battle tend to make one harsh and cruel, then the counterbalancing military culture of compassion and fellowship may help renew and preserve the remaining emotional connections to others. If a defendant's record demonstrates a person already violent or sadistic or if the defendant later fails to acknowledge responsibility and guilt, fails to see those he or she killed or harmed as "insiders," or fails to "come clean" to his or her commanders, sympathy seems less fitting. Specialist Charles Graner's ten-year sentence might be explained this way, as may also be the life sentence (later reduced to twenty-five years)[139] given to Sergeant Michael P. Williams for three execution-style killings of Iraqi prisoners.[140] In both of these cases, the defendants' own comrades testified against them; there was no defense based on "good military character."[141] In cases like Bagram, where interrogators employed interrogation techniques that were more or less officially sanctioned but were ultimately inhumane, defendants have not received stiff sentences, perhaps because their commanders recognize the sacrifice of honor they made for us and for our purposes.

In showing appropriate mercy in war-related cases, we acknowledge that in approving methods of waging war that are likely to bring about the dishonor of honorable service members, we are shamed. Is this cheap mercy, out of racism and a culpable lack of concern for victims? It is not necessarily. If we truly see the moral degradation of our own (formerly honorable) service members as our fault, then mercy is a finding of complicity, putting us all on trial.

That was the conclusion reached by the Vietnam vets who testified before the Dellums committee. All had eventually come to the conclusion that the war they fought was wrong and that their careless attitudes toward Vietnamese civilians were also deeply wrong. Many of them were clearly haunted by their own participation and conduct and the horrible deeds they had done. But because they knew how it felt to see the world in this way—as a combat zone between "us" and everyone else—they were not "quick to judge." In short, they were not supporting Lieutenant Calley because they were presently racists and did not care about the lives of the Vietnamese but because they understood that his racism was part of his training, that it had "creeped into" his mind, as it had theirs, and was difficult to eradicate. Many, many of those who testified before the Dellums committee had never told their stories publicly before, because they were afraid of being treated as the "monster" Calley had been portrayed to be. They would only tell others who had been there, who would "understand," who could witness the wrong as wrong with compassion. Ilario Pantano, a veteran of the Iraq War, sums it up, "No real soldier wants their actions recorded for posterity. I didn't want my family to know. I didn't want my children to learn about bloodlust and fear and shit and killing. There was nothing good in it. There was nothing good that came out of war. You didn't come back more. You came back less."[142]

Given our recognition that our policies promote the moral degradation of soldiers in war, should we go farther and exonerate, rather than merely extend leniency to, service members who are guilty of war-related crimes but whose records reflect that their moral blindness, racism, and inhumanity was a product of the demands of war? This point of view is supported by the fact that modern warfare inevitably devastates the civilian population—old and young alike. In the context of modern warfare—fought from computer terminals by drones controlled remotely, where "you don't have to look at the corpses, you don't have to listen to the women and kids crying,"[143] and, often, no discerning judgment intervenes before violence—"'criminal' warfare,'" defined as knowing or intentional slaughter of civilians, is "inevitable."[144] As Pantano puts it, "chivalry is for museums."[145]

The contested question of when an interrogator, a guard, or an infantry-
man has crossed the line of honor is, for most deaths in war, irrelevant, and in
view of the mass destruction and death that even "conventional" warfare now
causes, it begins to seem a mere quibble around the edges.[146] Most suffer and
die lingering deaths without anyone judging up close whether they are civilian
or soldier, child or adult, armed or unarmed, threatening or friendly. Some veterans assert that "fighting fair" entails losing. If, indeed, the law of war that demands lives but not souls has been outstripped, is it madness to call to account
the few "grunts" who still have to fight it in all its real gore and danger, rather
than those who sit at the joystick? If "obdurate indifference" is the measure of
wrong, is the obdurate indifference of the bomber, the commander, and the citizens who scream for blood perhaps even more culpable than the anguished violence of the grunt who kills out of fear, the pain of loss, and retaliation?

Certainly it does seem as though we need a better legal paradigm of accountability for commanders (even presidents and citizens), not only for
crimes done at their bidding, but for those carried out under their acquies-
cence.[147] But we cannot eliminate the responsibility of the grunt. As I said earlier, to deny the possibility of individual responsibility in this context would be
disastrous, for it would also fail to recognize and honor those who manage to
resist the temptations of rage and revenge, resist the claimed necessity of ille-
gality, and act with only appropriate force. It would also criminalize the conduct of those whose humanity leads them to disobey "illegal" orders, and it
would dilute our understanding of right action. Amnesty, or a forgetting of the
crime, is not the answer. We must face the wrong as wrong. Hannah Arendt also
rejects the idea of legal "communal responsibility" in her examination of Nazi
butcher-bureaucrat Eichmann: "No matter through what accidents of exterior
or interior circumstances you were pushed onto the road of becoming a criminal, there is an abyss between the actuality of what you did and the potentiality
of what others might have done."[148] To fail altogether to face the wrong in judging is wrong.[149] But that does not eliminate the possibility of mercy.

So we are left with an apparent futility: to convict and forgive. The oddness
of this stance is not at all so strange from our new perspective on punishment.
If punishment is the experience of the wrong as wrong, then the conviction
may allow for that experience. The agonizing statements of many of these
young veterans are some evidence, at least, of the deep self-loathing and rebit-
ing trauma of remorse. When James Barker pled guilty to the rape of a fourteen-year-old and to conspiring in the murder of her parents and her six-year-
old sister, he stated, "I want the people of Iraq to know that I did not go there to

do the terrible things that I did . . . I do not ask anyone to forgive me today. To live there, to survive there, I became angry and mean. I loved my friends, my fellow soldiers, and my leaders, but I began to hate everyone else in Iraq."[150]

The "forgiveness" we may offer in these cases is the settlement made with a community that cannot ignore the fact that these crimes were committed by citizens of honor whom the community itself trained to be "obdurately indifferent" so they could kill.[151] The proper response may not be blame but something more akin to the voice of a Greek chorus. As Raimond Gaita puts it,

> Nearly everyone is vulnerable to the tendency to believe that severe moral appreciation must run together with blame. But there are voices in our culture that speak of different possibilities. Sophocles' Oedipus the King shows how moral severity may take the form of pity. The chorus does not blame Oedipus . . . It pities the evil-doer he became . . . Its severe pity holds him fast in serious moral response—it holds him *responsible to* the evil-doer he has become—insisting that he face the full meaning of it.[152]

George Fletcher reaches a similar conclusion in his essay on collective guilt. He suggests that "mitigating the penalties of those who commit horrendous crimes" may be appropriate where a people is responsible for generating "a climate of moral degeneracy" and "betrays its duty to create circumstances of moral action," in "a kind of treason by the nation against its loyal citizens."[153] Even Eichmann, says Fletcher, ought to be judged in the context of his immersion in a community that persistently denied the humanity of the Jewish people.

Perhaps, in the last analysis, we must be open to the possibility of seeing these torturers, killers, and rapists as human tragedies, not inhuman monsters, or we risk losing our own souls, too. When Simon sits with the SS soldier, "some kind of mysterious grace seems to have passed between these two young men."[154] Each seems to see beyond the categories imposed by ideology, war, hierarchy, and race hate, to see the infinite other.[155] It was not a moment of condescending pity on either side but a mutual recognition "without thinking, simply as a matter of course."[156] A work of grace happens. Matthew Fox suggests that Simon's lifelong hunt for other Nazi war criminals was galvanized by that moment. In any event, he was afterward able to bring forward the memory of wrong as wrong with the compassion of a witness, not the fear and hatred of a victim. Albert Speer, convicted Nazi war criminal, speaks of Simon's "eyes" "that reflected all the murdered people, eyes that have witnessed the misery, degradation, fatalism, and agony of your fellow human beings," yet "those eyes are not filled with hatred; they remain warm and tolerant and full of sympathy for the misery of others." He thanks Simon for his "clemency, humanity, and goodness."[157]

Common both to mercy and to remorse is this ability to see the face of the other—whether victim or criminal—outside and beyond the categories of prejudice and rules. Karl, though blinded before by the Nazi rhetoric, finally saw the "face" of the young boy who jumped from the second story; Simon saw the "face" of the nearly faceless SS soldier. Seeing "the enemy" as human, whether within or without our ranks, is still humanly possible, in glimpses and moments, and that may be our only redemption.

One cannot be open to the truth of the victim's suffering unless one is at the same time open to the truth of the offender's humanity. The witness to the wrong of wrong must see both. The "face" or "being-with" we share is before crime, before victims and offenders. True mercy in the sublime judgment becomes the flip side of true remorse; it is rare to point to, hard to "prove," perhaps beyond any intentional doing, but nonetheless the "matter of course" at the ground of human and humane ethics—the "face-to-face" or "being-with" that grounds all of law and ethics. Mercy may not be called for in all cases but should not be categorically excluded in any. Each case must be "faced," and each must be an ethical experience that does not prejudge what might happen to the parties in the course of the encounter.

> Shortly after liberation, a Jewish death-camp survivor is "given" a seventeen-year-old wounded Nazi soldier on whom she can take her revenge. Instead she bandages his wounds and sends him to the POW camp. When asked why, she replies, "How could I kill him—he looked into my face and I looked into his."[158]

> Well, there was this kid. I sat there and I had fed the kid all day, and he was walking along the dike, and he said hello to us and while the squad leader—well, he grabbed the kid and started beating him up. He put a .45 up to his head and then he cocked the hammer and he said, "Was there VC in his village last night?" And the kid said, "No, there wasn't." Then we beat him up and then I realized that he wasn't going to tell us that his father was in their village last night. Were they going to tell us that their husbands were there? That's all I have to say.[159]

Conclusion: Fallen Angels

Retributive justice's great strength has been its promise of nobility, derived from its kanticism. It gives meaning to the pain of punishment (and thereby to the wrong itself), it limits and rationalizes revenge, and it treats offenders with dignity. Retributivism also keeps mercy at bay, primarily by arguing that mercy is demeaning and unequal. Yet all of these strengths depend on the premise that human nature is, at core, the ability to follow universal rules of reason.

I have argued that the promises of retributivism are based on a false understanding of the nature of being human and, consequently, on a false assumption that reason is the glue and ground of community and responsibility. I conclude that perfect retributive justice is unattainable and disconnected from our true nature and that human dignity requires not "just deserts" but humble, clement judgment and a renewal of our human being as being-with. Instead of punishment as "just deserts," I imagine punishment as the work of remorse and compassion, which is a shared painful memory of wrong as wrong. The pain of the victim's fear and despair and the offender's remorse call for testimony and confession before a compassionate and merciful witness. Out of this encounter of remorse and compassion comes the completion of punishment as merciful settlement.

Stated this way, these ideas are abstractions, in need of concrete examples and the knowing-how that is tied to emotion and experience. In chapters 5 and 6, I provided some concrete examples of merciful settlement at work, but to give the emotional tenor and experience of this new ground of punishment and mercy is harder. I draw on the skills of two great novelists in this concluding chapter to provide at least vicarious experience. The first part of the conclusion draws on Alexandre Dumas' novel *The Count of Monte Cristo* to dramatize the limits of both victim-centered and retributive theories of justice. The second part of the conclusion draws on J. M. Coetzee's novel *Disgrace* to dramatize the way in which an offender who comes to remember the wrong as wrong can reach a settlement of renewed being-with, outside a retributive or Kantian paradigm of will, choice, and rules. Both novelists show us their protagonists (victim, then offender) as "fallen angels" who reconcile themselves in the course of the novels to their own finite humanity.

I. THE ACCOUNTING OF THE COUNT

Alexandre Dumas' intriguing character Edmond Dantès is a victim who has the luxury of unlimited time, wealth, and power to avenge himself against his wrongdoers. He is able to create, as his name suggests, his own personal Inferno. His vengeance, carefully conceived, is intended and executed to be retributive justice, as I will argue. However, Dumas shows us this retribution— even by a good man against those who clearly deserve it—not as justice but as a mistake that almost costs Dantès his soul.

As we meet him, Dantès is a valiant, honest, open, generous, trusting sailor, about to become the captain of his own ship and to marry the woman he loves. But he has a premonition that all will not be well: "I cannot think that man is meant to find happiness so easily! Happiness is like one of those palaces on an enchanted island, its gates guarded by dragons. One must fight to gain it; and, in truth, I do not know what I have done to deserve the good fortune of becoming Mercédès' husband" (34).[1] Sure enough, Dantès' enemies plot against him. Danglars, the greedy and jealous ship's bursar, fears that Dantès' captaincy will destroy his opportunity to continue embezzling from Morrel, the ship's owner. Fernand, who is in love with Dantès' beautiful fiancée Mercédès, wants to stop the marriage (without a direct confrontation with Dantès). Their confederate, the greedy Cadarousse, will be happy to keep their plot quiet in exchange for a bottle of wine and the power to blackmail them both.

Danglars knows that Dantès is to deliver a letter from the exiled Bonaparte. Dantès does not know the contents of the letter, and undertook the commission only at the request of his dying captain. But Dantès' naive sense of duty gives Fernand and Danglars a convenient excuse to denounce him to the local authorities. Dantès is arrested at his betrothal feast and brought before the ambitious assistant public prosecutor, Villefort. The young prosecutor is struck by the coincidence that he, too, was summoned from his own betrothal feast to hear the case. His first impulse of fellow feeling, however, is soon smothered by more ambitious thoughts, as he composes on this theme a "philosophical analogy" "designed to elicit applause" in his future father-in-law's salon (55). Convinced of Dantès' ignorance and innocence, Villefort is about to release Dantès. But just as he is gathering his hat and gloves, he learns from Dantès that the Bonapartist who was to receive this treasonous letter is his own father, Noirtier. To preserve his career, Villefort burns the incriminating letter and consigns Dantès to the island prison Chateau D'If. The bewildered Dantès finds himself in a dungeon, completely ignorant of who is responsible for his fate.

Dantès' suffering in the dungeon is a progressive loss of ignorance and innocence. When first interviewed by Villefort, Dantès declares that if his enemies "were to be among my friends, I should rather not know who they are, so as not to be obliged to hate them," and he is so very ironically urged by Villefort to "always see clearly how one stands" (56). Dantès begins his time in Chateau D'If with pride and hope that his innocence will be discovered. After time, he "came to doubt his own innocence." He "fell from the summit of his pride and prayed, not to God, but to men; God is the last refuge" (114). Finally, having "exhausted every human resource," Dantès "turned to God" (115). When, despite his prayers, he remains a prisoner, "fury followed asceticism. Edmond's curses made his jailer start back in horror. He dashed himself against the walls of his prison and raged" (115). Then, he remembered the informer's letter. "He decided that it was human hatred and not divine vengeance that had plunged him into this abyss. He doomed these unknown men to every torment that his inflamed imagination could devise, while still considering that the most frightful were too mild and, above all, too brief for them: torture was followed by death, and death brought, if not repose, at least an insensibility that resembled it" (115–16). The thought of death, finally, brings Dantès to try suicide.

Dantès loses more than his future, his fiancée, and his freedom. We are told that he loses his pride and self-confidence. Like many victims, he even doubts his own innocence.[2] He grovels before his jailors with no sense of dignity. Finally, he loses his faith in God and his very will to live. His misfortune is so great and so undeserved that he later tells his mentor and fellow prisoner, Abbe Faria, that he wishes he could blame men for it, "so that I may no longer blaspheme against God" (139).

Dantès suffers because he cannot understand his fate, because it does not accord with his vision of a just universe. There are three ways to understand his misfortune. One possibility is that he deserves it. He is somehow, inexplicably, guilty, and he should die.[3] A second possibility is that there is *no* sense to his suffering. His world has been turned upside down; chaos, not cosmos, reigns; and God must be dead. But this idea is intolerable. The third possibility is that others are to be blamed. If this is so, then he can still have hope for the universe to be placed back in balance through his enemies' fall. As explained by the trauma literature in chapter 4, anger will mask his fear of senselessness.[4] Revenge will be the remedy, because revenge will put the world back in order.[5] Revenge will be Dantès' proof of the existence of God.

As Dantès is suffering these thoughts and feelings and slowly dying of self-imposed starvation, he discovers the Abbe Faria tunneling toward his cell. Dantès' hope is revived; his fellow feeling is restored. Faria becomes his teacher, mentor, and prison father. Faria also helps him discover the identity of his enemies. As Dantès thinks over the truth, he "made a fearful resolution" and swore "a terrible oath" (144). Faria is worried: "I regret having helped you in your investigation . . . I have insinuated a feeling into your heart that was not previously there: the desire for revenge" (145).

As the familiar story goes, Faria dies in prison, leaving Dantès a map to an immense treasure and a means of escape. Faria hopes that Dantès will use it for good, but Dantès plans to use it to harm his enemies. He considers his deliverance a sign that he is to become, in Dumas' recurring image, an avenging angel of Providence—the means by which God will restore the balance of right and wrong. Dantès wants "to be Providence, because the thing that I know which is finest, greatest and most sublime in the world is to reward and punish" (477).

Dantès now has the power and mission of an ideal avenger. How does he choose to use this power? First, he gathers information about his targets. He follows the careers of Danglars and Fernand, learning of all Danglars' ill-gotten gains and of Fernand's ill-gotten honor, carefully gathering evidence and witnesses to all their crimes. He confirms from the greedy Cadarousse that Danglars and Fernand are responsible for denouncing him to Villefort, and he learns of the loyalty of his former employer, Morrell.

Then, he spends years making a study of forms of punishment. After having "made a comparative study of executions in different parts of the world" (332), Dantès decides that "death may be a torment, but it is not an expiation" (332), and that there are "crimes for which the impalement *à la turque,* or Persian burial alive, or the whips of the Iraqis would be too mild" (333). He seeks not merely the suffering or death of his enemies but something "slow, deep, infinite and eternal" (333). He does not seek merely to kill his enemies or torture them or even procure their own imprisonment. Instead, he spends nearly ten years more in self-denial, stalking them and making elaborate plans for the perfect revenge.

The reader is drawn into the captivating power of Dantès, now resurrected as the Count of Monte Cristo, whose ancestors, quips journalist Beauchamp, "might have owned Calvary" (389). He constructs punishments exquisitely tailored to each of his enemies, though each has the following elements: (1) each enemy suffers a kind of rebound of his own character upon himself; (2) each loses that for which he committed the crimes against Dantès; (3) each suffers public humiliation; and (4) each, in the end, knows that his downfall is due to Dantès. As we will see, each of these elements of Dantès' revenge looks more like a perfected offender-centered retributive justice than the victim-centered vengeance that would "stand by the victim," grant restitution to the victim, or reestablish the victim's self-esteem or social standing through the offender's humiliation.

The first and most interesting aspect of Dantès' revenge is that he takes great pains to bring upon his enemies the "natural" consequences of their own evil characters. He makes them, in effect, live by their own law. This is the measure of classic retributive justice, not the vengeance measure of making the enemy suffer as the victim did.[6] Dantès does not demand that his revenge be exactly measured by the extent of his own suffering and loss. None of his enemies are cast into the Chateau D'If. None of them undergo years of starvation or privation. Most importantly, none of them suffer the moral vertigo of not understanding why they are suffering. On the contrary, Dantès makes very sure they see their suffering as punishment, not misfortune.

Dantès' punishments are precisely the rebound of his enemies' actions, become universal law. For Fernand, the cowardly soldier, who is afraid to challenge Dantès for Mercédès' love directly and who betrays Dantès' offer of friendship, Dantès orchestrates a public accusation of treason, exposing Fernand's claims to honorable military service as false. His wife and son then desert the deserter. For Danglars, the greedy banker, Dantès turns his own scheme of trading on public secrets against him, bankrupting him and publicly humiliating him by exposing a potential rich son-in-law as a pretender and thief (like his would-be father-in-law). Danglars is then captured by greedy bandits at Dantès' instigation and suffers near starvation and extortion. For Cadarousse, Dantès turns his own blackmail against him, causing him to be shot by his own confederate. For Villefort, the ambitious and compassionless prosecutor, Dantès arranges a public exposure of the crimes he has so bloodlessly committed in order to achieve his position, as well as inducing his equally ambitious wife to commit murder within Villefort's own family. His wife's ambition, fostered by Villefort's own ambition, brings about his downfall. To the reader's keenest satisfaction, the plunderer is plundered, the traitor betrayed, the blackmailer blackmailed, and the ambitious deposed by ambition. Each suffers the law of his own making; each experiences the universal ricochet of his own character.

Retributive justice also requires the forfeiture of ill-gotten gains, the disgorgement of that for which the crime was committed. This measure is different from the measure of civil damages, which are designed to restore the victim to his or her previctimized position. A victim-centered, revenge-based paradigm would suggest restitutionary remedies rather than forfeiture. But Dantès does not take any restitution from his enemies: Danglars' gold is given away to hospitals, and Dantès does not even reclaim the love of Mercédès. Instead, the loss suffered by each of his enemies is that by which and for which their crimes were committed—the tools of crime and their ill-gotten gains. Fernand loses Mercédès, his honor, and then, most precious to a coward, his life. The greedy Danglars loses his fortune. Cadarousse, the blackmailer, is shot in the back by his friends. Villefort, who attained his own position by cool, rational calculation, loses his heir, his status, and, most precious of all, his reason. The count gains nothing tangible from all this but, on the contrary, spends a large fortune bringing it about. His only gain is the satisfaction of seeing justice done.

The public humiliation aspect of Dantès' revenge seems at first to be in accord with victim-centered theories of punishment. Villefort's crime is uncovered in court, Fernand's is uncovered at the legislative assembly, and Danglars is publicly embarrassed at his daughter's engagement party. (Cadarousse is not publicly humiliated.) Jean Hampton's argument,[7] adopted by and extended by others, that the public punishment of an offender "brings him down" and thereby restores the dignity he robbed from the victim, would suggest that public exposure is essential to punishment. Victims are to have standing in court, to be able to be present and speak, to be able to witness the punishment. The necessity of publicity is less obvious from the standpoint of retributivism.

Yet at none of these moments of public exposure does Dantès reveal himself in public as the triumphant victim, and he is personally present at only the engagement party. In fact, he is careful *not* to be present at the accusations of Fernand or Villefort. If the shaming of his enemies is meant somehow to enable him to publicly reassert his own dignity, Dantès does not seem to require this. He has already created a high social character for himself as the Count of Monte Cristo. He does not even bother to clear his true name in public—even in the end, when his revenge is complete. Instead, he reveals his true identity before no one except his enemies and his close friends, even though neither his enemies nor his close friends had a false opinion of his character to dispel. It seems that the public event of humiliating his enemies is not for the purpose of raising the status or clearing the name of Dantès, as a victim-centered view might suggest.

There is another account to be given here, however. The public exposure of his enemies is necessary not to restore Dantès' honor but to unmask the criminals. Here, Dantès presents the character of a public prosecutor, acting on behalf of the universal Law and bringing the Truth to actuality, as Hegel would have it. Indeed, Hegel tells us that it is only through the institution of justice, where crime is perceived to be not against an individual but against an entire community, that Law can come into play in the world, can be seen and felt and lived. The public exposure of Dantès' enemies is the very opposite of a private vendetta discharged by a discreet duel or shadowy murder, and, indeed, Fernand and Albert blame him for not seeking revenge privately. They believe the public exposure to be officious on Dantès' part. But Dantès here transcends the personal and plays the part of Providence—absolute justice come to earth.

But surely, one might argue, the final aspect of Dantès' revenge is victim-centered, for in each case, Dantès makes himself personally known to his enemy as the agent of his downfall. Surely this is the moment of his triumphing over them, showing his equality with them at last. Even here, however, the victim-centered paradigm is at best incomplete, for the point of Dantès' last interview with his offenders does not seem to be to gain a personal triumph over them (though that is what happens in part), to make them crawl and beg for mercy, to establish dominance and mastery, or even to reassert his own equality. Instead, each of these moments of revelation is primarily a moment of conversion. The sheer improbability of Dantès' return strikes into his enemies' hearts a fear, not of Dantès, but of God. Each sees his own fate, his own life, as under the power of a higher order and a higher justice. Each understands his punishment as just and deserved, and each has the opportunity to repent.

In his last moments, Cadarousse declares to Dantès (disguised as Abbe Busoni), "If there was any divine justice, you know as well as anyone that there are people who would be punished, but who are not" (804). "There is no God, there is no Providence. There is only chance" (805). Dantès replies, "There is both Providence and God . . . The proof is that you are lying there, desperate, denying God, and I am standing before you, rich, happy, healthy and safe, clasping my hands before the God in whom you try not to believe" (805). Cadarousse demands, "But who are you then?" (806). When Dantès then reveals his real name to Cadarousse, he cries, "Oh, God, forgive me for denying You! You do indeed exist, You are the father of men in heaven and their judge on earth" (806).

Fernand comes to Dantès to challenge him to a duel. But when Dantès reveals who he really is, "a face rejuvenated by the joy of revenge, a face that you must have seen often in your dreams since your marriage . . . to my fiancée Mercédès" (877), Fernand, "his head thrown back, his hands held out, his eyes staring, watched this dreadful spectacle in silence" (877). Then with a "heart-rending cry: 'Edmond Dantès!'" (877), Fernand stumbled to his carriage and rode home to commit suicide.

Even the vestige of personal triumph, however, is gone when Dantès confronts Villefort. Villefort has already felt his downfall as "the hands of a vengeful God" (1018). But when Dantès reveals his identity, it is Villefort's turn to accuse, for both his wife and son are dead. "'You are Edmond Dantès!' cried the crown prosecutor, gasping the count by the wrist, 'Then, come with me!' . . . he said, showing the count the bodies of his wife and child. 'There! Look! Are you fully revenged?'" (1024). Dantès turns pale. Villefort curses Dantès, but then "the veins of his temples swelled with boiling ferments that tried to burst the narrow vault of his skull and drown his brain in a deluge of fire" (1025), and Villefort goes mad, digging in the garden for his missing son.

Finally, when Dantès reveals himself to Danglars, he first asks Danglars to repent "of the evil you have done" (1066). Dantès then forgives him, revealing that he is "the one whom you sold, betrayed and dishonoured . . . the one on whom you trampled in order to attain a fortune . . . the one whose father you condemned to starvation, and the one who condemned you to starvation, but who none the less forgives you, because he himself needs forgiveness—I am Edmond Dantès!" (1066). Danglars "gave a single cry and fell, prostrate" in supplication (1066).

The revelation of Dantès as the agent of punishment is, in part, a way to demonstrate to his offenders that they did not get away with anything. As in the retributivist demand that a defendant understand not only *that* he or she is being punished but *why* he or she is being punished, Dantès' revelation of his identity gives the suffering of his enemies a meaning and a sense: it is divine retribution, not mere revenge. Indeed, when Villefort's son is poisoned, Dantès blanches: he does not want to be "revenged"; he wants justice. He fears he has gone too far.

In sum, what Dantès, the ideal victim, desires is not revenge but justice. It would be hard to distinguish the vengeance Dantès inflicts from the retributivism of Hegel or Kant. The retributivist imagines the offender confronting the universal law of his or her own making, suffering the rebound of his or her own character. Like Dantès, the retributivist sees this occurring in a public forum, where all can witness the actualization of justice, the coming to appearance of law. Falsity is replaced with truth, appearance with actuality. As in the conversion of Cadarousse, the existence of God is proved by the appearance of justice. Chaos is abolished; cosmos is reestablished.

So Dantès, as ideal victim, does not merely want to watch his enemies suffer and die, nor does he want restitution or a public parade reaffirming his honor. It is not enough to give Dantès back riches, security, social position, or even happiness. He wants, thirsts for, longs for, and suffers for justice. He wants his enemies to live by their own law and to understand themselves as bound by reason, to understand their fate as deserved, to see that they are living in a world where justice prevails. Only justice can banish Dantès' doubts about the meaning of it all. Only justice can prove the existence of God.

But as Villefort's final accusation makes clear, Dumas does not leave us with this triumphant conclusion. He does not allow us to be so completely comfortable. There is a darker side to this revenge as justice. To fully understand the character of this darker side, Dumas first asks us to contrast an older form of vengeance.

Unlike Dantès' search for vengeance, which carries a metaphor of balancing the universal order, other characters in the novel seek vengeance in order to restore honor or cleanse pollution. Robert Solomon perceptively notes that revenge plays on three metaphors: debt, balance, and pollution. The debt metaphor requires a "paying back" of like for like; the balance metaphor, a "felt need to put the world back into balance"; and the pollution metaphor, a "cleansing."[8] The former two are both reflected in Dantès' vengeance, though "balance" predominates. The "count" is concerned with accounting,[9] as he tries to balance the scales of cosmic justice. But the pollution metaphor is reflected in a different understanding that crime "dishonors" the victim; the avenger is required to purify the family to restore honor. The count, by contrast, uses the language of honor seldom, and he dismisses the conventional form of honor vengeance, dueling, as sufficient only for insult, but not for crime (333–34). Still, the book is full of honor avengers, including Dantès' chargé d'affaires, Bertuccio, who has sworn vengeance against Villefort for refusing to prosecute the assassination of his brother. Dantès also consorts with and perhaps even invites vengeance outlaws to shelter on Monte Cristo.[10]

The pollution metaphor is most explicit in the story of Rita, a long aside told to Albert and Franz by their innkeeper. A bandit, Cucumetto, captures the young girl Rita while she awaits her love, Carlini. When he discovers her plight, Carlini arranges for Rita to be ransomed, instead of gang-raped by the band of outlaws as is the "common law" (297). But Cucumetto betrays him, rapes Rita, prevents Carlini at gunpoint from aiding her, and then consigns her to "satisfy the lusts of the whole band" (295). Carlini appears to give up his defense of Rita, but while the others are drawing lots for their turn with her, he forestalls them by stabbing Rita in the heart. When her father arrives with the ransom, Carlini offers his life for hers: "If I was wrong, avenge her" (299). The father replies, "you did well" (299). He embraces Carlini, and together they bury Rita's body. Afterward, the father hangs himself. The clear message here is that crime pollutes; it is better to die than to be a victim.

The nature of honor is difficult to understand from a modern perspective. Trisha Olson gives the most penetrating insight into it when she writes,

> In contrast to modern accounts of the nature of wrong, the medieval person experienced wrong as a sullying of another's honor and dignity. It could be no other way. In a world where identity is not individualistic, but tied to, and dependent upon, our various relationships with others then a rupturing and blackening of a relationship is a blackening of both the wrongdoer and the one wronged. The idea of the psychology of the individual came at the end of the twelfth century. Until that time, the world was a place of deeds and those deeds took place between persons shaping, elevating or degrading the appearance of each. Hence, the feud commanded respect. It said that one was not "timid" and would take action to restore his reputation (*fama* being the touchstone of whether one dwelled in a state of honor or shame).[11]

Only later is honor translated into a metaphysical, untouchable Kantian dignity or a Hegelian will that cannot be touched by crime. But Dumas' novel literally straddles the ancien régime and the modern one, covering the period of the French Revolution, the rise and fall of Napoleon, and the Restoration. The culture of honor still persists, but the state refuses to recognize it. Legal justice fails twice, then, argue Dumas' Corsican characters—once in failing to avenge and twice in killing the avengers. Honor killings are driven underground and, in the process, become ambiguous.

The ambiguity of vengeance is highlighted several times in the book. For example, when Bertuccio asks Villefort for justice when his brother is murdered, Villefort refuses to consider the killing a murder, rather than a revenge:

saying, "There are disasters in every revolution ... Your brother was a victim of this one. It's unfortunate, but it doesn't mean that the government owes your family anything. If we were to try all the cases of reprisals that the supporters of the usurper carried out on those of the king when they were in power, then it could well be that your brother would be condemned to death. What happened was entirely natural, it's the law of retaliation ... He lived by the sword and he died by the sword" (427). But Bertuccio responds "you are wrong, Monsieur. He lived by the sword, but he died by the dagger" (427). Bertuccio then declares a vendetta against Villefort.

The ambiguity of revenge is also underscored later, when Bertuccio tells the count how he stabbed (and believed he had killed) Villefort and stole a box he thought contained treasure. Dantès says, "It seems you committed a modest little murder, combined with robbery" (430). But Bertuccio says, "No, Excellency, ... it was a vendetta, combined with reparation" (430). Perhaps Dantès is only toying with Bertuccio here, but the distinction between vendetta and murder has become fraught with doubt, as avengers jump from the murk behind pillars or bushes and stab their unarmed victims in the back.

Dueling, with its clear, gentlemanly rules of fairness, seems to have been, in part, a way of clarifying the distinction between murder and vengeance. Villefort's father, Noirtier, for example, produces a document arguing that his killing of General Epinay was fair and just, because the death was the outcome of a duel and therefore not a murder. But although Dantès is willing to fight a duel over an insult (and "more or less certain of killing my opponent" [333]), he does not believe a duel gives satisfaction of greater wrongs: "You consider yourself revenged because you ... put a bullet in his head, after he has turned your mind to delirium and your heart to despair? Come, come! ... He is often the one ... purged in the eyes of the world and in some sense pardoned by God. ... No, No, ... in return for a slow, deep, infinite, eternal pain, I should return as nearly as possible a pain equivalent" (333).

Dantès seems a modern hero, then, who seeks something more than restored honor. He may also be more cruel, for the avenger of honor does not torture but merely kills to cleanse. Dantès, however, takes vengeance to a metaphysical level. The wrong is a cosmic disharmony, not only a personal pollution. He is no longer Dantès the sailor but the Count of Monte Cristo— Calvary's own accountant.

In a gripping encounter with Villefort, who is described as "a living statue of the Law" (472), the Count of Monte Cristo explains how superior divine justice is to mere human justice, which is limited "by mountains or rivers, or by a change in customs or by a difference of language" (476). He declares that he is one of the agents of Providence, "whom God has set above office-holders, ministers, and kings" (474) and whose mission is to reward and punish (477). Repeatedly, Dantès asserts that he is an agent of divine justice, perfect justice, justice untainted by the usual foibles of the human justice, so "inadequate as a consolation" (333): "I have my own justice, high and low, which suspends no sentences and hears no appeals, which merely condemns or pardons" (275). He rescues innocent men from execution, befriends worthy bandits, and seeks out the evil that escapes human administration.

But for all his being "millionaire and adroit" (334), his plans do not go smoothly. Because of his careful instigation (perhaps even criminal solicitation) of Villefort's wife to poison all who stand in the way of her son's inheritance, Dantès' friend Maximilien almost loses his love, Villefort's daughter Valentine. Dantès does not foresee that when Villefort's wife finally poisons herself at Villefort's command, to spare him from infamy, she will also poison her young son. Dantès "realized that he had exceeded the limits of vengeance, he realized that he could no longer say, 'God is for me and with me'" (1024). When Dantès discovers he has unwittingly caused his friend Maximilien's love to be poisoned through Villefort's wife, he cries like "a wounded lion" (888): "God punishes the most boastful and the most detached of men for their indifference to the frightful scenes that He displays before them. . . . I, who, like the fallen angel, laughed at the evil that men do . . . now I myself am bitten by that serpent whose progress I was observing" (889). He also comes to respect Fernand's son, Albert, who he planned to kill and whose prospects he has ruined, and he wonders how he can give back "the happiness I have taken away" from this innocent man (991).

For all his careful and thorough planning, for all his investigations, Dantès still is not omniscient or omnipotent. His justice is not perfect; his aim goes astray. He causes the innocent to suffer with the guilty; he unbalances the cosmic scales. The prophecy of Albert's sober friend Franz, that "the one who pours himself a cup of vengeance is likely to drink a bitter draught" (334), is true after all. Dantès cannot know or control the consequences of his actions; indeed, both the count's rewards and punishments rebound in unanticipated ways throughout the book.[12] Neither rewards nor punishments can be confined to their targets.

Recognizing the imperfection of even his better justice, Dantès struggles to balance the scales. He spares Danglars' life "because he himself needs forgiveness" (1066), and he brings Maximilien and Valentine safe to each other: "I consider that restitution is a weight thrown back into the scales in the opposite tray from the one where I cast evil" (1072). In the end, he even plans to commit suicide "to punish" himself for the wrongs he has done on his path to perfect justice (1076).

But there is an even deeper question for Dantès. It is possible that he has not only unbalanced the scales but he has been "sacrilegious" and should never have sought to play the part of Providence at all (1036). Perhaps God is not on his side. Or worse, perhaps God does not exist. He seeks constantly for evidence that he is meant to pursue this path, for signs from God that he is in the right (1043, 1072). Yet, after his aim goes astray, after Mercédès begs for her son's life, after she refuses his offer of financial help, he doubts his mission. He has seen revenge as the proof of God's existence. Justice is a way to avoid blasphemy, a way to keep his faith. But what if he is wrong? He agonizes, "Ah, I shall have to become a fatalist, after fourteen years of despair and ten years of hope had made me a believer in Providence" (855).

There is something weak and heretical about a faith that requires human enemies in order to avoid losing faith in God. We blame humans for our suffering, so we can make sense of it. Understood this way, justice becomes a kind of revenge against our own mortality, a revenge against chaos, a foil against facing the frightening thought that there is no sense we can make of it all.[13] This background demand for a divine justice that we can make sense of is itself a demand that God be reasonable and that reason be God. We want an all-powerful reason, one that cannot pass away, one that is never defeated or changed. So our idea of divine justice as something that is "infinite and eternal" can even reach the past and wrap it in a justification from the future, uniting past and future in a timeless balance.

This unchanging justice is inevitably at war with the flux and finitude we are. We exist in time and yet long to control it, stop it, rewind it, fix it, change it, erase it, complete it. As Nietzsche put it, "'It was': thus is the Will's teeth-gnashing and lonesomest tribulation called. Impotent towards what hath been done—it is a malicious spectator of all that is past . . . This, yea, this alone is revenge itself: the Will's antipathy to time, and its 'It was.'"[14] The revenge against time, of course, is the ultimate revenge against our own mortality and therefore against life itself.

Dantès admits to being an enemy of time. He says he has only three adversaries: distance, time, and mortality (476). His immense fortune allows him to overcome the first two, but he worries that he will die before his mission is accomplished. Dantès races against his own mortality in trying to make the past present again. At first, it seems he is successful, as ghosts rise all around him: Villefort's dead infant son is dramatically resurrected; Haydee, thought dead, comes back to haunt Fernand; Valentine is miraculously restored to life; and, of course, Dantès himself is a ghost, come back from the grave. Dantès battles time, torquing it to his will, stopping and reversing and twisting it to achieve a "slow, deep, infinite, and eternal" justice.

Justice, for the Count of Monte Cristo, is the search for a perfectly rational, perfectly fair, perfectly meaningful universe. But we are not perfect, and neither is our world. The fanatical quest for justice (and for humans to blame) may mask a disquieting and unsettling truth that the world does not make sense to us, that there is no easy explanation for why bad things happen to good people. It may also manifest a certain self-hatred and inability to reconcile ourselves to the uncertainty and mystery that come with being finite.[15] We, like Dantès, wish to defeat time.

Does Dantès, the avenged victim, achieve peace and closure at last? It certainly seems so, as he sails off into the sunrise with his new young bride, Haydée. Yet Dumas is careful to tell us that the peace he achieves at last is not due to his vengeance. Indeed, the end of his vengeance was, according to his plan, to be closure by death. He expected to finish his mission and then commit suicide. In his suffering in prison, Dantès loses his youth, his family, his freedom, his future. He also loses his pride and his dignity. But in honing himself for vengeance, he realizes that he has lost something more. He explains to Mercédès, "From then on, that fortune seemed to me a holy vocation . . . Not an hour of calm . . . I loaded my weapons . . . making my body used to the most violent exercise and my soul to the roughest shocks, teaching my arm to kill, my eyes to see suffering and my mouth to smile at the most dreadful of spectacles. Kind, trustful and forgiving as I was, I made myself vengeful, secretive, and cruel—or rather, impassive like fate itself" (1034). Vengeance does not give him back his humanity; instead, he becomes, like Villefort, a "man of bronze" and a "hammer of God" (475).

Villefort's own "conversion" makes the point as well. The professional prosecutor, the statue of the law, the man "like granite" (427), who has cut his own name off[16] in order to serve as a detached and ambitious professional, discovers that his own wife has been poisoning his family. "Today," he tells himself, "the man who is to hold the sword of justice must strike wherever the guilty one may be" (1001). "Impassive" (1003), he interrogates his wife, asking, "Where do you keep the poison that you habitually use?" (1003). His trick question is that of an experienced interrogator, intentionally lacking in foundation. She asks whether she is to reply "to my husband or to the judge?" "To the judge, Madame, to the judge!" he replies. "I have been put on earth to punish" (1005), he tells her, and despite her pleas as his wife and the mother of his son, he declares, "I will denounce you with my own lips and arrest you with my own hands" (1006). "The man who is to hold the sword of justice," however, is Monte Cristo, and, ironically, Villefort becomes defendant rather than prosecutor when he arrives in court that day. His past crime of attempted infanticide is revealed as he attempts to prosecute his own unknown son for murder. Like Cadarousse, he sees this as the vengeance of God (1018). Suddenly he is struck by the brutality of his conduct toward his wife: "He had just assumed the role of implacable judge with this woman, condemning her to death" (1020). For the first time, he considers mercy to be a "good deed" (1021) and rushes home to pardon her, but it is too late; his wife and son are dead, and "this man, who had never felt pity for anyone, went to seek out the old man, his father, just so that in his weakness he might have someone to whom to tell his misfortune and someone with whom to weep" (1023).

The implacable avenger is heartless. The peace that vengeance gives is the peace of not feeling anything, the peace of death. The closure is the closure of having one's heart "torn out" (854). Vengeance does not heal, it cauterizes. As Villefort so ironically prophesies at the beginning of the novel, "we do not repair wrongs, but avenge them, that is all" (46).

So how does Dantès achieve his happiness in the end, if not through retribution? It is precisely because he has not managed to tear out his heart. He is still capable of loving Faria and staying with him until his death. He is still capable of being moved by Mercédès' plea for Albert's life. He is still capable of loving Maximilien and Haydée and of forgiving Danglars.

The counterpoint to Dantès' quest to balance the scales of justice is the character of Mercédès. For Dantès, the proof of God's existence is justice, but for Mercédès, the proof of God's existence is, as her name itself suggests, mercy. When Dantès returns, Mercédès alone recognizes him, and her first greeting is a blessing "from the bottom of my heart" (410). When Mercédès' son Albert challenges Dantès to a duel to recover the family's honor, Mercédès comes to beg Dantès to spare her son's life. She asks him to "forgive . . . for my sake, forgive, for I love you still!" (851). Her plea is much like that of Villefort's wife, and Dantès' initial answer is much like his: "Disobey God, who roused me up to punish it! Impossible, Madame, impossible!" (851). But Mercédès persists: "As long as I have known you I have worshipped your name and respected your memory. My friend, do not ask me to tarnish that noble and pure image which is constantly reflected in the mirror of my heart" (851–52). Dantès is moved by her words, and he agrees not to harm Albert, though he believes it will mean his own death and, more important, the failure of justice, which is to him as though "God had extinguished the sun and with His foot dashed the world into eternal night" (853). But in Mercédès' view, Dantès' willingness to end his pursuit of vengeance is "fine, it is great, it is sublime" (853) and proves "there is a God above us" (853). She says, "I have nothing further to ask of God . . . I have rediscovered you as noble and great as ever" (854).

At their final meeting, Dantès apologizes to Mercédès for causing "all your misfortunes" (1032) and explains that vengeance made him an unfeeling agent of fate. "Enough, Edmond!" she says, "you may believe that the only person to recognize you was also the only one who could understand" (1034). She forgives him—without "the glimmer of a reproach" (1032). Dantès, still trying to even the score, offers to give Mercédès back her half of Fernand's fortune, if she will agree. But she will not choose: "I am no longer a thinking creature. God has so shaken me with storms that I have lost my will. . . . Since I am alive, He does not want me to die. If He sends me any succour, it will be because He wants it, and I shall accept" (1035). But Dantès is horrified by her answer: "That is not how God should be worshipped. . . . He wants us to understand and debate His power: that is why He gave us free will" (1035). But Mercédès is horrified in her turn: "Don't speak like that to me. If I believed that God had given me free will, what would remain to save me from despair!" (1035).

In the end, Dantès is saved not by vengeance but by a new love, Haydée's love. It is love he feels he does not deserve. Love that will give him both happiness and pain. He "accept[s] [his] fate" whether the gift of a new love will be "a reward or punishment" (1076). He tries to sort out whether this gift is a final proof of his right to seek revenge. But at last, he gives up the quest for a perfect balance and asks Maximilien to pray for "a man who, like Satan, momentarily thought himself the equal of God and who, with all the humility of a Christian, came to realize that in God's hands alone reside supreme power and infinite wisdom. These prayers may perhaps ease the remorse that he takes with him in the depth of his heart" (1077). He no longer asks for justice as proof of cosmos or even for understanding, only "hope" (1077). Like Mercédès, he has at last reconciled himself to not knowing, to not understanding, and thereby to a faith based not on justice but on love.

The Count of Monte Cristo demonstrates that revenge and retribution may not be so far apart; victims long for more than the suffering of their enemies or the restoration of what they have lost. They long to make sense of their own suffering. They long to see right prevail over wrong, cosmos over chaos, God over chance. But justice should not be demanded as a proof of the existence of God. Rather, justice only papers over such questions. Dumas is careful to tell us, "Human justice is inadequate as a consolation: it can spill blood for blood, that's all. But one must only ask it for what is possible, not for anything more" (333). Like Nietzsche, Dumas cautions us not to chase after justice as a philosopher's godlike universal reason, which may be not only inhuman but inhumane. Instead, he counsels humility, which bears itself out in hopeful settlement, mercy, and love.

II. GRACE IN DISGRACE

The final narrative I will draw on in conclusion is J. M. Coetzee's novel *Disgrace*.[17] It is most often cited in articles *against* mercy, for, as I will discuss here, it dramatizes the difficulty in making remorse a necessary prerequisite for leniency in a formal justice proceeding. Nonetheless, the novel as a whole is a depiction of the work of punishment as a gift of merciful, undeserved settlement, or what can be called an "act of grace." It shows us how one can come to see justice—not as a perfect balancing of cosmic scales but a humble settlement of a wrong experienced as such within a human world, where we all begin in medias res and are part of a plot that both precedes and succeeds us. In its expression of humility and its acknowledgment of the *given* of human being-in-and-with, the book allows one to "live" the movement from reason to grace that I have been arguing for here.

The protagonist of *Disgrace*, David Lurie, is a divorced and superannuated professor of romantic poetry in a postapartheid, post-Nietzschean South Africa. He is a man who lives in a world of erotic fantasy and Platonic ideals, a world that is fleeing away, along with his own sexual powers. His students do not know who Lucifer is and are embarrassed by words like *passion*. His world, a "literature" department replaced by "communications," has been "technologized" and "rationalized": "Although he devotes hours of each day to his new discipline, he finds its first premise, as enunciated in the Communications 101 handbook, preposterous: 'Human society has created language in order that we may communicate our thoughts, feelings and intentions to each other.' His own opinion, which he does not air, is that the origins of speech lie in song, and the origins of song in the need to fill out with sound the overlarge and rather empty human soul" (3–4).

As Lurie tells his students, his dilemma (along with Wordsworth and

Byron) is this: "We cannot live our daily lives in a realm of pure ideas, cocooned from sense-experience. The question is not, How can we keep the imagination pure, protected from the onslaughts of reality? The question has to be, Can we find a way for the two to coexist?" (22). Like Nietzsche, like Heidegger, like Levinas, Professor Lurie is living with the remnants of the "real world" of reason, which has, as Nietzsche says, now become a myth. All that is left is sense experience, barren without the patina of a romantic sensibility. Kant's pure reason, Hegel's world spirit, the romantic notion of the sublime—a philosopher's god, in other words—is dead. In such a world, what can right and wrong, good and bad, ugly and beautiful, and true and false mean? If we no longer have those distinctions, what can punishment or mercy be?

Lurie struggles to live in his ideal world, but it keeps being snatched away. His illusion of erotic connection with a prostitute, Soraya, dissipates as soon as he sees her on the street with her sons, when "the little boys become presences between them" (6). The erotic ideal is dispelled by the real, now become tawdry and businesslike. He then seduces a young student, Melanie, with the Shakespearean line that "a woman's beauty does not belong to her alone ... She has a duty to share it" (16). She makes love with him unwillingly, passively; indeed, he "almost" rapes her, enraptured and captivated by his own aesthetic pleasure in her "perfect" beauty. She misses classes, misses the midterm, drops out of school. He feels only vaguely responsible for her "breathing presence," still caught up in his ideal "to keep her alive in her archetypal, goddesslike form" (22). He is later surprised to discover that she "takes things to heart" (37).

In teaching Byron's poem *Lara*, Lurie finds himself describing Lucifer to his class, an eerie reflection of himself: a "thing of dark imaginings," with a "mad heart" and "secret pride / To do what few or none would do beside," which would both lead him to do good and "mislead his spirit equally to crime" (33). He explains to his students that Byron invites us "to understand and sympathize [with Lucifer]. But there is a limit to sympathy. For though he lives among us, he is not one of us. He is exactly what he calls himself: a *thing*, that is, a monster ... It will not be possible to love him, not in the deeper, more human sense of the word. He will be condemned to solitude" (34).

These words are prophetic within the novel. Lurie is called before the academic discipline committee for his relationship with Melanie. He wishes only to plead guilty and "be shot" rather than "be fixed." He will not change "his nature" or "his temperament." He later explains to his daughter that he once "despaired" for a dog he had seen who had been so repeatedly beaten for his acts of lust that "at the smell of a bitch it would chase around the garden with its ears flat and its tail between its legs, whining, trying to hide" (90). The spectacle was "ignoble" because "the poor dog had begun to hate its own nature . . . At that point it would have been better to shoot it" (90).

Lurie's ex-wife tells him not to expect sympathy from the committee: "No mercy, not in this day and age" (44); "The whole thing is disgraceful from beginning to end. Disgraceful and vulgar too" (45). Lurie faces the committee, as Lucifer would, "with vanity," even though he knows that is a "dangerous" attitude. He pleads guilty to the charges and asks for his sentence. The academic committee, however, wants not to shoot him but to "fix" him. They ask whether he has sought counseling. He replies, "I am beyond the reach of counseling" (49). When he explains that he was "a servant of Eros" (52), the committee seizes on this as a potential excuse of "ungovernable impulse" (52). But Lurie will have none of that: "It was far from ungovernable. I have denied similar impulses many times in the past, I am ashamed to say" (52). The committee wants a "sincere" acknowledgment that he was wrong, a statement that "comes from his heart" (54). He objects, "And you trust yourself to divine that, from the words I use—to divine whether it comes from my heart?" (54). An angry committeewoman, looking for some "mention of the pain he has caused" or acknowledgment of "the history of exploitation of which this is part" (53), responds, "We will see whether you express contrition" (54). Lurie is disgusted: "Confessions, apologies: why this thirst for abasement?" (56).

When the school newspaper asks whether he regrets what he did, he responds defiantly that he was "enriched by the experience" (56). He objects, "Before that secular tribunal I pleaded guilty, a secular plea. That plea should suffice. Repentance is neither here nor there. Repentance belongs to another world, to another universe of discourse" (58). Later, he explains to his daughter: "It reminds me too much of Mao's China. Recantation, self-criticism, public apology. I'm old-fashioned, I would prefer simply to be put against a wall and shot. Have done with it . . . These are puritanical times. Private life is public business. Prurience is respectable, prurience and sentiment. They wanted a spectacle: breast-beating, remorse, tears if possible . . . The truth is, they wanted me castrated" (66). His daughter replies, "It isn't heroic to be unbending" (66).

Lurie wants to hold on to his ideals, his romantic nature. He refuses to be castrated, to let go of the only god left to him, Eros. He stubbornly continues to see his affair as something beautiful, enriching, though wrong. The *Shadenfreude* of the committee and its desire to "fix" him is not grace or mercy but annihilation, disgrace, abasement, the completion of the nihilism of rationalization that will see everything shorn of the ideal, that will have a "soulless image on the eye / That had usurped a living thought / That never more could be" (21). The committee's brand of "mercy" is demeaning, a denial of his manhood, his responsibility; it is the mercy of the Grand Inquisitor. He prefers simple Kantian justice, simple punishment, a simple paying back. He is satisfied to lose his job, his pension, his benefits, rather than lose his "nature." He will move away, write an opera instead. He does not want their "compromise." He chooses the "solitude" of Lucifer. But Lurie's attempt to take the high road of Kantian dignity does not succeed. That is not how the story ends.

In the novel, Lurie is changed. He is punished. He is, fictively, castrated. He does, eventually, confess and apologize, "from the heart," even bowing his head to the floor before Melanie's mother and sister. He does "let go" of his gods and even his own ideas of Kantian nobility. Somewhere in the bleakness of a world shorn of these ideals, a world of violence and hatred but also of people who take on duties of friendship after only a cup of tea, he finds grace. How does this transformation, this "work" of punishment, happen?

After Lurie is cast down from his haven at the university by "taking his punishment" and refusing to "express remorse," he moves in with his daughter Lucy, who is farming alone in the Eastern Cape. From this moment, Lurie and Lucy, Lucy and Lurie, form a kind of yin-yang pairing in the novel. To occupy his time, Lucy suggests that Lurie help her friend Bev, an unattractive woman who runs the local dog shelter. He is suspicious: it sounds like community service. But Lucy reassures him: the dogs will not care what his intentions are (77). He does not have to be changed. At first, he finds it hard to be moved by "cheerful" and "well-intentioned" animal welfare people. They make him want to "rape and pillage, or kick a cat." Lucy objects, "[Dogs] are part of the furniture, part of the alarm system. They do us the honour of treating us like gods, and we respond by treating them like things" (78). Lurie responds, "The Church Fathers had a long debate about them, and decided they don't have proper souls . . . Their souls are tied to their bodies and die with them." Lucy retorts, "I'm not sure that I have a soul. I wouldn't know a soul if I saw one" (79).

Lurie's cocksure attachment to "intention," to "soul," to his "principles," and to his own free will and masculinity are soon overthrown. Three black men come to Lucy's farm, overpower Lurie, beat him, burn him (though not with the immortal fire of Eros), lock him in the bathroom, and rape Lucy, with a brutality and hatred that sears and deadens her. Lurie tries to explain to her, "It was history speaking through them . . . It may have seemed personal, but it wasn't. It came down from the ancestors." She replies, "That doesn't make it easier. The shock simply doesn't go away. The shock of being hated, I mean. In the act" (156). Her dogs cannot protect her; they are shot, "contemptible, yet exhilarating, probably, in a country where dogs are bred to snarl at the mere smell of a black man" (110). Lurie, knocked on the head and locked in the bathroom, is powerless as well. He can do nothing to save her, nothing to comfort her. He is an "Aunt Sally," emasculated. Even afterward, Lucy must care for *him*; he can do nothing for *her*. But he feels lucky to have escaped with his life, unlike the dogs (98). No longer does he prefer to be shot than castrated.

Lurie cannot understand why his daughter refuses to leave the farm after this horrendous experience. He thinks she must be accepting some universal punishment on behalf of all the history of white exploitation. But Lucy does not live for ideas (105, 112). She "is adaptable" and lives "closer to the ground" (210). She only knows that she feels dead after the attack, and she must find her life there again, for if she leaves, she will leave in defeat. She bends and bends. She gives up her farm to Petrus, once her worker, her "boy" and her "dog-man," but now her powerful black neighbor and protector. In the end, she, a lesbian, even agrees to the humiliation of being known as Petrus's third wife, in order to receive his protection for herself and the yet-unborn child of her rape. She comes to see her rapists as "tax collectors," as part of the price she must pay for the past, for living on this ground. All of this is, of course, an eerie echo of Lurie's own words to Melanie: she does not own herself; she has a duty to share her body, to "increase" (16). Lucy vows to have the child, to love him, to be a good mother and a good person. Out of hatred and dirt and nothing, she will bring life and love. She is a farmer. She tells Lurie, "Yes, I agree, it is humiliating. But perhaps that is a good point to start from again. Perhaps that is what I must learn to accept. To start at ground level. With nothing. Not with nothing but. With nothing. No cards, no weapons, no property, no rights, no dignity . . . yes, like a dog" (205).

In the aftermath of Lurie's pain and despair and humiliation, his true "disgrace," regard for the dogs he is "serving" at the shelter takes him by surprise. His witnessing of Lucy's suffering enables him to be open in a new way to the suffering and to the love of others, even the "soulless" dogs, devoid of Kantian reason. He befriends an old abandoned female bulldog, who cannot, like he has done, go live with her children. He feels sorry for goats that the neighbor is planning to slaughter and has tied up where they cannot graze. He helps at the clinic, hauling away the euthanized dogs and incinerating them himself, so their dead bodies will not be beaten with shovels into a "more convenient shape" by the workers there. He moves from god to dog, a "dog-man"—from "reasonable man" to thing, from soul to life, from ideal to real. He thinks, "Curious that a man as selfish as he should be offering himself to the service of dead dogs . . . He saves the honour of corpses because there is no one else stupid enough to do it" (146). Like his description of Lucifer, the fallen angel, halfway between man and God, he has a "mad heart" and does "what few or none would do" (33). He is a "dog-man," "a thing of dark imaginings," given no mercy, unloved and unlovable, left in solitude—but not quite. His romantic ideal is turned on its head. He begins to unify the ideal and the real, the human and the animal, life and death, honor and dishonor; he begins to find grace in disgrace, love in the unlovely. He goes to bed with Bev, the ugly woman at the shelter, and in a role reversal of his relation with Melanie, "has let her do everything she has felt a need to do," "without passion but without distaste either" (150).

Lucy's rape and his own powerlessness in the face of it, his "witnessing" with Lucy of the wrong as wrong, and his growing connection to the dogs at the shelter propel Lurie at last to see his wrong to Melanie as a wrong. He goes to Melanie's father to "say what is in his heart." He explains that "she struck up a fire in me" (166). The father invites him to "break bread"—the traditional ceremony of reconciliation. Lurie almost backs out, but Melanie's father insists, "We'll be all right! We will do it! . . . You have to be strong!" After dinner, Lurie can bear the pretense of politeness no longer. He needs to say something more. He tells Melanie's father that it might have worked out except that he was "lacking the lyrical." He apologizes for "what I took your daughter through," for "the grief I have caused you and Mrs. Isaacs," and he asks for "your pardon" (171). The father replies, "The question is, what does God want from you, besides being very sorry? Have you any ideas, Mr. Lurie?" (172). Lurie "pick[s] his words carefully."

> Normally I would say . . . that after a certain age one is too old to learn lessons. One can only be punished and punished. But perhaps that is not true, not always. I wait to see. As for God, I am not a believer, so I will have to translate what you call God and God's wishes into my own terms. In my own terms, I am being punished for what happened between myself and your daughter. I am sunk into a state of disgrace from which it will not be easy to lift myself. It is not a punishment I have refused. I do not murmur against it. On the contrary, I am living it out from day to day, trying to accept disgrace as my state of being. Is it enough for God, do you think, that I live in disgrace without term? (172)

Melanie's father asks, "Why do you think you are here? . . . Who did you really come to speak to?" The question makes Lurie dislike Melanie's father: "He does not like this man, does not like his tricks." But he goes into the next room, where Melanie's mother and sister are sitting. Despite his situation, he is aware of their womanly attractiveness. He knows they are his "potential victims," part of a long history of men exploiting women in which he and they are implicated and entangled, along with his own daughter. He responds to this knowledge with an act of contrition: "With careful ceremony he gets to his knees and touches his forehead to the floor. Is that enough? He thinks. Will that do? If not, what more?" (173).

It is only a gesture, but somehow it is enough. Lurie begins to write his opera again, but it is now transformed. A middle-aged, ugly woman becomes his romantic heroine, calling to her lover Byron from his grave: "The halt helping the lame, for want of better" (183). In confronting the wrong as wrong, Lurie becomes his victim, a woman, shorn of his ideal of beauty, who takes things to heart. In the end, "it is not the erotic that is calling to him after all, nor the elegiac, but the comic . . . the voice that strains to soar away from the ludicrous instrument but is continually reined back, like a fish on a line" (184–85). His art will not raise him from disgrace, return him "triumphant to society" (214). He only hopes that "there will dart up, like a bird, a single authentic note of immortal longing" or, if not, that his heroine will forgive him for having brought her back to life (214). He thinks of all the women in his past: "*Enriched:* that was the word the newspapers picked on to jeer at. A stupid word to let slip, under the circumstances, yet now, at this moment, he would stand by it . . . By each of them he was enriched, and by the others too, even the least of them, even the failures. Like a flower blooming in his breast, his heart floods with thankfulness" (192).

Lurie is not alone after all, nor is he unloved. There is a lame dog at the pound whose "period of grace is almost over." The dog has adopted him, has come to love him, would die for him. Perhaps even the dog's howl will have a place in his opera. He will give the dog all he can in the way of love and honor, the halt helping the lame, after he has brought him through death, after "the soul is out" (219), the body burned up, the gift given up again.

Those who are "bankrupt," who have "nothing," who "give everything up," who start from the "ground," like dogs, learn to be thankful; they learn to accept the gift, the grace. Giving up our gods of philosophy that rank us as little lower than the angels, full of power, reason, and will, we are able to see for the first time what is given—world, things, the Other. We "dog-men" bend, bow, accept, receive—even grace, love, life, death. True thinking, says Heidegger, is thanking. Without the Kantian god, genuine punishment is no longer a simple price paid to keep our vaunting reason, our puissance, our Kantian godlike responsibility for our actions. We cannot really "own" or pay for our actions in this way; they escape us, overwhelm us, reverberate through history and generations, like the rebound of race hate and sexual exploitation, like war and revenge. Coetzee tells us that genuine punishment is the remembrance, in pain, of wrong as wrong, an overturning of our perspective from that of offender to victim, an utter humiliation of our own sense of mastery and control and the abyss of remorse and dis-grace. But in that pain and through the compassion it engenders, we are given the gift, the mercy, the grace, of a renewed connection with all people and all things—a merciful settlement.

Coetzee, it seems, offers us an account of punishment and grace intertwined but also an account of art, the work in which he reveals what punishment and grace are. These are revealed not in the sublime or the elegiac or the tragic but, as he says, in the comic, which brings us close to things, so we can see their moles and bunions. Comedy is humble. For the recipient of grace, Coetzee gives us an aging roué in a white skullcap, sitting under an umbrella in a dirty yard, playing a banjo to a lame dog. Yet his portrait is beautiful. Collingwood, in *Outlines of a Philosophy of Art*, suggests something similar: "In true beauty there is always present not so much sublimity itself as a transmuted form of sublimity; the mind is not so much overwhelmed with the shock of an unexpected glory as touched to a calm solemnity . . . And there is also present not so much a frankly comic element as an element of sublimated comedy, laughter softened into that smile with which we all naturally contemplate beauty."[18] Described here is a unity, perhaps, of ideal and reality, in which human nature is not divine or tragic but given, vulnerable, finite, humble, and not to be taken too seriously.

In Coetzee's novel, as in this book, punishment, grace, and mercy are brought together as settlement, based on an encounter with another "from the site of trauma,"[19] which provides an experience of the wrong as wrong. Punishment is not just deserts but a settlement rendered in uncertainty and humility, in which the "halt help the lame." There may be no triumph of universal law, no rebalancing of the cosmos, no restoration of "free will," but settlement allows for trust, thanks, hope, loyalty, and, perhaps transient, love. Being-with can be restored, and for humans, that is justice. And mercy. Indeed, that is what it is to be human.

Notes

INTRODUCTION

1. Anselm of Canterbury, *Proslogion*, in *A Scholastic Miscellany: Anselm to Ockham*, ed. Eugene R. Fairweather (Philadelphia: Westminster Press, 1956), 78, 81.

2. See Marty Slaughter, "Sublime Mercy," *Journal of Law, Culture, and Humanities* 6 (forthcoming, 2010).

3. See Austin Sarat, *Mercy on Trial: What It Means to Stop an Execution* (Princeton: Princeton University Press, 2005).

4. See chapter 3.

5. Dan Markel, "Against Mercy," *Minnesota Law Review* 88 (2004): 1421. Rachel E. Barkow connects the demise of mercy to the rise of the administrative state and the application of its formal principles to criminal law, in "The Ascent of the Administrative State and the Demise of Mercy," *Harvard Law Review* 121 (2008): 1333–65.

6. Kathleen Dean Moore, *Pardons: Justice, Mercy, and the Public Interest* (New York: Oxford University Press, 1989).

7. Jeffrie G. Murphy, "Mercy and Legal Justice," in *Forgiveness and Mercy*, by Jean Hampton and Jeffrie G. Murphy (Cambridge: Cambridge University Press, 1988). Murphy's position is modified to some degree in *Getting Even: Forgiveness and Its Limits* (New York: Oxford University Press, 2003) (it may sometimes be right to forgive those who are repentant), but epistemological worries control in "Remorse, Apology, and Mercy," *Ohio State Journal of Criminal Law* 4 (2007): 423, 444 (remorse is too easy to fake). A somewhat broader view is taken in P. E. Digeser, *Political Forgiveness* (Ithaca: Cornell University Press, 2001) (arguing that governments have standing to extend mercy, but not in cases of murder or where the victim has not had a chance to forgive).

8. Martha Minow, *Between Vengeance and Forgiveness: Facing History after Genocide and Mass Violence* (Boston: Beacon Press, 1999).

9. Martha C. Nussbaum, "Equity and Mercy," in *Sex and Social Justice* (New York: Oxford University Press, 2000); Martha C. Nussbaum and Dan M. Kahan, "Two Conceptions of Emotion in the Criminal Law," *Columbia Law Review* 96 (1996): 270. For another brief summary of the main positions in this debate, see Stephen P. Garvey, "Questions of Mercy," *Ohio State Journal of Criminal Law* 4 (2007): 321.

10. John Braithwaite, *Restorative Justice and Responsive Regulation* (New York: Oxford University Press, 2002); John Braithwaite and Philip Pettit, *Not Just Deserts: A Republi-*

can Theory of Criminal Justice (New York: Oxford University Press, 1990); Margaret Urban Walker, *Moral Repair: Reconstructing Moral Relations after Wrongdoing* (New York: Cambridge University Press, 2006). For a comprehensive history and bibliography of the restorative justice movement, see Dennis Sullivan and Larry L. Tifft, eds., *Handbook of Restorative Justice* (New York: Routledge, 2008).

11. There have been efforts to demonstrate the consonance of restorative justice with traditions of particular communities, religions, or nations, however. See James W. Zion and Robert Yazzie, "Navajo Peacemaking: Original Dispute Resolution and a Life Way," in Sullivan and Tifft, *Handbook of Restorative Justice,* 151–60; Dirk J. Louw, "The African Concept of *Ubuntu* and Restorative Justice," in ibid., 161–73; Michael L. Hadley, "Spiritual Foundations of Restorative Justice," in ibid., 174–87. But restorative justice ideas remain in tension with traditional theories of punishment, and a philosophical basis for the movement has not yet been given. See Stephen P. Garvey, "Restorative Justice, Punishment, and Atonement," *Utah Law Review,* 2003, 303 (making this point about restorative justice theories).

12. See, e.g., Minow, *Between Vengeance and Forgiveness.*

13. Clarence Thomas, "Crime and Punishment—and Personal Responsibility," *National Times* (September 1994): 31, reprinted in Sanford Kadish and Stephen Schulhofer, *Criminal Law and Its Process: Cases and Materials,* 6th ed. (New York: Little, Brown, 1995), 1032, 1034.

14. See R. A. Duff, *Punishment, Communication, and Community* (Oxford: Oxford University Press, 2001).

CHAPTER 1

1. Cf. Bernard Harcourt, *Against Prediction: Profiling, Policing, and Punishing in an Actuarial Age* (Chicago: University of Chicago Press, 2006).

2. Philippe Nonet, "In the Matter of *Green v. Recht*," *California Law Review* 75 (1987): 363; Marianne Constable, "Genealogy and Jurisprudence: Nietzsche, Nihilism, and the Social Scientification of Law," *Law and Social Inquiry* 19 (1994): 551; Brian Tamanaha, *Law as a Means to an End: Threat to the Rule of Law* (New York: Cambridge University Press, 2006); Steven D. Smith, *Law's Quandary* (Cambridge, Mass.: Harvard University Press, 2007).

3. Ronald Dworkin, *Taking Rights Seriously* (Cambridge, Mass.: Harvard University Press, 1977).

4. Immanuel Kant, *Fundamental Principles [Grundwerk] of the Metaphysic of Morals,* trans. T. K. Abbott (Buffalo: Prometheus, 1987) (further cites, to *Groundwork,* are in the text).

5. Antonin Scalia, "The Rule of Law Is a Law of Rules," *University of Chicago Law Review* 56 (1989): 1175; Frederick Schauer, "Is the Common Law Law?" *California Law Review* 77 (1989): 455; Larry Alexander and Emily Sherwin, *The Rule of Rules: Morality, Rules, and the Dilemmas of Law* (Durham: Duke University Press, 2001) (arguing that rules are necessary but carry a price: "The very imperfections [in moral reasoning] that require us to have rules will require that the rules themselves be blunt and thus at least

occasionally immoral in application. And therein lies the dilemma of rules, and we believe, the dilemma of law itself").

6. Herbert Wechsler, "Toward Neutral Principles of Constitutional Law," in *Principles, Politics, and Fundamental Law* (Cambridge, Mass.: Harvard University Press, 1961), 4.

7. M'Naghten's Case, 10 Cl. & F. 200, 8 Eng. Rep. 718 (House of Lords, 1843).

8. George P. Fletcher ("The Storrs Lectures: Liberals and Romantics at War: The Problem of Collective Guilt," *Yale Law Journal* 111 [2002]: 1499, 1551) links this move from "cause" to "intention" in the evolution of criminal law doctrine directly to the influence of a misinterpretation of Kant.

9. See Meir Dan-Cohen, *Harmful Thoughts: Essays on Law, Self, and Morality* (Princeton: Princeton University Press, 2002), 236.

10. See Fletcher, "Storrs Lectures" (noting that the shift in criminal law from focus on results to intentions could be traced to a "persistent misreading of Kant's moral philosophy" that "tends to support this metamorphosis of criminal law" by reading "intention" for "will").

11. Immanuel Kant, *Critique of Pure Reason*, trans. Norman Kemp Smith (New York: St. Martin's Press, 1965), 29.

12. Hannah Arendt, *Lectures on Kant's Political Philosophy*, ed. Ronald Beiner (Chicago: University of Chicago Press, 1982), 4, 13, 26–27; Shai Lavi, "Crimes of Action, Crimes of Thought: Arendt on Reconciliation, Forgiveness, and Judgment," in *Thinking in Dark Times: Hannah Arendt on Ethics and Politics*, ed. Roger Berkowitz, Jeffrey Katz, and Thomas Keenan (New York: Fordham University Press, 2010), 229, 234. See also Desmond Manderson, *Songs without Words: The Aesthetic Dimensions of Justice* (Berkeley: University of California Press, 2000) (arguing that law is a form of aesthetic judgment).

13. Immanuel Kant, *The Critique of Judgment*, trans. J. H. Bernard (Amherst, N.Y.: Prometheus, 2000), 16.

14. Kant, *Judgment*, 39–41. Hannah Arendt explains, "The faculty of thinking, however, which Kant . . . called *Vernunft* (reason) to distinguish it from *Verstand* (intellect [or understanding]), the faculty of cognition, is of an altogether different nature. The distinction, on its most elementary level and in Kant's own words, lies in the fact that 'concepts of reason serve us to conceive [*begreifen*—grasp, comprehend], as concepts of the intellect serve us to apprehend perceptions' . . . In other words, the intellect (*Verstand*) desires to grasp what is given to the senses, but reason (*Vernunft*) wishes to understand its *meaning*. Cognition, whose highest criterion is truth, derives that criterion from the world of appearances in which we take our bearings through sense perceptions, whose testimony is self-evident, that is, unshakeable by argument and replaceable only by other evidence. As the German translation of the Latin *perceptio*, the word *Wahrnehmung* used by Kant (what is given me in perceptions and ought to be *true* [*Wahr*]) clearly indicates, truth is located in the evidence of the senses. But that is by no means the case with meaning and the faculty of thought, which searches for it; the latter does not ask what something is or whether it exists at all—its existence is always taken for granted—but *what it means for it to be*" (*The Life of the Mind* [New York: Harcourt,

1978], 57, quoting Kant, *Critique of Pure Reason,* B367). See also Paul Guyer, *Kant and the Claims of Taste* (Cambridge: Cambridge University Press, 1997), 31.

15. Lloyd L. Weinrib, *Legal Reason: The Use of Analogy in Legal Argument* (New York: Cambridge University Press, 2005); Edward H. Levi, *An Introduction to Legal Reasoning* (Chicago: University of Chicago Press, 1962); Marianne Constable, "On the (Legal) Study Methods of Our Time: Vico Redux," *Chicago Kent Law Review* 83 (2008): 1303, 1323 ("law still lets poets dig up another way with words"). Analogical reasoning is currently under attack in the academy, though as Weinrib points out, not in legal practice. See, e.g., Alexander and Sherwin, *Rule of Rules;* Scott Brewer, "Exemplary Reasoning: Semantics, Pragmatics, and the Rational Force of Legal Argument by Analogy," *Harvard Law Review* 109 (1996): 923. This "new formalism" is itself based on a "kanticism" that misses much of the real Kant as well as a fear of uncertainty in the law. The model of legal and ethical reasoning adopted in this book, after the turn to Heidegger, is analogical reasoning, which I have argued is the main form of ethical reasoning available to finite human beings whose best understandings are grounded in a knowing-how rather than a knowing-that. I also point out that we live very comfortably with legal uncertainty, as we do with every other form of uncertainty. The continuum of cases of "clearly right" shading into "clearly wrong" is ubiquitous for us, both legally and ethically, all the time. See, e.g., Linda Ross Meyer, "When Reasonable Minds Differ," *New York University Law Review* 71 (1996): 1467; idem, "Why Barbara, Celarent, Darii, and Ferio Flunk Out of Law School: Comment on Scott Brewer, 'On the Possibility of Necessity in Legal Argument,'" *John Marshall Law Review* 34 (2000): 77; idem, "Is Practical Reason Mindless?" *Georgetown Law Journal* 86 (1998): 647, 664–65.

16. See Lavi, "Crimes of Action," 233: "Judgment for Arendt is the ability to act not according to rules, but in an unmediated response to the singularity of the case at hand."

17. Ronald Dworkin, *Law's Empire* (Cambridge, Mass.: Harvard University Press, 1986).

18. Friedrich Nietzsche, *Twilight of the Idols,* trans. R. J. Hollingdale (New York: Penguin, 1979), 40 ("how the [true] world became a myth").

19. See Guyer, *Kant and the Claims of Taste,* 34 (pleasure in the beautiful "accustoms us to disinterested enjoyment in general and thus prepares us for the more difficult task of joyfully superseding personal interests in the way that morality can often require").

20. See Philippe Nonet, "What Is Positive Law?" *Yale Law Journal* 100 (1990): 667. See Roger Berkowitz, *The Gift of Science: Leibnitz and the Modern Legal Tradition* (New York: Oxford University Press, 2005) (exploring the problem and irony of "justifying" positive law through an intellectual history of Leibnitz and the codification movement).

21. See, e.g., Jennifer L. Culbert, *Dead Certainty: The Death Penalty and the Problem of Judgment* (Stanford: Stanford University Press, 2008) (demonstrating the movement of nihilism in the Supreme Court's death penalty jurisprudence as the ideal of reason erodes).

22. See Jed Rubenfeld, *Freedom and Time: A Theory of Constitutional Self-Government* (New Haven: Yale University Press, 2001).

23. Despite our current practice of detaining the possibly dangerous (sex offenders and terrorists) without trial, despite parole practices that determine sentences based on statistical likelihood of reoffending, and despite strict liability for immigration crimes

(see Jeffrey A. Meyer, "Authentically Innocent: Juries and Federal Regulatory Crimes," *Hastings Law Journal* 59 [2007]: 137), we still have trouble stomaching the execution of the innocent regardless of its deterrent effect, and we still imagine that punishments, at least by and large, should fit the crime, not the likelihood of reoffense. But as Keally McBride argues, "The links between crime and punishment, and between punishment and redemption, have been severed. Those in prison often feel that their incarceration was random, therefore unjust. Dozens of people engage in similar criminal activities yet are not caught and sentenced" (*Punishment and the Political Order* [Ann Arbor: University of Michigan Press, 2007], 55).

24. See Marty Slaughter, "Sublime Mercy," *Journal of Law, Culture, and Humanities* 6 (forthcoming, 2010).

CHAPTER 2

1. James R. Martel's wonderful book *Love Is a Sweet Chain: Desire, Autonomy, and Friendship in Liberal Political Theory* (New York: Routledge, 2001) reminds us that even Locke, Rousseau, and Hobbes did not believe that reason alone could serve as the "glue" of social arrangements and that each struggled with whether it was possible for some form of emotional attunement or attachment, modeled on charity, friendship, or an expansive and "indifferent" godly love, to play a role in the formation and "glue" of political community.

2. See Larry May, *Sharing Responsibility* (Chicago: University of Chicago Press, 1992), 2–4; George P. Fletcher, "The Storrs Lectures: Liberals and Romantics at War: The Problem of Collective Guilt," *Yale Law Journal* 111 (2002): 1499, 1551 (making a sophisticated argument for a qualified theory of collective guilt); Meir Dan-Cohen, *Harmful Thoughts: Essay on Law, Self, and Morality* (Princeton: Princeton University Press, 2002), 209–24 (also arguing for a "constitutive" theory of self and responsibility based on slightly different philosophical progenitors). For Dan-Cohen, "for the will to serve as a responsibility base it need not be free in the metaphysical, anti-determinist sense . . . Responsibility for voluntary actions simply marks them as constituents of the self . . . Transposing voluntarist responsibility into the constitutive framework also opens up the possibility that candidates other than the will may be eligible as potential constituents of the self and therefore as bases of responsibility" (213). The piece that Heidegger adds to this assessment is an explanation of why we are "constituted" by prevailing accounts of responsibility—grounding responsibility in being-in and being-with as the foundation of being human.

3. See Martin Heidegger, *Being and Time*, trans. John Macquarrie and Edward Robinson (New York: Harper and Row, 1962), 74–75, 78–90. Heidegger claims, "Knowing is a mode of Dasein founded upon Being-in-the-world. Thus Being-in-the-world, as a basic state, must be Interpreted *beforehand*" (90). See also Hubert Dreyfus, *Being-in-the-World: A Commentary on Heidegger's "Being and Time," Division I* (Cambridge, Mass.: MIT Press, 1991).

The term *Being* is conventionally capitalized in this usage because all nouns are capitalized in German and because, in English translation, this convention easily distinguishes the philosophical term *Being* from the present participle of the verb *to be*. Its capitalization should not be read to suggest any otherworldly quality. In comparison, the capitalization of *Other*, from Levinas's French, does intend to convey an importance and sublimity, though, according to Levinas, not divinity.

4. Heidegger, *Being and Time*, 84.

5. Ibid., 88.

6. Ibid., 246–47.

7. "The kind of dealing which is closest to us is as we have shown, not a bare perceptual cognition, but rather than kind of concern which manipulates things and puts them to use; and this has its own kind of 'knowledge'" (ibid., 95).

8. "Only something which is in the state-of-mind [*Befindlichkeit*] of fearing (or fearlessness) can discover that what is environmentally ready-to-hand [*Zuhanden*] is threatening. Dasein's openness to the world is constituted existentially by the attunement of a state-of-mind . . . *Existentially, a state-of-mind implies a disclosive submission to the world, out of which we can encounter something that matters to us* . . . Even the purest θεωρία [theory] has not left all moods behind it" (ibid., 176–77).

9. Martin Heidegger, *Nietzsche: Will to Power as Art*, trans. David Farrell Krell (San Francisco: Harper and Row, 1979), 99.

10. The structure of logic and ethical deliberation itself is temporal: "But if deliberation is to be able to operate in the scheme of the 'if-then,' concern must already have 'surveyed' a context of involvements and have an understanding of it. That which is considered with an 'if' must already be understood *as something or other* . . . The schema 'something as something' has already been sketched out beforehand in the structure of one's pre-predicative understanding. The as-structure is grounded ontologically in the temporality of understanding" (Heidegger, *Being and Time*, 411).

11. Lloyd L. Weinrib, *Legal Reason: The Use of Analogy in Legal Argument* (New York: Cambridge University Press, 2005); Edward H. Levi, *An Introduction to Legal Reasoning* (Chicago: University of Chicago Press, 1962); Steven J. Burton, *Judging in Good Faith* (Cambridge: Cambridge University Press, 1992); Melvin Aron Eisenberg, *The Nature of the Common Law* (Boston: Harvard University Press, 1988); David A. Strauss, "Common Law Constitutional Interpretation," *University of Chicago Law Review* 63 (1996): 877; Guido Calabresi, *A Common Law for the Age of Statutes* (Boston: Harvard University Press, 1982); Cass R. Sunstein, "On Analogical Reasoning," *Harvard Law Review* 106 (1993): 741. My account of analogical reasoning, though owing much to the preceding sources, differs in being grounded explicitly in the philosophy of Wittgenstein and Heidegger. The textual discussion that follows this note is a shorter version of themes that appear in many of the following articles: Linda Ross Meyer, "Nothing We Say Matters: Teague and New Rules," *University of Chicago Law Review* 61 (1994): 423, 465–76; idem, "When Reasonable Minds Differ," *New York University Law Review* 71 (1996): 1467; idem, "Why Barbara, Celarent, Darii, and Ferio Flunk Out of Law School: Comment on Scott Brewer, 'On the Possibility of Necessity in Legal Argument,'" *John Marshall Law Review* 34 (2000): 77; idem, "Is Practical Reason Mindless?" *Georgetown Law Journal* 86 (1998): 647, 664–65; idem, "Unruly Rights," *Cardozo Law Review* 22 (2000): 1. For a recent defense of common law reasoning in the context of constitutional theory, see Douglas E. Edlin, *Judges and Unjust Laws: Common Law Constitutionalism and the Foundations of Judicial Review* (Ann Arbor: University of Michigan Press, 2008).

12. Another example may be found in literary criticism. For example, T. S. Eliot ("Tradition and the Individual Talent," in *The Sacred Wood and Major Early Essays* [Mineola, N.Y.: Dover, 1998], 28) wrote, "No poet, no artist of any art, has his complete meaning alone. His significance, his appreciation is the appreciation of his relation to the dead poets and artists. You cannot value him alone; you must set him, for contrast and comparison, among the dead. I mean this as a principle of aesthetic, not merely historical, criticism. The necessity that he shall conform, that he shall cohere, is not one-sided; what happens when a new work of art is created is something that happens simultaneously to all the works of art which preceded it. The existing monuments form an ideal order among themselves, which is modified by the introduction of the new (the really new) work of art among them. The existing order is complete before the new work arrives; for order to persist after the supervention of novelty, the *whole* existing order must be, if ever so slightly, altered; and so the relations, proportions, values of each work of art toward the whole are readjusted; and this is conformity between the old and the new. Whoever has approved this idea of order, of the form of European, of English literature, will not find it preposterous that the past should be altered by the present as much as the present is directed by the past. And the poet who is aware of this will be aware of great difficulties and responsibilities." I am grateful to Max Simmons for this reference.

13. See Ludwig Wittgenstein, *Philosophical Investigations,* trans. G. E. M. Anscombe (New York: Macmillan, 1953); Steven Winter, "Transcendental Nonsense, Metaphoric Reasoning, and the Cognitive Stakes for Law," *Pennsylvania Law Review* 137 (1989): 1105, 1156–59; Stanley Fish, "Normal Circumstances, Literal Language, Direct Speech Acts, the Ordinary, the Everyday, the Obvious, What Goes without Saying, and Other Special Cases," in *Is There a Text in This Class? The Authority of Interpretive Communities* (Cambridge, Mass.: Harvard University Press, 1982).

14. "We never really perceive a throng of sensations, e.g., tones and noises, in the appearance of things . . . Rather we hear the storm whistling in the chimney, we hear the three-motored plane, we hear the Mercedes in immediate distinction from the Volkswagen. Much closer to us than all sensations are the things themselves. We hear the door shut in the house and never hear acoustical sensations or even mere sounds. In order to hear a bare sound we have to listen away from things, divert our ear from them, i.e., listen abstractly" (Martin Heidegger, "Origin of the Work of Art," in *Poetry, Language, Thought,* trans. A. Hofstadter [New York: Harper and Row, 1971], 26).

15. "But even in this characterization does one not start by marking out and isolating the 'I' so that one must then seek some way of getting over to the Others from this isolated subject? To avoid this misunderstanding we must notice in what sense we are talking about 'the Others.' By 'Others' we do not mean everyone else but me—those over against whom the 'I' stands out. They are rather those from whom, for the most part, one does *not* distinguish oneself—those among whom one is too . . . By reason of this with-like [*mithaften*] Being-in-the-world, the world is always the one that I share with Others. The world of Dasein is a with-world [*Mitwelt*]. Being-in is Being-with Others" (Heidegger, *Being and Time,* 154–55).

16. Immanuel Kant, *Fundamental Principles of the Metaphysic of Morals,* trans. T. K. Abbott (Buffalo, N.Y.: Prometheus, 1987), 29–30.

17. See Marc Miller, "The Foundations of Law: Sentencing Equality Pathology,"

Emory Law Journal 54 (2005): 271 (arguing that the "formal equality" stressed in the federal sentencing guidelines is not "true" equality, which is more contextual).

18. See Jed Rubenfeld, *Freedom and Time: A Theory of Constitutional Self-Government* (New Haven: Yale University Press, 2001) (arguing for a temporally extended account of democracy).

19. See Marianne Constable, *Just Silences: The Limits and Possibilities of Modern Law* (Princeton: Princeton University Press, 2005), 4 (sometimes silence means "we do not need signs as such to pass along . . . everyday practices or tradition").

20. See also Miller, "Foundations of Law" (drawing on Martha Fineman's work to argue for the "inherently contextual nature of equality" and applying that insight to criticize the "formal equality" of mandatory minimum penalties and the "context-free sentencing policy" of the federal sentencing guidelines).

21. "Perhaps the distinction of this age consists in the fact that the dimension of grace has been closed. Perhaps this is its unique dis-grace" (Martin Heidegger, "Letter on Humanism," trans. E. Lohner, in *Philosophy in the Twentieth Century*, ed. William Barrett and Henry D. Aiken (New York: Random House, 1962), 3:294. The passage also states: "The thinking that runs counter to 'values' does not state all that one declares 'values'— 'culture,' 'art,' 'science,' 'human dignity,' 'world,' and 'God'—is worthless. One should rather come to understand that it is exactly through the characterization of something as 'value,' that it loses its dignity. This is to say that through the estimation of something as a value, one accepts what is evaluated only as a mere object for the appreciation of man. But what a thing is in its Being is not exhausted by its being an object, much less when the objectivity has the character of value. All valuing, even when it values positively, subjectivises the thing. It does not let beings be, but makes them valuable as the object of its action. The extravagant effort to demonstrate the objectivity of values does not know what it is doing. When one proclaims 'God' as altogether 'the highest value,' this is a degradation of the essence of God. Thinking in values here and in general is the greatest blasphemy that can be thought of in the face of Being. To think counter to values, therefore, does not mean to beat the drum for the worthlessness and nullity of the existent, but means to bring—against the subjectivization of the existent as mere object—the clearing of the truth of Being before thought" (292–93).

22. See ibid., 300: "Thought attends to the clearing of Being by putting its speaking of Being into language as the dwelling of existence. Thus thought is an action. But an action that is superior at the same time to all practice. Thinking surpasses doing and producing, not through the magnitude of its performance, nor through the consequences of its activity, but through the humbleness of its achievement that it accomplishes without result."

23. See Martin Heidegger, *The Question Concerning Technology, and Other Essays*, trans. W. Lovitt (New York: Harper Perennial, 1982), 26–27 ("man . . . exalts himself to the posture of lord of the earth. In this way the impression comes to prevail that everything man encounters exists only insofar as it is his construct. This illusion gives rise in turn to one final delusion: It seems as though man everywhere and always encounters only himself . . . *In truth, however, precisely nowhere does man today any longer encounter himself, i.e., his essence* [i.e., we do not see ourselves as *Dasein*, finite, receptive, and "given" a world]").

24. Levinas makes this very clear in his assertion that ethics is prior to religion. We are not aspects of God, and submersion into a divine being is just as worrisome as submersion into a totalitarian state: "The ethical relation is defined, in contrast with every relation with the sacred, by excluding every signification it would take on unbeknown to him who maintains that relation. When I maintain an ethical relation I refuse to recognize the role I would play in a drama of which I would not be the author or whose outcome another would know before me; I refuse to figure in a drama of salvation or of damnation that would be enacted in spite of me and that would make game of me. This is not equivalent to a diabolical pride, for it does not exclude obedience. But obedience precisely is to be distinguished from an involuntary participation in mysterious designs in which one figures or which one prefigures" (Emmanuel Levinas, *Totality and Infinity: An Essay on Exteriority*, trans. Alphonso Lingis [Pittsburgh: Duquesne University Press, 1969], 79). Heidegger might respond that Levinas's insistence on the primacy of human autonomy violates the "respect for the limits which have been set upon human thought" (*Humanism*, 294) and refuses to acknowledge its "givenness."

25. "Nothing is more direct than the face to face, which is droiture itself" (Levinas, *Totality and Infinity*, 78); "The eyes break through the mask—the language of the eyes, impossible to dissemble. The eye does not shine; it speaks. The alternative of truth and lying, of sincerity and dissimulation, is the prerogative of him who abides in the relation of absolute frankness which cannot hide itself" (ibid., 66).

26. Donald Davidson, "Actions, Reasons, and Causes," in *Essays on Actions and Events* (New York: Oxford University Press, 1980).

27. Emmanuel Levinas, *Existence and Its Existents*, trans. Alphonso Lingis (Pittsburgh: Duquesne University Press, 2001), 85.

28. Levinas, *Totality and Infinity*, 86–87.

29. Ibid., 75.

30. Emmanuel Levinas, *Otherwise than Being, or Beyond Essence*, trans. Alphonso Lingis (Pittsburgh: Duquesne University Press, 1998), 18.

31. Desmond Manderson, *Proximity, Levinas, and the Soul of Law* (Montreal: McGill-Queens University Press, 2007), 77. Manderson believes, however, that ethics nonetheless leaves a "trace" in law of its call, which makes possible the ethical development of law.

32. Jill Stauffer, "Productive Ambivalence: Levinasian Subjectivity, Justice, and the Rule of Law," in *Essays on Levinas and Law: A Mosaic*, ed. Desmond Manderson (New York: Palgrave, 2009), 80–81. Stauffer's account of Levinas calls not for a "reversal" (78) of law and ethics, but an always unresolved troubling of law by ethics.

33. See Julia Ponzio, "Politics Not Left to Itself," in *Levinas, Law, Politics*, ed. Marinos Diamantides (New York: Routledge-Cavendish, 2007), 35–48. Ponzio explains that "the political role *par excellence* must be assigned to the Feminine because it is, as we have seen above, the human possibility of the exposed position, of recognition without justification that is forgiveness. To expose essence, to expose the space in which all is justified should include recognising that justice does not have in itself its own justification, and that it can, in turn, signify the possibility of a dialogue that is not ratification of a position, the possibility of asking non-rhetorical questions" (47). See also Marty Slaughter, "Levinas, Mercy, and the Middle Ages," in Diamantides, *Levinas*,

Law, Politics, 49–65. Slaughter writes, "Thus, while love and forgiveness do not belong to the order of [ideal] justice, they ground it. For Levinas, justice must not be simply the operation of a system of law or, even worse, the imposition of power. It must rest on ethical persons—those who experience responsibility and compassion for others and can transform this into (equitable) judgments, ameliorate punishment, and when necessary reform the law" (51).

34. Levinas's insistence that being-with take priority over being-in may make this move impossible within his philosophical system. But I also do not believe that an understanding of "being-in-with" leads to a totalizing transparency with totalitarian dangers, precisely because law is temporal (and therefore humble), not universal.

35. Kant's understanding of the sublime as the hidden or infinite is muted but not absent in Heidegger. A work of art, for Heidegger, is itself the tension between earth (concealing) and world (opening): "The world is the clearing of the paths of the essential guiding directions with which all decision complies. Every decision however, bases itself on something not mastered, something concealed, confusing; else it would never be a decision. The earth is not simply the Closed but rather that which rises up as self-closing" ("Origin of the Work of Art," 55). This "appearance of the self-closing" in Heidegger comes very close to echoing (and perhaps is a reinterpretation of) the Kantian sublime—that which *appears* as *beyond* our knowing. This, too, is Levinas's account of our encounter with the other—an encounter with an infinite other whom we cannot know but yet still encounter as "face"—appearing as beyond our knowing.

Heidegger also speaks of the Dionysian, or the *Befindlichkeit* of *Rausch,* usually translated as "rapture." For Heidegger, beauty is the shining forth of things in the truth of their being, which is what is at work in a work of art: "This shining, joined in the work [of art], is the beautiful. Beauty is one way in which truth occurs as unconcealedness" (ibid., 56). Rapture, usually assigned to the Dionysian, or sublime, is rethought in Heidegger as the mode of *Befindlichkeit* that reveals beauty. Heidegger writes, "Rapture as a state of feeling explodes the very subjectivity of the subject. By having a feeling for beauty the subject has already come out of himself; he is no longer subjective, no longer a subject. On the other side, beauty is not something at hand like an object of sheer representation. As an attuning, it thoroughly determines the state of man. Beauty breaks through the confinement of the 'object' placed at a distance, standing on its own, and brings it into essential and original correlation to the 'subject.' Beauty is no longer objective, no longer an object. The aesthetic state is neither subjective nor objective. Both basic words of Nietzsche's aesthetics, rapture and beauty, designate with an identical breadth the entire aesthetic state, what is opened up in it and what pervades it" (*Nietzsche: Will to Power,* 123). See also Martin Heidegger, "Dialogue on Language," in *On the Way to Language,* trans. Peter D. Hertz (New York: Harper and Row, 1982), 44–46, where the Japanese word *Iki* is called "the breath of the stillness of luminous rapture" and contains "nothing of stimulus and impression." In this last essay, however, the English word *rapture* translates *Entzücken,* not *Rausch.*

36. "Then, all presence would have its source in grace [*Anmut*], in the sense of the pure delight [*Entzücken*] of the calling stillness" (Heidegger, "Dialogue on Language," 44).

37. Anthony V. Baker, "Slavery and Tushnet and Mann, Oh Why? Finding 'Big Law' in Small Places," *Quinnipiac Law Review* 26 (2008): 691.

38. Slaughter, "Levinas, Mercy, and the Middle Ages," 52.

39. See Enguist v. Oregon Department of Agriculture, 128 S.Ct. 2146, 2154 (2008): "There are some forms of state action, however, which by their nature involve discretionary decisionmaking based on a vast array of subjective, individualized assessments. In such cases the rule that people should be 'treated alike, under like circumstances and conditions' is not violated when one person is treated differently from others."

40. Kathleen Dean Moore, *Pardons: Justice, Mercy, and the Public Interest* (New York: Oxford University Press, 1989).

41. See also David Dolinko, "Some Naive Thoughts about Justice and Mercy," *Ohio State Journal of Criminal Law* 4 (2007): 349, 354; Carla Ann Hage Johnson, "Entitled to Clemency: Mercy in the Criminal Law," *Law and Philosophy* 109 (1991): 109.

42. See John Tasioulas, "Repentance and the Liberal State," *Ohio State Journal of Criminal Law* 4 (2007): 487 (retributive justice itself requires attention to the particular and case-by-case adjudication of guilt); James Sterba, "Can a Person Deserve Mercy?" *Journal of Social Philosophy* 10 (1979): 11.

43. See Mary Sigler, "Mercy, Clemency, and the Case of Karla Faye Tucker," *Ohio State Journal of Criminal Law* 4 (2007): 455, 486 ("a person who lacks the virtue of mercy has a flawed, possibly corrupt, character"); Heidi Hurd, "The Morality of Mercy," *Ohio State Journal of Criminal Law* 4 (2007): 389 (mercy is a virtue and indeed constitutive of relationships of love and friendship but is not appropriate in criminal punishment; still, because one's character cannot be divided, we will see "spillover" effects in the criminal justice system if it is run by loving friends); Josh Dressler, "Hating Criminals: How Can Something That Feels So Good Be Wrong?" *Michigan Law Review* 88 (1990): 1448; George W. Rainbolt, "Mercy: An Independent, Imperfect Virtue," *American Philosophical Quarterly* 27 (1990): 169; Lyla H. O'Driscoll, "The Quality of Mercy," *Southern Journal of Philosophy* 21 (1983): 229, 230–31 ("a just person need have no sympathy or good will toward others, and might be petty, querulous and vindictive in exercising his rights; miserly and irascible in fulfilling his duties, obligations and commitments; unfailingly harsh in the bargains he strikes; and willing to exploit for his benefit any weakness or disadvantage suffered by others").

44. Stephen Kershnar, "Mercy Retributivism and Harsh Punishment," *International Journal of Applied Philosophy* 14 (2000): 209, 222; Daniel Statman, "Doing Without Mercy," *Southern Journal of Philosophy* 32 (1994): 331, 339 ("a court that lets its feelings of sorrow and compassion determine its sentence betrays its role as a court of *justice*").

45. Herbert Morris, "Murphy on Forgiveness," *Criminal Justice Ethics* 7 (1988): 15.

46. "Disjunctive Desert," *American Philosophical Quarterly* 20 (1983): 357.

47. See Steven Sverdlik, "Justice and Mercy," *Journal of Social Philosophy* 16, no. 3 (1985): 36.

48. Claudia Card, "On Mercy," *Philosophical Review* 81 (1972): 182; Lyla H. O'Driscoll, "The Quality of Mercy," *Southern Journal of Philosophy* 21 (1983): 229, 230–31; Andrew Brien, "Utilitarianism and Retributivism," *Philosophia* 24 (1995): 493 (mercy is the resistance to a temptation to be harsher than overall utility requires and may temper "cruelty,

indifference, irrational rule-worship, apathy, bigotry, and ignorance" as well as being an occasional act-utilitarian exception to a rule-utilitarian punishment).

49. R. A. Duff, " Justice, Mercy, and Forgiveness," *Criminal Justice Ethics* 9 (1990): 51; idem, "The Intrusion of Mercy," *Ohio State Journal of Criminal Law* 4 (2009): 361.

50. Hurd, "Morality of Mercy"; Kershnar, "Mercy Retributivism"; Dan Markel, "Against Mercy," *Minnesota Law Review* 88 (2004): 1421; P. Twambley, "Mercy and Forgiveness," *Analysis* 36 (1976): 84.

51. O'Driscoll, "Quality of Mercy," 246. See also Twambley, "Mercy and Forgiveness" (mercy has its place in civil, not criminal, court; for an unrepentant criminal, mercy is an insult if the criminal feels he or she has done no wrong to begin with). Early work by Jeffrie G. Murphy took this position (see "Forgiveness, Mercy, and the Retributive Emotions," *Criminal Justice Ethics* 7 [1988]: 3), but his view is now much more nuanced.

52. N. E. Simmonds, "Judgment and Mercy," *Oxford Journal of Legal Studies* 13 (1993): 52.

53. Morris, "Murphy on Forgiveness."

54. In *Being and Time,* Heidegger breaks *Dasein* into three moments, which correspond to past, present, and future. The past is our "thrownness" or mood or *Befindlichkeit*—that is, where we find ourselves. *Verstand,* or understanding, is the second moment—where we stand in the sense of seeing what reveals itself to us and accepting what is given by our past and the possibilities the past enables for us. *Rede* is the third moment, which is the path that language (understood not as a tool of communication but as the sense/meaning the world makes for us) calls us forward to. I expand on this in chapter 4.

55. Heidegger, *Being and Time,* 329.

56. H. G. Liddell and Robert Scott, *An Intermediate Greek-English Lexicon* (Oxford: Clarendon, 1986), 881 (under the listing for χαρα). See Euripides, *Alcestis,* line 1124.

CHAPTER 3

1. Leo Zaibert makes this point in *Punishment and Retribution* (Burlington, Vt.: Ashgate, 2006): 1.

2. "To be sure, 'that' it is made is a property also of all equipment that is available and in use. But this 'that' does not become prominent in the equipment; it disappears in usefulness. The more handy a piece of equipment is, the more inconspicuous it remains that, for example, such a hammer is and the more exclusively does the equipment keep itself in its equipmentality" (Martin Heidegger, "Origin of the Work of Art," in *Poetry, Language, Thought,* trans. A. Hofstadter [New York: Harper and Row, 1971], 65).

3. See, e.g., J. Q. Wilson, "Penalties and Opportunities," in *A Reader on Punishment,* ed. Anthony Duff and David Garland (New York: Oxford University Press, 1994): 174–209, at 204 ("I believe the wisest course of action for society is to try simultaneously to increase both the benefits of non-crime and the costs of crime, all the while bearing in mind that no feasible change in either part of the equation is likely to produce big changes in crime rates").

4. For an ironic take on this theory, see J. C. Oleson, "The Punitive Coma," *California Law Review* 90 (2002): 829. See also Frank Zimring and Gordon Hawkins, *Incapaci-*

tation: Penal Confinement and the Restraint of Crime (New York: Oxford University Press, 1995); Leonard Long, "Rethinking Selective Incapacitation: More at Stake than Controlling Violent Crime," *UMKC Law Review* 62 (1993): 107 (making Kantian objections to incapacitation theory).

5. Harry Elmer Barnes, *The Story of Punishment* (Boston: Stratford, 1930), 265–70; E. Rotman, "Beyond Punishment," in Duff and Garland, *Reader on Punishment,* 284–305.

6. Joel Feinberg, "The Expressive Function of Punishment," in Duff and Garland, *Reader on Punishment,* 71–91; T. Mathiesen, "General Prevention as Communication," in ibid., 221–37. For a related set of theories, see Jean Hampton, "The Moral Education Theory of Punishment," in *Punishment,* ed. A. J. Simmons et al. (Princeton: Princeton University Press, 1995), 112–42; Herbert Morris, "A Paternalistic Theory of Punishment," *American Philosophy Quarterly* 18 (1981): 263, reprinted in Duff and Garland, *Reader on Punishment,* 92; R. A. Duff, *Punishment, Communication, and Community* (Oxford: Oxford University Press, 2001); Dan Markel, "Are Shaming Sanctions Beautifully Retributive?" *Vanderbilt Law Review* 54 (2001): 2151; Christopher Bennett, *The Apology Ritual: A Philosophical Theory of Punishment* (Cambridge: Cambridge University Press, 2008); Robert Justin Lipkin, "Punishment, Penance, and Respect for Autonomy," *Social Theory and Practice* 14 (1988): 87. These last theorists, following Hampton and Morris, do not consider their theories to be utilitarian. The "communication" in punishment is, in their view, inherent in the punishment itself, not a further purpose to be served that could be served some other way—for example, through advertising. I will consider communication theories of this sort in more detail later in this chapter, as they are the closest contemporaries to the Hegelian tradition that I discuss, along with Stephen P. Garvey, "Punishment as Atonement," *UCLA Law Review* 46 (1999): 1801.

7. Herbert Morris, "Persons and Punishment," in *On Guilt and Innocence: Essays in Legal Philosophy and Moral Psychology* (Berkeley: University of California Press, 1976), 31–88.

8. John Braithwaite and Philip Pettit, *Not Just Deserts: A Republican Theory of Criminal Justice* (New York: Oxford University Press, 2002).

9. George P. Fletcher, *With Justice for Some: Victims' Rights in Criminal Trials* (Reading: Addison Wesley, 1995).

10. H. L. A. Hart, *The Concept of Law* (Oxford: Clarendon, 1961), 80–81.

11. See Joseph Raz, *Practical Reason and Norms* (Oxford: Oxford University Press, 1990), 150–52. Of course, to take this point seriously is to recognize that "cruel and unusual punishment" becomes a nonsensical phrase, for a justified harm could hardly be termed "cruel." But as Zaibert (*Punishment and Retribution*) points out, many constitutional conundrums would be made easier if we were to read this phrase as "cruel and unusual treatment" instead: we would not have to struggle with definitions of punishment that link it to legislative intent (for example, sex offender civil commitment statutes, prison rape, and Megan's Law are not punishment, according to the Court, at least in part because they are not "intended to be," and so, however cruel or unusual, the Eighth Amendment does not apply to them). In any case, we should not let the language of the Eighth Amendment or its often very confused interpretation by the Court drive our philosophical account of punishment any more than we should allow phrases like "no ex post facto laws" drive us to a positive law account of law for similar reasons.

12. Zaibert, *Punishment and Retribution,* 33. Blaming involves (1) believing that X is a bad thing; (2) believing that X is an action of B's; (3) believing that B is a moral agent; (4) believing that there are no excuses, justifications, or other circumstances that preclude blame; (5) believing that the world would be better had B not done X; (6) believing that the world would be better if something would happen to B to offset B's Xing; and (7) that B's Xing tends to make A feel something negative like outrage, indignation, or resentment (ibid., 31).

13. Zaibert, *Punishment and Retribution,* 31.

14. G. W. F. Hegel, *Philosophy of Right,* trans. T. M. Knox (Oxford: Clarendon, 1952), para. 99. The right cannot be injured, and the victim cannot be injured in her personhood, only in her embodiment: "Only the will which allows itself to be coerced can in any way be coerced" (ibid., para. 91). Hence, the "wrong" (as opposed to the harm) only has any actual existence in the will of the offender.

15. Hegel, *Philosophy of Right,* para. 100.

16. Ibid., para. 220.

17. Philippe Nonet understands sanction from Hegel's entire philosophical system as itself the working out or actualization of spirit. If man is the work (*Wirklichkeit*) of spirit, then crime and sanction are intimately related as the actualization of freedom (crime as the vaunting pride of breaking from all ground and trying to become god), which necessarily fail (as our "creations" or deeds fail to actualize our true freedom, which cannot be captured in a finite world) and enchain us instead (as Raskolnikov discovers in *Crime and Punishment*). Our failure to enact our infinite freedom in a finite world causes us to despair at our finitude and the imperfection of our efforts (the reversal of pride) and to submit our will once again to the universal law beyond our will. We come to see our place in the eternal self-actualization/self-crucifixion of spirit, itself a perspective that forgives (fore-gives—shows us the necessity and giveness of the cycle of wrong and its sanction as part of our essence). Crime and its sanction, then, are part of the work of spirit itself, as it comes again and again to finitude. In Hegel's metaphysics, law comes to appearance as universal law, only through crime and its sanction. See Philippe Nonet, "Sanction," *Cumberland Law Review* 25 (1994): 489.

18. Michael S. Moore, "The Moral Worth of Retribution," in *Responsibility, Character, and the Emotions,* ed. Ferdinand Schoeman (Cambridge: Cambridge University Press, 1987), 179–219.

19. Ibid., 215.

20. Immanuel Kant, *The Philosophy of Law,* trans. W. Hastie (Edinburgh: T. T. Clark, 1887), 198.

21. Fyodor Dostoevsky, *The Brothers Karamazov,* Norton Critical Edition (New York: W. W. Norton, 1976), 237.

22. Paul Campos, "The Paradox of Punishment," *Wisconsin Law Review,* 1992, 1931.

23. Braithwaite and Pettit, *Not Just Deserts.* See also Margaret Urban Walker, *Moral Repair: Reconstructing Moral Relations after Wrongdoing* (Cambridge: Cambridge University Press, 2006).

24. Braithwaite and Pettit, *Not Just Deserts,* 165: "We think that retributivists face a difficult choice. They can refuse to give a rationale for the desert-constraints they invoke, as many natural rights theorists refuse to give a rationale for rights. In that case

they certainly cannot be accused of covert consequentialism but their attachment to the constraints in question looks arbitrary; fundamental natural rights are difficult enough to stomach, fundamental natural deserts look wholly unpalatable. Alternatively, retributivists can offer a rationale for their favoured constraints, in the fashion of the theorists reviewed in this section [Hampton, Nozick, Morris, Sher, etc.]. In that case they may succeed in making the constraints look more attractive but their retributivism begins to look questionable; they begin to look like consequentialists who want to promote the factor quoted in the rationale and who defend the constraints as means for generally promoting it."

25. This point is powerfully made by many writers, including Michael Moore ("Moral Worth of Retribution"); Jeffrie G. Murphy, "Marxism and Retribution," reprinted in *A Reader on Punishment,* ed. R. A. Duff and D. Garland (New York: Oxford University Press, 1994), 44–70; and Bennett, *Apology Ritual,* 74–100.

26. Jean Hampton and Jeffrie Murphy, *Forgiveness and Mercy* (Cambridge: Cambridge University Press, 1988); Jean Hampton, "Correcting Harms versus Righting Wrongs: The Goal of Retribution," *UCLA Law Review* 39 (1992): 1659. See also George P. Fletcher, "The Place of Victims in the Theory of Retribution," *Buffalo Criminal Law Review* 3 (1999): 51.

27. Robert C. Solomon, "Justice v. Vengeance," in *The Passions of Law,* ed. Susan Bandes (New York: New York University Press, 1999), 144.

28. George P. Fletcher, *With Justice for Some: Victims' Rights in Criminal Trials* (Reading: Addison Wesley, 1995). Utilitarian victim-oriented theories are also prevalent. Alon Harel and Gideon Parchomovsky argue that the purpose of criminal punishment should be fairly providing protection against crime to victims, not calculating the wrongfulness or culpability of the offender ("On Hate and Equality," *Yale Law Journal* 109 [1999]: 507). The law and economics literature and the game theory literature have been most explicit in arguing that revenge is a necessary part of maintaining norms. See Ward Farnsworth, "The Economics of Enmity," *University of Chicago Law Review* 69 (2002): 211 (some manifestations of enmity may help maintain norm compliance); Robert Axelrod, *The Evolution of Cooperation* (New York: Basic Books, 2006), 122–23; Robert H. Frank, *Passions within Reason: The Strategic Role of the Emotions* (New York: W. W. Norton, 1988), 29–37; Edna Ullmann-Margalit and Cass R. Sunstein, "Inequality and Indignation," *Philosophy and Public Affairs* 30 (2002): 337, 345 ("Indignation frequently inclines people to sacrifice, by punishing, at their own expense, people who have behaved unfairly . . . Indignation may turn out to have strategic advantages, and in a way that bears directly on acting against inequality"). But see Jon Elster, "Norms of Revenge," *Ethics* 100 (1990): 862 (arguing that following a revenge norm is not rational); Alan P. Hamlin, "Rational Revenge," *Ethics* 101 (1991): 374 (arguing that following a revenge norm is rational if honor is valuable). Therapeutic jurisprudence writings have argued that punishment should be, at least in part, a way for victims to achieve closure and peace. But see Susan Bandes, "When Victims Seek Closure: Forgiveness, Vengeance, and the Role of Government," *Fordham Urban Law Journal* 27 (2000): 1599.

29. Doug Janicik, "Allowing Victims' Families to View Executions: The Eighth Amendment and Society's Justifications for Punishment," *Ohio State Law Journal* 61 (2000): 935 ("Right to view statutes implement a private form of vengeance that has

been authorized by the state . . . They are actually the means legislatures have used to channel the vengeance of those who believe that victims' rights do not go far enough").

30. See Douglas Evan Beloof, "The Third Model of Criminal Process: The Victim Participation Model," *Utah Law Review,* 1999, 289.

31. See Paul G. Cassell, "Barbarians at the Gates? A Reply to the Critics of the Victims' Rights Amendment," *Utah Law Review,* 1999, 479.

32. Marc Galanter and David Luban, "Poetic Justice: Punitive Damages and Legal Pluralism," *American University Law Review* 42 (1993): 1393.

33. Hampton, "Correcting Harms," 1659. See also David Sachs, "How to Distinguish Self-Respect from Self-Esteem," *Philosophy and Public Affairs* 10 (1981): 346–60 (arguing that even if the victim's intrinsic worth is untouched, the victim's self-esteem may be injured).

34. Hampton, "Correcting Harms," 1672–74.

35. Ibid., 1678.

36. Ibid.

37. Ibid.

38. Ibid., 1687.

39. Punishment is so characterized by Dan Kahan, for example, in his defense of shaming penalties in "What Do Alternative Sanctions Mean?" *University of Chicago Law Review* 63 (1996): 591. Kahan later repudiated part of this argument, in "What's Really Wrong with Shaming Sanctions?" *Texas Law Review* 84 (2006): 2075.

40. Section 5.05(1) of the Model Penal Code reads, "Except [when conduct charged is so inherently unlikely to result in crime and public danger] attempt, solicitation and conspiracy are crimes of the same grade and degree as the most serious offense which is attempted or solicited or is an object of the conspiracy."

41. Sanford Kadish, Carol Steiker, and Stephen Schulhofer, *Criminal Law and Its Process: Cases and Materials,* 8th ed. (New York: Aspen, 2007), 544–45.

42. The Federal Sentencing Guidelines make this clear for all drug and financial crimes (the more drugs or money involved, the more time should be served) and for crimes resulting in injury or death.

43. See, e.g., United States v. Balint, 258 U.S. 250 (1922); United States v. Dotterweich, 320 U.S. 277 (1943).

44. United States v. Dotterweich, 320 U.S. 277 (1943); United States v. Park, 421 U.S. 658 (1975). But see State v. Guminga, 395 N.W.2d 344 (Minn. 1986) (refusing, under the Minnesota Constitution, to allow vicarious criminal liability).

45. Bernard Williams, *Moral Luck* (Cambridge: Cambridge University Press 1981), 20–39. Williams points out that our kanticism cannot account for the agent regret, even remorse, we feel even when we are not at fault for bad consequences we involuntarily cause, and he suggests this is a reason for reaching beyond Kantian ethics. For the more traditional reaction to moral luck, see H. L. A. Hart, *Punishment and Responsibility: Essays in the Philosophy of Law* (Oxford: Clarendon, 1968), 129–31 (arguing from a Kantian standpoint that punishment should not vary by the contingency of result).

46. Michael S. Moore, "The Independent Moral Significance of Wrongdoing," *Journal of Contemporary Legal Issues* 5 (1994): 237, 272–80.

47. See, e.g., Morris, "Paternalistic Theory of Punishment"; M. Walker, *Moral Repair;*

Bennett, *Apology Ritual* ("What this book sets out, therefore, is a retributive theory of punishment, but one that pays attention to the challenge presented by restorative justice. In the end I agree with those who argue that there is a legitimate public interest in censuring crime. However, I argue that in order to do its job such censure has to be *symbolically adequate*. And I argue that the appropriate symbols are to be found in the practice of apology . . . My defence of retributivism is distinctive because I claim that retributive reactions are necessary to do justice *to the offender* . . . In the absence of punishment we would be failing to respect the status of the offender as a moral agent); Markel, "Shaming Sanctions," 2151 ("the retributive relationship . . . is less interested in expressing condemnation to the world and more interested in communicating the message of opprobrium to the offender").

48. Duff, *Punishment, Communication, and Community.* Duff distinguishes "expressive punishment" from "communicative punishment" on the ground that "expression requires only one who expresses . . . By contrast, communication requires someone to or with whom we try to communicate . . . and appeals to the other's reason and understanding—the response it seeks is one that is mediated by the other's rational grasp of its content" (79–80). This distinction, for Duff, avoids the problem of "expressing condemnation" to the community at large as a merely utilitarian goal of punishment.

49. Duff, *Punishment, Communication, and Community,* 121.

50. Lewis Carroll, *Through the Looking Glass* (New York: Random House, 1946), 94 ("'When I use a word,' Humpty Dumpty said in a rather scornful tone, 'it means just what I choose it to mean, neither more nor less'"). A nice exchange is also reported in George H. Smith, "Of the Certainty of Law and the Uncertainty of Judicial Decisions," *American University Law Review* 23 (1889): 699, 702–3: "The principle is well illustrated by the story of the Roman emperor, who was reproved by a distinguished grammarian for the use of an incorrect term, but justified by one Capito, on the ground that the unlimited power and will of the sovereign itself made the term correct. 'Capito is a liar, Caesar,' was the reply; 'you can make a Roman citizen, but you cannot make a Latin word.'"

51. Hubert Dreyfus, *Being-in-the-World: A Commentary on Heidegger's "Being and Time," Division I* (Cambridge, Mass.: MIT Press, 1991), chapter 12.

52. "Communication is never anything like a conveying of experiences, such as opinions or wishes, from the interior of one subject into the interior of another" (Martin Heidegger, *Being and Time,* trans. John Macquarrie and Edward Robinson [New York: Harper and Row, 1962], 205).

53. See John Tasioulas, "Repentance and the Liberal State," *Ohio State Journal of Criminal Law* 4 (2007): 488 ("feelings of guilt . . . are painful experiences that present his action as wrongful.").

54. See, e.g., J. K. Rowling, *Harry Potter and the Prisoner of Azkaban* (Danbury: Scholastic, 2001), 290 (Harry feels remorseful after only a word from Lupin but resentful toward Snape's punishment of "detention"); Jonathan Stroud, *The Amulet of Sarakand* (New York: Mirimax/Hyperion, 2003), 232 ("If his master's torrent of anger had merely numbed him, these few words from Mrs. Underwood, laced as they were simply with quiet disappointment, pierced Nathaniel to the marrow. His last vestiges of self-control failed him. He raised his eyes to her, feeling tears prickle against the cor-

ners"); Fyodor Dostoevsky, *Crime and Punishment*, trans. Jessie Coulson (Oxford: Oxford University Press, 1980) (Raskolnikov feels no remorse despite his imprisonment until he finally responds to Sonya's love). This may signal a problem with "righteous anger" theories of judgment. Anger is a narrowing emotion: it sees only the offense and not the person. See Robert C. Solomon, *The Passions: Emotions and the Meaning of Life* (Indianapolis: Hackett, 1993), 226-29. We respect and listen to those who care about us, not those who see in us only a wrongdoer.

55. Duff, *Punishment, Communication, and Community*, 120.

56. The potential for Duff to slip into an expressivist mode is especially obvious in his discussion of why we should not grant leniency for remorse. He argues that such discounts are a bad idea because they encourage false shows of remorse (120) and do not allow an offender to show sincerity in the way "required to reconcile herself with the political community" (119). The danger here, of course, is that the theory turns into an expressive theory, relying on the *public's* perspective of whether a penance has been adequately served and the crime adequately denounced. The value of stressing the confrontation with the offender, in order to preserve the offender's moral personhood and own moral conscience, seems to elide easily into a more utilitarian account of whether the public has been adequately "appeased." John Tasioulas avoids this pitfall by allowing for mercy for the already-repentant offender. "Repentance and the Liberal State."

CHAPTER 4

1. *Werke* may be understood as Heidegger's reinterpretation of Hegelian *Wirklichkeit*, often translated as "actuality" and, in both thinkers, signaling a coming to presence of truth.

2. Model Penal Code § 2.02.

3. See also Jill Stauffer, "Productive Ambivalence: Levinasian Subjectivity, Justice, and the Rule of Law," in *Essays on Levinas and Law: A Mosaic*, ed. Desmond Manderson (New York: Palgrave, 2009), 78 ("Instead of an original freedom, Levinas posits an absolute subjection to a responsibility it is not possible to choose or refuse").

4. Judith Shklar makes a similar point in her book *Faces of Injustice* (New Haven: Yale University Press, 1992).

5. The idea that responsibility may overflow traditional mens rea categories or Kantian "choice" and be connected instead with a preexisting relation to others has been recognized by others. See, e.g., Herbert Morris, "Nonmoral Guilt," in *Responsibility, Character, and the Emotions*, ed. Ferdinand Schoeman (Cambridge: Cambridge University Press, 1987), 240 ("We may have great difficulty finding a philosophically satisfying account of personal identity. It is, however, a principal assumption underlying one's ever being guilty. We assume such identity; we take responsibility for what we have done and view ourselves, the guilty person, as the self-same person responsible for wrongdoing. Now, if we accept the legitimacy of identificatory ties moving not just to ourselves when we acted in the past—our not having changed in any relevant way—can we not also find it acceptable that individuals establish those identificatory ties with others and that they may do this without irrationality?"); Jeffrie G. Murphy, "Shame Creeps through Guilt and Feels Like Retribution," *Law and Philosophy* 18 (1999): 327, 332-34 ("We typically feel

our most intense guilts, not because of abstract and formal violations of authoritative rules, but because we see vividly the harm that we have inflicted on others by such violations" [or even absent such violations] "because [we] have deeply betrayed and disappointed" others we care about).

6. See Margaret Urban Walker, *Moral Repair: Reconstructing Moral Relations after Wrongdoing* (Cambridge: Cambridge University Press, 2006), 99: "Rules of etiquette . . . may seem like purely conventional stipulations. To the extent that rules of etiquette invest particular actions . . . with meanings such as respect, gratitude, tact, or deference, however, to abandon them may be to express an offensive, insulting, or provocative attitude"; Sarah Buss, "Appearing Respectful: The Moral Significance of Manners," *Ethics* 109 (1999): 795–826.

7. Samuel H. Pillsbury, "Crimes of Indifference," *Rutgers Law Review* 49 (1996): 105.

8. Manderson (*Proximity, Levinas, and the Soul of the Law* [Montreal: McGill-Queens University Press, 162) quotes this apt phrase from Justice Kirby's dissent in the Australian case *Modbury Triangle Shopping Centre v. Anzil*, 176 A.L.R. 411, 434 (2000) (refusing to hold an employer liable for criminal acts suffered by an employee in a dark parking lot, even when the employer failed to fix lighting after notice).

9. See Pillsbury, "Crimes of Indifference"; Samuel H. Pillsbury, *Judging Evil: Rethinking the Law of Murder and Manslaughter* (New York: New York University Press, 2000), 161–89; idem, "Speaking the Language of Evil," in *Minding Evil: Explorations of Human Iniquity*, ed. Margaret Sönser Breen (New York: Rodopi, 2005).

10. Shklar, *Faces of Injustice*.

11. See Pillsbury, "Speaking the Language of Evil."

12. See Pillsbury, "Crimes of Indifference."

13. Meir Dan-Cohen has articulated a broader concept of responsibility based on "ascriptivism," a view that associates responsibility with more flexible boundaries of the self (and what the self "takes on" responsibility for or must "take on" responsibility for in order to be the sort of "self" one sees oneself as being). See Dan-Cohen, "Responsibility and the Boundaries of the Self," *Harvard Law Review* 105 (1992): 959; idem, *Harmful Thoughts: Essays on Law, Self, and Morality* (Princeton: Princeton University Press, 2002), 236. The insight that responsibility is not only grounded in mens rea but includes some sorts of unintended consequence constitutive of oneself influenced my views here. However, from this perspective, Dan-Cohen argues further that "revisionary practices" of forgiveness, repentance, and pardon are ways of "redrawing" the borders of the self to exclude responsibility for past wrongs. Some crimes, he argues, are unforgivable precisely because excluding one's responsibility for them would deny too much of one's self to continue to be the same self. See his "Revising the Past: On the Metaphysics of Forgiveness, Repentance, and Pardon," in *Forgiveness, Mercy, and Clemency*, ed. Austin Sarat and Nasser Hussein (Stanford: Stanford University Press, 2007), 117. I disagree that "revisionary practices" exclude responsibility so much as "settle" it, as I explain later in this chapter. It seems to me that remembering and continuing to *own* the wrong is an essential part of both punishment and mercy.

14. See Jeffrey A. Meyer, "Authentically Innocent: Juries and Federal Regulatory Crimes," *Hastings Law Journal* 59 (2007): 137.

15. Hannah Arendt, *The Human Condition* (New York: Anchor Books, 1958), 140–41.

See also Jill Stauffer, "Seeking the Between of Vengeance and Forgiveness: Martha Minow, Hannah Arendt, and the Possibilities of Forgiveness," *Theory and Event* 6 (2002): 1 (reading Arendt to suggest that "here is a possibility: forgiveness is a way of rendering the past the past. It attends to the possibility inherent in the term 'future,' the time-to-come that enables humans to create things anew rather than dragging their way through a determined universe. Because revenge is never-ending, it *is* a determined universe, until forgiveness or some like measure puts an end to this by acting unexpectedly to stop the cycle. Thought in this way, forgiveness is the possibility of a new order").

16. Dan Kahan, "What Do Alternative Sanctions Mean?" *University of Chicago Law Review* 63 (1996): 591.

17. Philippe Nonet, "Sanction," *Cumberland Law Review* 25 (1994): 489, 502.

18. Friedrich Nietzsche, *On the Genealogy of Morals* (second essay, section 3), trans. Walter Kaufmann and R. J. Hollingdale (New York: Vintage, 1967), 61.

19. I assume, in this chapter, that we are discussing the most serious crimes. Forgiveness of small delicts is our daily fare; it is the nature of punishment and of forgiveness or mercy in cases of serious injury that seem hardest to understand, so it is these cases I discuss both here and in subsequent chapters.

20. Cathy Caruth, "Trauma and Experience," in *Trauma: Explorations in Memory*, ed. Cathy Caruth (Baltimore: Johns Hopkins University Press, 1995).

21. Ibid., 11. See also Shoshana Felman, "Education and Crisis," in Caruth, *Trauma*, 45 ("Within the context of these dialogic interviews, many of these Holocaust survivors in fact narrate their story *in its entirety* for the first time in their lives, awakened to their memories and to their past both by the public purpose of the enterprise (the collection and the preservation of first-hand, live testimonial evidence about the Holocaust), and, more concretely, by the presence and involvement of the interviewers, who enable them for the first time to believe that it is possible, indeed, against all odds and against their past experience, to tell the story and *be heard*, to in fact *address* the significance of their biography—to *address*, that is, the suffering, the truth, and the necessity of this impossible narration—to a hearing 'you,' and to a listening community . . . for a historical experience which annihilated the very possibility of address").

22. Rabbi Baruch G. reported, "I will never forget the first time I was beaten up and that really got to me, not so much the, not so much the, the pain from the beating, but the mental anguish. Instead of telling me how to put bricks together, had to be placed a certain way in order for them to be stacked up, he simply went over and beat me for it, without [my] knowing why. I couldn't even cry. When I came home, this is when I burst out crying. Animal! And I was, I was conscientious. I had to go to work. I knew one thing. I had to do the best I can—[it was] forced labor. But why? I mean, what right? What? It was incomprehensible to me" (Fortunoff Video Archive for Holocaust Testimonies, at http://www.library.yale.edu/testimonies/excerpts/baruchg.html).

23. Henry Krystal, "Trauma and Aging," in Caruth, *Trauma*, 82.

24. Ibid.

25. Felman, "Education and Crisis," 58 (quoting student). See also ibid., 19 ("the texts that testify do not simply *report facts* but, in different ways, encounter—and make us encounter—*strangeness*").

26. Felman, "Education and Crisis," 16.

27. Krystal, "Trauma and Aging," 87.

28. Theodore Eisenberg, Stephen P. Garvey, and Martin T. Wells, "But Was He Sorry? The Role of Remorse in Capital Sentencing," *Cornell Law Review* 83 (1998): 1599.

29. Sigmund Freud, *Beyond the Pleasure Principle* (New York: W. W. Norton, 1961): 24.

30. Cathy Caruth, *Unclaimed Experience: Trauma, Narrative, and History* (Baltimore: Johns Hopkins University Press, 1996), 4.

31. J. M. Coetzee, *Disgrace* (New York: Penguin Putnam, 1999), 156. I discuss this novel at length in this book's conclusion.

32. See M. Walker, *Moral Repair*, 102–7, arguing that victims tend to adapt to bad treatment and need "some community of moral judgment that provides a reference point" (103) to avoid being, literally, "demoralized" (107). See also Martha Minow, "Breaking the Cycles of Hatred," in *Breaking the Cycles of Hatred: Memory, Law, and Repair* (Princeton: Princeton University Press, 2002), 16 ("For victims and survivors, failure to deal with the incidents wreaks its own damage: painful secrets can lead to a freezing of individuals' capacities to love and act. Unaddressed trauma can produce wounded attachments to devastation itself and contribute to what psychologists call the intergenerational transmission of trauma . . . The question, then, is not whether to remember, but how").

33. See Sharon Lamb, "The Psychology of Condemnation: Underlying Emotions and Their Symbolic Expression in Condemning and Shaming," *Brooklyn Law Review* 68 (2003): 929 (arguing that resentment and condemnation often overlay unconscious fear and vulnerability); Austin Sarat, "When Memory Speaks: Remembrance and Revenge in *Unforgiven*," in Minow, *Breaking the Cycles of Hatred*, 254 ("Vengeance . . . depends on memory, but not all memory serves vengeance equally. *Unforgiven* tells this story of remembrance and revenge by relying on a humanist narrative in which the memory of direct experience quells vengeance while monumental memory incites it").

34. Robert C. Solomon, *The Passions: Emotions and the Meaning of Life* (Indianapolis: Hackett, 1993), 289 ("self-accusation and punishment," are "much like guilt (Jean-Paul Sartre's *The Flies* underscoring the point that the nagging, buzzing, biting annoyances are self-inflicted)"). Solomon calls remorse "extremely self-indulgent emotion, more concerned with its esteem in its own eyes than with the victims of its folly." He finds shame a morally better response, because it acknowledges the possibility of expiation and atonement (payment), whereas remorse finds the wrong beyond expiation and calls for pardon, seemingly cheating punishment. However, in my view, shame seems the less morally sensitive response, because what triggers the emotion is one's loss of reputation and standing "in public," not an appreciation of the harm one has caused. See Jeffrie G. Murphy, "Shame Creeps through Guilt and Feels Like Retribution," *Law and Philosophy* 18 (1999): 327; Dan Markel, "Are Shaming Sanctions Beautifully Retributive?" (Arguing that guilt, not shame, is the properly moral emotion in this context, though Murphy is more optimistic about the potential for shame to induce guilt than is Markel.)

35. "Remorse is radically individuating of the victim and also of the person who has wronged her" (Raimond Gaita, *The Philosopher's Dog: Friendships with Animals* [New York: Random House, 2005], 170).

36. See chapter 6.

37. Remorse "implies a degree of empathic pain on the part of one who has caused

the fracture" (H. Cox, "Repentance and Forgiveness: A Christian Perspective," in *Repentance: A Comparative Perspective*, ed. A. Etzioni [Lanham, Md.: Rowman and Littlefield, 2000], 24).

38. Ian McEwan, *Atonement* (New York: Anchor Books, 2003).

39. Ibid., 272.

40. Martin Heidegger, *Being and Time*, trans. John Macquarrie and Edward Robinson (New York: Harper and Row, 1962), 185.

41. See, e.g., Martha C. Nussbaum, "Equity and Mercy," in *Sex and Social Justice* (Oxford: Oxford University Press, 1999), 161, suggesting that Aristotle's discussion of equity as the corrective for written law requires "a forgiving attitude" (*suggnômê*, or "judging with"), which Aristotle then connects with sympathy or compassion. Nussbaum elaborates, quoting Aristotle's *Rhetoric*, "To perceive the particular really accurately, one must not simply be concerned with retribution. One must, in addition, judge *with* the agent who has done the alleged wrong . . . see things from that person's point of view . . . Recognizing the burden of these 'human things,' the equitable judge is inclined not to be 'zealous for strict judgment in the direction of the worse,' but to prefer merciful mitigation"; Nir Eisikovits, *Sympathizing with the Enemy: Reconciliation, Transitional Justice, Negotiation* (Boston: Brill, 2010).

42. In "Education and Crisis," Felman describes the traumatic response of her class after they watched video testimony from the Fortunoff Video Archive for Holocaust Testimonies. To alleviate this trauma, the students needed to meet together and talk it through—to put it into language.

43. The uncanny experience of confession narrated by Simon Wiesenthal in *The Sunflower: On the Possibilities and Limits of Forgiveness* (New York: Schocken, 1998) and its traumatic influence on him throughout his life comprise an excellent example. I discuss this book in more detail in chapter 6.

44. Krystal, "Trauma and Aging," 89.

45. Edmund (Pat) Brown, with Dick Adler, *Public Justice, Private Mercy: A Governor's Education on Death Row* (New York: Weidenfeld and Nicolson, 1989), 17.

46. See, e.g., Kahan, "What Do Alternative Sanctions Mean?" (arguing that punishment must have a social meaning of condemnation of crime).

47. Fred E. Inbau, John E. Reid, Joseph P. Buckley, Brian C. Jayne, *Criminal Interrogation and Confessions*, 4th ed. (New York: Aspen, 2004), 242, 255. The interrogator-as-friend ploy may be more effective with younger offenders or more serious crimes, however. See Richard A. Leo, "Criminal Law: Inside the Interrogation Room," *Journal of Criminal Law and Criminology* 86 (1996): 266.

48. Felman, "Education and Crisis," 58.

49. John Knowles, *A Separate Peace* (New York: Bantam, 1960), 108–9 (Phineas begins grooming Gene for the Olympics that Phineas had hoped to participate in himself, before Gene caused his injuries).

50. See Vladimir Jankelevitch, *Forgiveness*, trans. Andrew Kelley (Chicago: University of Chicago Press, 2005), 120–21 ("Of course, forgiveness is very much a type of 'despair,' in the sense that remorse is a despair. Despair would not be despair, but rather a theatrical *disperato*, if it squinted toward redemption of which it is perhaps the forerunner and if it were counting on this forerunner as if on a promise").

51. Caruth, *Unclaimed Experience*, 8.

52. See ibid., 25–56, a beautiful meditation on the sharing of trauma through a discussion of the film *Hiroshima Mon Amour*.

53. See Jeffrie Murphy, *Getting Even: Forgiveness and Its Limits* (New York: Oxford University Press, 2003), 35 ("When I am wronged by another, a great part of the injury—over and above any physical harm I may suffer—is the insulting or degrading message that has been given to me by the wrongdoer: the message that I am less worthy than he is, so unworthy that he may use me merely as a means or object in service to his desires and projects . . . If the wrongdoer sincerely repents, however, he now joins me in repudiating the degrading and insulting message").

54. See Arendt, *The Human Condition*, 140–41.

55. G. W. F. Hegel, "Who Thinks Abstractly?" in *Texts and Commentary*, trans. Walter Kaufmann (New York: Anchor Books, 1966), 117 ("A murderer is led to the place of execution. For the common populace he is nothing but a murderer. Ladies perhaps remark that he is a strong, handsome, interesting man. The populace finds this remark terrible: What? A murderer handsome? How can one think so wickedly and call a murderer handsome; no doubt, you yourselves are something not much better! . . . This is abstract thinking: to see nothing in the murderer except the abstract fact that he is a murderer, and to annul all other human essence in him with this simple quality").

56. "On a reasonable view of human understanding, though, we cannot escape recognizing the fallibility of our moral vision, and so a margin of uncertainty about our standards or the ways we apply them" (M. Walker, *Moral Repair*, 66).

57. This becomes retributivism's difficulty. How much pain is deserved as a penalty? Do we measure desert in subjective pain? How else do we measure it? Is how that pain is experienced by the offender relevant to the calculus of desert? If it is not, why not? What other measure of pain is relevant to individual desert? These problems are well explained by Adam J. Kolber in "The Subjective Experience of Punishment," *Columbia Law Review* 109 (2009): 182. He argues that if the penalty must fit the crime, then that means equal pain, but pain is a subjective experience, so penalty must vary by individual experience, or we implicitly acknowledge that the penalty is really for the community's satisfaction and is not measured by equivalence with desert from the offender's point of view. See also Kenneth W. Simons, "Retributivists Need Not and Should Not Endorse the Subjectivist Account of Punishment," *Columbia Law Review Sidebar* 109 (2009): 1 (arguing that retributivists can measure desert in "objective terms," such as "deprived liberty and outside relationships").

58. Cf. Nonet, "Sanction," 521–22.

59. "Pain first appears in the light of spirit, when man sees himself as the existing self, and is born in his humanity. But then it is miscast at once as the curse by which man is condemned to the labor of spirit in existence, and must suffer the seemingly insuperable contradiction of his insatiable craving in futile striving for the good. This is the onset of man's revolt against pain in the madness of his desperate will to extinguish suffering" (ibid., 517).

60. The experiences of victim-offender mediation bear this out: "Certain 'ingredients' seem particularly important in conferences where forgiveness is one of the goals. One is reframing, in which the victim sees the offender in a broader context than the of-

fense. Hearing the offender's story of upbringing and the circumstances surrounding the crime can go far in helping the victim see a human being across the table. On the seeking forgiveness side of this issue, a sincere apology and a willingness to make amends seem particularly important" (Robert D. Enright and Bruce A. Kittle, "Forgiveness in Psychology and Law: The Meeting of Moral Development and Restorative Justice," *Fordham Urban Law Journal* 27 [2000]: 1621). Lack of compassion can preempt it. See Douglas B. Ammar, "Forgiveness and the Law—a Redemptive Opportunity," *Fordham Urban Law Journal* 27 (2000): 1583 ("the wife of the victim ranted about race issues and obviously saw our client not as a fifteen-year-old child, but as a black man").

61. P. E. Digeser, *Political Forgiveness* (Ithaca: Cornell University Press, 2001); M. Walker, *Moral Repair,* 179 (only the victims can forgive: "Secondary and tertiary victims ought to be respectful and circumspect about exercising even their proper prerogatives to forgive when the primary victim does not forgive, lest they imply a lack of regard for the victim's loss and suffering, or a lack of support for the victim's task of repairing her own moral confidence, trust, and hopefulness"); Minow, "Breaking the Cycles of Hatred," 18 ("Forgiveness cannot be arrogated from the survivors without inflicting a new victimization. As human rights activist Aryeh Neier warns, when governments or their representatives 'usurp the victim's exclusive right to forgive his oppressor,' they fail to respect fully those who have suffered").

62. Cf. Joanna North, "The 'Ideal' of Forgiveness: A Philosopher's Exploration," in *Exploring Forgiveness,* ed. Robert D. Enright and Joanna North (Madison: University of Wisconsin Press, 1998), 20 (arguing that for forgiveness to have moral value, it must be an active process and not a "mere cessation of hostile feelings").

63. I do not explicitly consider apology separately here, in part because I am not sure that I know yet what apology adds to confession and the willingness to undertake a sacrifice for settlement. Does an apology require more than saying "I did wrong and I am remorseful"? If not, then apologies look a lot like what I am calling confessions. Does an apology require saying "I wish the act undone" or "I promise not to do it again"? Does "I am sorry" say more than "I am remorseful"? Can one apologize to a community representative or just to the victim? Must apologies be public or ritualized in some way? These questions must wait for another time. For recent insightful treatments, see Bennett, *The Apology Ritual,* and Danielle Celermajer, *The Sins of the Nation and the Ritual of Apologies* (New York: Cambridge University Press, 2009).

64. Many authors argue for categories of unforgivable crimes, especially murder. See, e.g., Digeser, *Political Forgiveness;* Cynthia Ozick's response in Wiesenthal, *Sunflower,* 219–20.

65. Jacques Derrida, "On Forgiveness," in *Forgiveness and Cosmopolitanism* (New York: Routledge, 2001), 32–38.

66. In a couple of recent examples, legal scholars thought the Second Amendment a dead letter, but now it lives again (*District of Columbia v. Henner,* 128 S.Ct. 2783 [2008]), and scholars thought that *Patterson v. New York* (432 U.S. 197 [1977]) spelled the end of *Mullaney v. Wilbur* (421 U.S. 684 [1975]), but the old precedent received new life, at least by analogy, in *Apprendi v. New Jersey* (530 U.S. 466 [2000]) and *United States v. Booker* (543 U.S. 220 [2005]).

67. See Malcolm Feeley, *The Process Is the Punishment* (New York: Russell Sage, 1979). Duff also understands the trial as a means of confronting the offender with his wrong.

See R. A. Duff, *Trials and Punishments* (Cambridge: Cambridge University Press, 1986), 75. But see Robert Justin Lipkin, "Punishment, Penance, and Respect for Autonomy," *Social Theory and Practice* 14 (1988): 87, 90 (arguing that trials are more like self-interested competitions than any dramatic confrontation).

68. Robert P. Burns, *A Theory of the Trial* (Princeton: Princeton University Press, 1999).

69. Robert Justin Lipkin ("Punishment, Penance, and Respect for Autonomy," 103 n. 22) suggests that to make a penance-oriented theory as a true sacrifice and offering by an offender, we must stop thinking of penance as coercive and "take the offender's autonomy much more seriously than is presently thought possible. The offender then must have a greater voice in the type and duration of his punishment . . . Compulsory arbitration may serve as a model for this type of sentencing. The autonomy of two parties—the state and the offender—is respected only when both agree on a solution to their conflict." If plea negotiations included the offender and were the result of real deliberation between prosecutor and defense counsel/offender (as they sometimes are), then Lipkin's suggestion is hardly revolutionary but rather commonplace.

70. See, e.g., Eisenberg, Garvey, and Wells, "'But Was He Sorry?'" (remorse does matter, though it may matter less when the crimes are "vicious" and "cold-blooded").

71. Cf. Jeffrie G. Murphy, "Remorse, Apology, and Mercy," *Ohio State Journal of Criminal Law* 4, (2007): 423, 444 (agreeing that remorse is important but doubting that we can use it in criminal sentencing because there is "too much chance of being made a sucker by fakery").

72. This is the objection voiced in Coetzee's novel *Disgrace*, discussed in this book's conclusion.

73. Melville's story *Billy Budd* stands as an example of how a mandatory penalty can be enforced in such a way as to ennoble an offender rather than degrading him, where the fault for the tragic sentence is understood to lie with our law's finite and clumsy inability to judge, rather than in the "desert" of the offender.

74. See Pillsbury, "Speaking the Language of Evil."

75. See, e.g., Leigh A. Payne, *Unsettling Accounts: Neither Truth nor Reconciliation in Confessions of State Violence* (Durham: Duke University Press, 2008), suggesting trials may be less effective than other institutions for allowing for confrontation and that the confrontation is not always immediately productive of reconciliation and peace but may be a long, though democratically fruitful, "contentious coexistence."

76. Braithwaite, Duff, Garvey, Walker, and others have sketched out what a reconciliatory sentencing system might look like on the ground, and as is pretty obvious, I have little to add. In most concrete ways, I agree with much they say. My goal here was merely to provide a sounder philosophical foundation, beyond our kanticism, for such proposals, not to offer a sentencing scheme of my own.

77. See Marc Miller, "The Foundations of Law: Sentencing Equality Pathology," *Emory Law Journal* 54 (2005): 271.

78. Ludwig Wittgenstein, *Philosophical Investigations*, trans. G. E. M. Anscombe (New York: Macmillan, 1953).

79. George Lakoff, *Women, Fire, and Dangerous Things: What Categories Reveal about the Mind* (Chicago: University of Chicago Press, 1987), 95–96.

80. See H. L. A. Hart, *The Concept of Law* (Oxford: Clarendon, 1961).

81. Sanford Kadish, Stephen Schulhofer, and Carol Steiker, *Criminal Law and Its Process: Cases and Materials*, 8th ed. (New York: Aspen, 2007).

82. See Pamela J. Utz, *Settling the Facts* (Toronto: Lexington, 1978).

83. See Linda Ross Meyer, "Rituals of Death: The Meaning of Last Words and Last Meals," available on the Social Science Research Network, Abstract 1480686, September 30, 2009, and forthcoming in *Who Deserves to Die? Constructing the Executable Subject*, ed. Austin Sarat and Karl Shoemaker (Amherst: University of Massachusetts Press, 2010).

84. I thank Jeffrie Murphy for bringing this beautiful novel to my attention.

85. Keally McBride makes the very important point that a liberal state imagines its legitimacy as deeply tied to its rationality and the *appearance* of rule-following reason. Punishment, she insightfully notes, becomes the necessary and most common everyday demonstration of this limited "power-only-by-the-rules." Punishment is also a way of explaining suffering as *deserved* and is an exemplar of our presumption of free will and personal responsibility. Retributive punishment makes the world *seem* just and the government *seem* legitimate. But McBride also notes that government "will inevitably fail in its attempts to accomplish these tasks." See McBride, *Punishment and Political Order* (Ann Arbor: University of Michigan Press, 2007), 55–57.

86. C. S. Lewis, *The Four Loves* (New York: Harcourt Brace, 1960), 27–28.

87. John Braithwaite, *Restorative Justice and Responsive Regulation* (New York: Oxford University Press, 2002); Austin Sarat, *Mercy on Trial: What It Means to Stop an Execution* (Princeton: Princeton University Press, 2005); James Q. Whitman, *Harsh Justice: Criminal Punishment and the Widening Divide between America and Europe* (New York: Oxford University Press, 2003); Anne-Marie Cusac, *Cruel and Unusual: The Culture of Punishment in America* (New Haven: Yale University Press, 2009). See also Moriah Balingit, "Nearly 500 Teens Serving Life Terms in Pennsylvania Prisons," *Pittsburgh Post-Gazette,* September 29, 2008 (pointing out that the United States has the highest rate of teenage life imprisonment in the world).

88. See Jonathan Simon, *Governing through Crime: How the War on Crime Transformed American Democracy and Created a Culture of Fear* (New York: Oxford University Press, 2007).

CHAPTER 5

1. P. E. Digeser, *Political Forgiveness* (Ithaca: Cornell University Press, 2001).

2. Daniel Kobil, "How to Grant Clemency in Unforgiving Times," *Capital University Law Review* 31 (2003): 227; idem, "Mercy in Clemency Decisions," in *Forgiveness, Mercy, and Clemency,* ed. Austin Sarat and Nasser Hussain (Stanford: Stanford University Press, 2007): 36.

3. Elizabeth Rapaport, "Retribution and Redemption in the Operation of Executive Clemency," *Chicago-Kent Law Review* 74 (2000): 1501.

4. Austin Sarat, *Mercy on Trial: What It Means to Stop an Execution* (Princeton: Princeton University Press, 2005).

5. Bob Egelko, "Law Students Show Inmate Is Innocent," *San Francisco Chronicle,* February 19, 2005, B-1.

6. P. E. Digeser and Joanna North rightly point out that it is more than slightly insulting to be "forgiven" for something that one did not do. See P. E. Digeser, *Political Forgiveness* (Ithaca: Cornell University Press, 2001); Joanna North, "The 'Ideal' of Forgiveness: A Philosopher's Exploration," in *Exploring Forgiveness,* ed. Robert D. Enright and Joanna North (Madison: University of Wisconsin Press, 1998).

7. See Stuart Banner, *The Death Penalty: An American History* (Cambridge, Mass.: Harvard University Press, 2002), 54–55 (providing examples of pardons for innocence in the early years of nationhood when there was no appellate process to correct trial errors); George Lardner Jr. and Margaret Colgate Love, "Mandatory Sentences and Presidential Mercy: The Role of Judges in Pardon Cases, 1790–1850," *Federal Sentencing Reporter* 16 (2002): 212 (giving many examples of trial judges supporting pardon requests when sentences required by statute seemed unjustly severe or when new evidence was discovered after trial).

8. Laurence Hammack, "Convicted Man Gets New Day in Court," *Roanoke Times,* May 15, 2005; Laurence Hammack, "Lawyer: Girl Now Says Man Did Abuse Her," *Roanoke Times,* February 12, 2005.

9. Carpitcher v. Commonwealth, 273 Va. 335, 641 S.E.2d 486 (2007).

10. Laurence Hammack, "Kaine Denies Clemency for Carpitcher," *Roanoke Times,* October 22, 2009.

11. See Lardner and Love, "Mandatory Sentences" (giving examples of pardons in 1790–1850 that were supported by trial judges because mandatory penalties seemed too harsh: "When these conscientious judges were confronted with harsh and unyielding laws, they didn't always wait for the president to ask them. They asked him"); Charles Shanor and Marc Miller, "Pardon Us: Systematic Presidential Pardons," *Federal Sentencing Reporter* 13 (2001): 139 (arguing for systematic pardons for crack cocaine users to address unfair disparities with sentencing structures for powder and crack cocaine offenses).

12. See Richard F. Celeste, "Executive Clemency: One Executive's Real Life Decisions," *Capital University Law Review* 31 (2003): 139–40 (Celeste, while governor of Ohio, granted clemency to twenty-five women who had already served at least two years, on the grounds of "repeated and severe abuse," willingness to obtain treatment, and willingness to do community service on issues of domestic violence).

13. See cases discussed in David Tait, "Pardons in Perspective: The Role of Forgiveness in Criminal Justice," *Federal Sentencing Reporter* 13 (2001): 134 (contrasting a jury's mercy in France in the euthanasia case of Anne Pasquiou with the Latimer case in Canada that forbade clemency at the jury or judge level in a euthanasia case where Parliament had established a mandatory penalty).

14. Austin Sarat and Nasser Hussain, "On Lawful Lawlessness: George Ryan, Executive Clemency, and the Rhetoric of Sparing Life," *Stanford Law Review* 56 (2004): 1307.

15. Sarah Kershaw, "California Gang Founder Loses Death Row Appeal," *New York Times,* December 13, 2005, A-27.

16. Kathleen Dean Moore, *Pardons: Justice, Mercy, and the Public Interest* (New York: Oxford University Press, 1989), 173–78. Trying to judge subjective painfulness, however, is very tricky, especially since inmates can "adapt" to prison to some extent. See John Bronsteen, Chris Buccafusco, and Jonathan Masur, "Happiness and Punishment," *University of Chicago Law Review* 76 (2009): 1037.

17. Dan Markel, "Against Mercy," *Minnesota Law Review* 88 (2004): 1421; P. E. Digeser, "Justice, Forgiveness, Mercy, and Forgetting: The Complex Meaning of Executive Pardoning," *Capital University Law Review* 31 (2003): 161, 171. See also Rapaport, "Retribution and Redemption."

18. Sarat and Hussain, "On Lawful Lawlessness."

19. Abraham Lincoln, *Lincoln: Speeches and Writings, 1859–1865*, ed. Don E. Fehrenbacher (New York: Library of America, 1989), 555–56.

20. See Daniel T. Kobil, "The Quality of Mercy Strained: Wresting the Pardoning Power from the King," *Texas Law Review* 69 (1991): 569; Shanor and Miller, "Pardon Us" (listing all the presidential pardons used to "heal sectional wounds," including pardons for various rebellions, those convicted under the alien and sedition acts, pirates who assisted in the War of 1812, Mormons involved in the Utah Rebellion, Confederate sympathizers, participants in the Philippine Insurrection, Vietnam-era violators of selective service laws, etc.).

21. Archbishop Desmond Tutu, foreword to Enright and North, *Exploring Forgiveness*; Martha Minow, *Between Vengeance and Forgiveness: Facing History after Genocide and Mass Violence* (Boston: Beacon Press, 1999). See also Leigh A. Payne, *Unsettling Accounts: Neither Truth nor Reconciliation in Confessions of State Violence* (Durham: Duke University Press, 2008) (comparing, contrasting, and analyzing transitional justice in South Africa, Argentina, Chile, and Brazil); Jon Elster, *Closing the Books: Transitional Justice in Historical Perspective* (Cambridge: Cambridge University Press, 2004) (analyzing transitional justice across historical contexts, from Athens through the French restorations, post–World War II and Nuremberg, post-Communism, and contemporary South Africa and Latin America).

22. Lars Waldorf, "Rwanda's Failing Experiment in Restorative Justice," in *Handbook of Restorative Justice*, ed. Dennis Sullivan and Larry Tifft (New York: Routledge, 2008), 425.

23. Lincoln, *Lincoln: Speeches and Writings, 1859–1865*, 416.

Theorists Love, Kobil, and Digeser have all emphasized the importance of this aspect of the pardon power. Professor Digeser would separate peacemaking from reconciliation, however, and would place the latter roughly where I put allegiance pardons. See Margaret Colgate Love, "The Pardon Paradox: Lessons of Clinton's Last Pardons," *Capital University Law Review* 31 (2003): 185; Kobil, "Quality of Mercy Strained"; P. E. Digeser, "Justice, Forgiveness, Mercy, and Forgetting," *Capital University Law Review* 31 (2003): 168. See also Digeser, *Political Forgiveness*.

There is a vast literature debating whether and how pardons in this context can actually attain peace. Most conclude that, not surprisingly, whether peace can be restored through pardoning depends on many factors. Two of the most recent and illuminating works are Payne's *Unsettling Accounts* and Elster's *Closing the Books*.

24. See also Margaret Colgate Love, "Of Pardons, Politics, and Collar Buttons: Reflections on the President's Duty to be Merciful," *Fordham Urban Law Journal* 27 (2000): 1483, 1487; Peter M. Shane, "Presidents, Pardons, and Prosecutors: Legal Accountability and Separation of Powers," *Yale Law and Policy Review* 11 (1993): 361, 403 (citing Lincoln/Johnson pardons of Confederate soldiers and Truman/Carter pardons of those who violated selective service laws); Kobil, "Quality of Mercy Strained," 571.

25. Michael J. Sandel, *Liberalism and the Limits of Justice,* 2nd ed. (Cambridge: Cambridge University Press, 1998).

26. Lincoln, *Lincoln: Speeches and Writings,* 572.

27. Interview with a commander at Camp Cropper, May 25, 2005.

28. Mark S. Umbreit, *Victim Meets Offender: The Impact of Restorative Justice and Mediation* (Monsey, N.Y.: Criminal Justice Press, 1994): 130.

29. Ibid., 132.

30. "Laws . . . cannot be framed on principles of compassion to guilt: yet justice, by the constitution of England, is bound to be administered in mercy: this is promised by the king in his coronation oath, and it is that act of his government, which is the most personal, and most entirely his own. The king himself condemns no man; that rugged task he leaves to his courts of justice: the great operation of his sceptre is mercy" (Blackstone, *Commentaries on the Laws of England,* vol. 4, chapter 31, p. 389 [Chicago: University of Chicago Press, 1979]).

31. Blackstone, *Commentaries on the Law of England,* vol. 4, 397–402.

32. 32 U.S. (7 Pet.) 150, 160–61 (1833).

33. 274 U.S. 480 (1926). Justice Holmes, of course, self-consciously took an approach to law based in "positive law" ("law for the bad man"), despairing of the law's having any deeper moral significance. He was a transitional and somewhat tragic figure, marking the Court's turn to a more technological understanding of law. See Yosal Rogat, "The Judge as Spectator," *University of Chicago Law Review* 31 (1964): 213.

34. Tait, "Pardons in Perspective."

35. This form of mercy echoes our medieval past. See Trisha Olson, "Of the Worshipful Warrior: Sanctuary and Punishment in the Middle Ages," *St. Thomas Law Review* 16 (2004): 473, 508–9 ("The warrior vowed to his lord loyalty and service, and the lord in return offered 'affectionate care' of his man and reward for his valor. These bonds denoted more than mutual self-interest. They were relations of friendship, loyalty, and deference whereby feelings ran so deep that in the Anglo-Saxon poem "The Wanderer" 'all joy . . . departed' upon the loss of one's lord . . . To be fidelis, in turn, was to be 'law-worthy.' Under-girding medieval law was not a theory of rights, but a network of trust and deference"); Pat McCune, book review, *Michigan Law Review* 89 (1991): 1661, 1671 ("For medieval English people, judgment—the establishment of social order through justice—always involved mercy. Justice was joined in the minds of people involved in the courts not with an abstract notion of reason, but with the practical values of forgiveness and restoration of the balance of relationships in the community . . . Reconciliation and forgiveness, not retribution, were for centuries the ideal means to maintain peace"); Marty Slaughter, "Sublime Mercy," *Journal of Law, Culture, and Humanities* 6 (forthcoming, 2010).

36. Bibas and Bierschbach ("Integrating Remorse and Apology") gesture to a "relational" approach to criminal responsibility instead of an "individual badness" approach and suggest opening up victim-offender mediation—even post-conviction. These authors do not suggest clemency but do see an important place for apology and reconciliation in mending the social bonds that are torn by wrongdoing. Their "relational" approach to crime might be justified and supported by the foundational change suggested here.

37. See George P. Fletcher, *Loyalty: An Essay on the Morality of Relationships* (New York: Oxford University Press, 1993), 21 ("The rooting of the self in a culture of loyalty enables individuals to grasp the humanity of their fellow citizens and to treat them as bearers of equal rights . . . Loyalty is a critical element in a theory of justice; for we invariably need some basis for group cohesion, for caring about others, for seeing them not as strangers who threaten our security but as partners in a common venture").

38. Edmund (Pat) Brown, with Dick Adler, *Public Justice, Private Mercy: A Governor's Education on Death Row* (New York: Weidenfeld and Nicolson, 1989), 15–16.

39. Benedict Carey, "For the Worst of Us, the Diagnosis May Be 'Evil,'" *New York Times*, February 6, 2005, F1, F4.

40. See Ian Ayres, *Supercrunchers: Why Thinking by Numbers Is the New Way to Be Smart* (New York: Bantam, 2007). If we operationalize sentencing by trying to predict recidivism, we do quite well statistically. The problem is, however, many of the most predictive and easily assessed factors tend to be ones that we cannot change ("static" rather than "dynamic") and that are morally objectionable, like race; for example, common predictive factors are marital status, gender, age, parents involved in crime, and offenses committed as a juvenile. See Paul Gendreau, Tracy Little, and Claire Goggin, "A Meta-Analysis of the Predictors of Adult Offender Recidivism: What Works," *Criminology* 34 (1996): 575, 576 (noting that "there is no disagreement in the criminological literature about some of the predictors of adult offender recidivism, such as age, gender, past criminal history, early family factors, and criminal associates"); Christopher Slobogin, "Dangerousness and Expertise Redux," *Emory Law Journal* 56 (2006): 275, 285 (describing a leading actuarial prediction device known as the "Violence Risk Appraisal Guide (VRAG)" and its principal reliance on "past misconduct, psychiatric diagnosis, substance abuse, age at the time of the offense, parental presence, and the gender of and harm to the victim," in addition to a psychosocial index known as the Psychopathy Checklist—Revised); Melinda D. Schlager and David J. Simourd, "Validity of the Level of Service Inventory—Revised (LSI-R) among African American and Hispanic Male Offenders," *Criminal Justice and Behavior* 34 (April 2007): 545 (noting that "while clinical judgment and structured assessment instruments are both commonly used in correctional practice, meta-analytic studies have shown that actuarial risk assessment instruments are superior to clinical judgments in the prediction of clinical outcome, including criminality") (collecting source citations); James Austin, Dana Coleman, Johnette Peyton, and Kelly Dedel Johnson, "Reliability and Validity Study of the LSI-R Risk Assessment Instrument, Final Report to the Pennsylvania Board of Probation and Parole" (January 9, 2003), 18, 22, at http://www.pccd.state.pa.us/pccd/lib/pccd/stats/lsi_r_final_report.pdf (listing key factors for predicting recidivism, including prior conviction history, arrest under age sixteen, drug problems, mental health problems, age at release, and mental status). So we can predict recidivism, in some studies, with about 75 percent accuracy, but in doing so, we fail to treat offenders as "sublime" and full persons, with whom a relationship is still in progress. We are frighteningly close to the film *Minority Report*'s negative utopia of the "Department of Pre-Crime."

41. Prosecutors and judges may or may not remember what is said at sentencing. For them, it is all too often a routine procedure that includes stock adversarial posturing.

But offenders remember. I was struck, when visiting a women's prison, by the many women who remembered the precise words the prosecutor or judge used to them when they were sentenced. Many cried at the memory, feeling that their lives and possibilities had been reduced in that moment to a criminal epithet.

42. See Love, "Pardon Paradox" (demonstrating that Clinton's misbegotten end-of-term pardons were partly the result of failing, because of time pressures, to check the facts in the clemency petitions, circumventing the usual Justice Department process, and thereby denying any appearance or actuality of equal opportunities to seek clemency).

43. Lincoln, *Lincoln: Speeches and Writings, 1859–1865*, 577.

44. Ibid., 494.

45. Ibid., 663.

46. Ibid., 499.

47. See Love, "The Pardon Paradox"; Kobil, "Quality of Mercy Strained"; Banner, *Death Penalty*.

48. See chapter 6.

49. See Claudia Card, "On Mercy," *Philosophical Review* 81 (1972): 182.

50. See California v. Brown, 479 U.S. 538 (1987).

51. Robert P. Burns, *A Theory of the Trial* (Princeton: Princeton University Press, 1999).

52. Martha C. Nussbaum, "Equity and Mercy," in *Sex and Social Justice* (New York: Oxford University Press, 2000): 154.

53. Cf. Larry May, *Sharing Responsibility* (Chicago: University of Chicago Press, 1992), 56 (arguing for a virtue of moral sensitivity that incorporates perceptiveness toward the needs or feelings of others, caring about the effects of one's actions, critical appreciation for the morally relevant features of the situation, and being moved to act to minimize harms and offenses of one's conduct); Nir Eisikovits, *Sympathizing with the Enemy: Reconciliation, Transitional Justice, Negotiation* (Boston: Brill, 2010).

54. See Markel, "Against Mercy."

55. See Payne, *Unsettling Accounts*, 283 ("The Abu Ghraib photographs graphically revealed what the formerly abstract consensus around [condoning] torture really meant. The Bush administration refused to label the acts portrayed in the photographs as 'torture,' using the language of 'humiliation' instead. But even the administration's defenders ignored the euphemism. Senator Bill Frist (Republican, Tennessee) remarked: 'What we saw is appalling'").

56. See Eisikovits, *Sympathizing with the Enemy.*

57. Michael Cuneo remarks, in his book on the Darrell Mease pardon, that what was missing from all the accounts of the case was Darrell himself. Cuneo sets himself the task in his book of making Darrell Mease real for us and therefore a possible object of understanding and compassion (*Almost Midnight*, 335). My experience in reading Cuneo's book is that once you get to know Darrell, it is indeed more difficult to be outraged by his pardon—even if others were more deserving. See also Patrick D. Healy, "After Coming Out, a Soap Opera Heroine Moves On," *New York Times*, February 24, 2005, E3 (describing how conservative viewers politically opposed to gay and lesbian relationships came to feel compassion for a lesbian character on a soap opera after following her story,

so that "the lesbian girl became the moral tent pole of our show"). See also Nussbaum, "Equity and Mercy" (arguing that a judge must take the point of view of a narrator).

58. See, e.g., Corey Rayburn, "To Catch a Sex Thief: The Burden of Performance in Rape and Sexual Abuse Assault Trials," *Columbia Journal of Gender and Law* 15 (2006): 473 ("When a rape is recounted through oral testimony, with limited physical evidence, it is likely to underwhelm a jury that has heard much better stories and seen much more convincing accounts of rape. The fact that the television or movie rapes may have been fictional does not mean a jury's conception of rape is not actively shaped by them . . . Fictional accounts can be more powerful because they are dramatized and sensationalized").

59. The issues from the standpoint of effective advocacy are well explored in Sarat and Hussain's "On Lawful Lawlessness," Anthony V. Alfieri's "Mercy Lawyers" (*North Carolina Law Review* 82 [2004]: 1297), and Daniel Kobil's "Mercy in Clemency Decisions."

60. Brown, *Public Justice, Private Mercy,* 83–84.

61. Douglas Hay, "Property, Authority, and the Criminal Law," in *Albion's Fatal Tree: Crime and Society in Eighteenth-Century England* (New York: Pantheon, 1975), 17.

62. Lieutenant Colonel W. G. Perdue "Scotch" Perdue, "Weighing the Scales of Discipline: A Perspective on the Naval Commanding Officer's Prosecutorial Discretion," *Naval Law Review* 46 (1999): 69.

63. Stephanos Bibas and Richard A. Bierschbach ("Integrating Remorse and Apology into Criminal Procedure," *Yale Law Journal* 85 [2004]: 114) would recharacterize these as something like my allegiance pardons, to recognize offenders who give over criminal allegiances to come over to "Team America." This would be an anti-utilitarian account of immunity, but insofar as the grant of immunity is contingent on (1) the fact that the person pardoned has valuable information or (2) success in prosecuting others, the immunity would still be "not on the merits." See also Alexandra Natapoff, "Snitching: The Institutional and Communal Consequences," *University of Cincinnati Law Review* 73 (2004): 645 (arguing that use of informants has extremely damaging consequences for communities that are already unstable, as informants continue to commit crimes with impunity and turn in only their enemies but not their friends).

64. Alwynne Smart ("Mercy," *Philosophy* 43 [1968]: 345) would include in this category clemency for offenders with dependents, on the ground that duties to the dependents (outside the merits of the case) would trump the duty to punish. Nigel Walker ("The Quiddity of Mercy," *Philosophy* 70 [1995]: 27–37) points out that Smart's acknowledgment here runs counter to her retributivism, since this idea of other duties trumping punishment looks suspiciously utilitarian. But I would argue that family concerns are not "extrinsic" to the case. These concerns demonstrate the level of the defendant's commitment to others and the pain that all parties, including the offender, would suffer because of separation, concerns that are "internal" to the case. I would categorize them as "compassion pardons."

65. Michael Cuneo, *Almost Midnight: An American Story of Murder and Redemption* (New York: Broadway Books, 2004), 292–93.

66. Ibid., 296–97.

67. Ibid., 310.

68. Nigel Walker ("Quiddity of Mercy") lists four "easy" cases of inappropriate mercy: personal gain, favoritism, whim, and superstition (e.g., the Christmas pardon). Spelling these out in particular cases, however, is much harder. Is pardoning out of fellow feeling or sympathy for "personal gain?" Is pardoning because of a religious conversion favoritism toward the religious? Is pardoning because of a sense of personal connection that cannot be elucidated a "whim" pardon? Is pardoning because the pope asks you to a "superstition" pardon? I do not believe it is so easy to exclude all these pardons categorically in this way.

69. Mark Strasser, "Some Reflections on the President's Pardon Power," *Capital University Law Review* 31 (2003): 141, 153 (refusal to grant pardons on the basis of race or sex would clearly be an abuse of presidential power).

70. Ohio Adult Parole Authority v. Woodard, 523 U.S. 272 (1998).

71. Linda Ross Meyer, "Unruly Rights," *Cardozo Law Review* 22 (2000): 1 (arguing for a dignity-based understanding of equal protection and other constitutional rights).

72. See Cuneo, *Almost Midnight,* 338 ("While not everyone in Darrell's home environs approved of the commutation, most of those with whom I spoke seemed unwilling to dismiss it as a mere accident of history. In the intensely religious culture of the Missouri Ozarks, there are no mere accidents. Events of every sort, but especially extraordinary ones, are believed to reverberate with divine purpose. To suggest otherwise would betray not only a lack of faith but an astonishing lack of imagination").

73. Ohio Adult Parole Authority v. Woodard, 523 U.S. 272, 289 (O'Connor, J., concurring in part and concurring in the judgment).

74. Nigel Walker ("Quiddity of Mercy") also argues that "merely whimsical or random" mercy is not acceptable.

75. P. S. Ruckman Jr. and David Kincaid, "Inside Lincoln's Clemency Decision Making," *Presidential Studies Quarterly* 29 (1999): 84–99.

76. Elster, *Closing the Books,* 4, quoting Plutarch *Solon* 20.1.

77. It was not an authority that Carnahan, a Baptist, was in any way bound to obey.

78. This is the military practice. See chapter 6.

79. See Sarat, *Mercy on Trial,* 32 ("Mercy and clemency always involve risks. Taking these risks means acknowledging the limits of law and justice, and of their ability to guarantee genuine moral deliberation rather than arbitrariness, fairness rather than discrimination").

80. Grant Gilmore, *The Ages of American Law* (New Haven: Yale University Press, 1977), 111.

81. No great degree of imagination is necessary here; the harsh, by-the-letter enforcement of habeas corpus or immigration law could provide many nonfictional examples.

82. Tom S. Wolfe, *A Man in Full* (New York: Simon and Schuster, 1998).

83. Ibid., 238.

CHAPTER 6

1. Simon Wiesenthal, *The Sunflower: On the Possibilities and Limits of Forgiveness* (New York: Schocken, 1998), 145 (comment by Matthew Fox).

2. Ibid., 149 (comment by Rebecca Goldstein).

3. Ibid., 219–20 (response by Cynthia Ozick).

4. Ibid., 216.

5. Ibid., 217.

6. See John Sarche, "Military Jury Recommends No Jail Time for Officer Convicted in Death of Iraqi General," *Stars and Stripes,* January 25, 2006.

7. Ilario Pantano, with Malcolm McConnell, *Warlord: No Better Friend, No Worse Enemy* (New York: Threshold Editions, 2006).

8. "Soldier Gets Six Months in Case of Drowned Iraqi," January 8, 2005, http://www.talkleft.com/new_archives/009260.html; "TA Badger, Platoon Leader Pleads Guilty in Iraq Case," Associated Press, March 14, 2005.

9. Alex Roth, "Bones May Be from Iraq," *San Diego Union-Tribune,* September 17, 2004; Major Mynda Ohman, "Integrating Title 18 War Crimes into Title 10: A Proposal to Amend the Uniform Code of Military Justice," *Air Force Law Review* 57 (2005): 1.

10. Alex Roth, "Marines Involved in Iraqi Abuse Frustrated after Their Convictions," *San Diego Union-Tribune,* December 13, 2004.

11. Tim Golden, "In U.S. Report, Brutal Details of 2 Afghan Inmate's Deaths," *New York Times,* May 20, 2005; idem, "The Bagram File: Revisiting the Case Years after 2 Afghans Died, Abuse Case Falters," *New York Times,* February 13, 2006.

12. Ohman, "Integrating Title 18 War Crimes"; Eric Schmitt, "Iraq Abuse Trial Is Again Limited to Lower Ranks," *New York Times,* March 23, 2006; Neil Lewis, "Court in Abuse Case Hears Testimony of General," *New York Times,* May 25, 2006; "Abu Ghraib Dog Handler Sentenced," *CBS News,* June 2, 2006.

13. Gidget Fuentes, "Two Marines Convicted of Prisoner Abuse," *Marine Times,* May 28, 2004; Sewell Chan, "Marine Sergeant to Face Court-Martial in Abuse," *Washington Post,* June 12, 2004; Ohman, "Integrating Title 18 War Crimes."

14. Bing West, "The Road to Haditha," *Atlantic Monthly,* October 2006, 95; Gayle Putrich, "A Dozen Marines May Face Courts-Martial for Alleged Iraq Massacre," *Marine Times,* May 25, 2006.

15. Paul von Zielbauer, "Investigator Recommends Courts-Martial for 4 Soldiers," *New York Times,* September 4, 2006, 8. One pled guilty, with a life sentence, to avoid the death penalty ("Iraq Soldier Given Life Rape Sentence," *Guardian,* November 17, 2006).

16. James Dao, "Ex-Soldier Gets Life for Iraqi Murders," *New York Times,* May 21, 2009.

17. Alex Roth, "U.S. Servicemen Found Guilty of Killings Often End Up Serving Little Time," *San Diego Union-Tribune,* June 11, 2006; Russell Carollo, "Soldier Convicted in 2004 Slaying of Iraqi Man Leaves Prison a Year Early: Daily News Probe of Cases Like This Showed Soldiers' Jail Sentences Usually Were Lighter than in Civilian Courts," *Dayton Daily News,* June 24, 2006; Tim Whitmire, "Short Sentences, Dismissals, Show Wartime Murder Prosecutions Hard," Associated Press, June 5, 2005; Golden, "Bagram File"; Schmitt, "Iraq Abuse Trial Is Again Limited"; Josh White, Charles Lane, and Julie Tate, "Homicide Charges Rare in Iraq War: Few Troops Tried for Killing Civilians," *Washington Post,* August 28, 2006, A1.

18. *By the Numbers: Findings of the Detainee Abuse and Accountability Project* (New York: Human Rights Watch and Center for Human Rights and Global Justice at New York University, 2006).

19. Michael Belknap, *The Vietnam War on Trial: The My Lai Massacre and the Court-Martial of Lieutenant Calley* (Lawrence: University Press of Kansas, 2002); Richard Hammer, *The Court-Martial of Lieutenant Calley* (New York: CM&G Press, 1971); John Sack, *Lieutenant Calley: His Own Story as Told to John Sack* (New York: Viking, 1971).

20. Gary Solis, *Son Thang: An American War Crime* (Annapolis: Naval Institute Press, 1997).

21. United States v. Goldman, 43 C.M.R. 711 (Army Bd. of Rev. 1970) (fining a soldier for failing to report these crimes). See also Colonel Jack Crouchet, *Vietnam Stories* (Boulder: University Press of Colorado, 1997), 70–82, 174–75, 130–35. The 1989 film *Casualties of War* (screenplay by David Rabe) is based on this crime. For another acquittal in a rape case during Vietnam, see Gary Solis, *Son Thang: An American War Crime* (Annapolis: Naval Institute Press, 1997), 103.

22. Gary D. Solis, "Military Justice, Civilian Clemency: The Sentences of Marine Corps War Crimes in South Vietnam," *Transnational Law and Contemporary Problems* 10 (2002): 59 (arguing that courts-martial in Vietnam treated crimes against the enemy very seriously, though many received clemency later through stateside pardon and parole authorities). By comparison, the *Washington Post* reported that in the first three years that we have been in Iraq, thirty-nine service members were formally accused of crimes in connection with civilian deaths; twenty-six were charged with murder, negligent homicide, or manslaughter; and twelve served prison time (White, Lane, and Tate, "Homicide Charges Rare in Iraq").

23. After Lieutenant Calley was court-martialed, many Vietnam veterans wanted Congress to hold hearings on the extent of other war crimes in Vietnam. They felt that Calley was being scapegoated for conduct that was pervasive and widespread. Congressional committees refused to hold these hearings, so a junior congressman, Ron Dellums of California, decided to chair informal hearings, attended by other members of Congress who were against the Vietnam War. These hearings are a remarkable read, for the soldiers' testimony is graphic, detailed, and moving, and they testify without any apparent concern for incriminating themselves.

24. *The Dellums Committee Hearings on War Crimes in Vietnam: An Inquiry into Command Responsibility in Southeast Asia,* ed. Citizens Commission of Inquiry (New York: Vintage, 1972), 32, 41, 85–86, 89, 93, 95, 144, 212, 231, 236, 240, 241, 248–49, 250, 252.

25. Ibid., 213, 135.

26. Ibid., 10, 40.

27. Ibid., 90.

28. Ibid., 32, 67 (part of training).

29. Ibid., 112–13, 218–19, 234, 238.

30. Ibid., 29, 32, 68, 92–93, 136–37, 144–46. One standard practice was to use a field telephone, which had two "hot" wires. This was known as "ringing up" a prisoner or "Bell Telephone Hour."

31. Ibid., 41, 168, 228, 251.

32. Ibid., 188–90, 211 (after a favorite platoon member had been killed by a booby trap).

33. Ibid., 60 and passim.

34. Ibid., 135.

35. Ibid., 111, 133–34, 232.

36. Ibid., 166, 178.

37. Ibid., 129.

38. Ibid., 137.

39. Ibid., 16, 146–47.

40. Ibid., 149.

41. Nick Turse and Deborah Nelson, "Civilian Killings Went Unpunished: Declassified Papers Show U.S. Atrocities Went Far Beyond My Lai," *Los Angeles Times,* August 6, 2006.

42. *American Military Culture in the Twenty-first Century: A Report of the CSIS International Security Program* (Washington, D.C.: Center for Strategic and International Studies, 2000), 13 (quoting Lieutenant General Paul Van Riper).

43. See Solis, *Son Thang,* 65.

44. Thomas E. Ricks, "Making the Corps," in *Semper Fi: Stories of the United States Marines from Boot Camp to Battle,* ed. Clint Willis (New York: Scribner, 2003), 11. See also Jill Schachner Canen, "JAG Edge: Proposed Changes for Military Lawyers Have Critics at Attention," *ABA Journal,* November 2003, 26 ("Most people do not understand how family-oriented the military and the JAG corps are," [Lee Schinasi] says. "The thing people really need to consider is the culture. It's what keeps good JAG officers on active duty"). One soldier explained how a father's court-martial will affect the military career of his daughter: "You have to understand how family-oriented the service is" (interview with J; all the interviews in this chapter took place in 2003–4 in New Haven, Connecticut).

45. Ricks, "Making the Corps," in Willis, *Semper Fi,* 19.

46. Marion F. Sturkey, *Warrior Culture of the U.S. Marines* (Plum Branch, S.C.: Heritage International Press, 2002), 155.

47. Ibid., 162.

48. *American Military Culture in the Twenty-first Century.*

49. Ibid.

50. Ibid., 8.

51. Ibid., 69–70.

52. A cultural liaison in public relations in Okinawa from 1993 to 1997 explained, "These people take this honor thing seriously"; "It's not like just all working at the same law school, it's about belonging—it's nice to have that sense of belonging"; "The downside is that everybody knows everything, people can be myopic about things, and the voice of dissent is not often heard or well-received" (interview with K, February 15, 2004).

53. Mark J. Osiel, "Obeying Orders," *California Law Review* 86 (1998): 939, 1055: "These bonds of camaraderie are sometimes described in terms that would warm the hearts of contemporary communitarians, if the context were less lethal. One former soldier reflects, for instance, that 'this confraternity of danger and exposure is unequaled in forging links among people of unlike desire and temperament.'"

54. Shannon E. French, *The Code of the Warrior: Exploring Warrior Values Past and Present* (Lanham, Md.: Rowman and Littlefield, 2005), 12. Mark Osiel points out that the

influence of "charismatic" leaders on the "primary group" in combat can generate loyalty either in the direction of chivalrous restraint or in the direction of atrocity (*Obeying Orders: Atrocity, Military Discipline, and the Law of War* [Piscataway, N.J.: Transaction, 2002], 223–30). Compare, for example, the stories of fine leadership in James R. McDonough's *Platoon Leader: A Memoir of Command in Combat* (New York: Ballantine, 1985) with the atrocities, discussed by Solis ("Military Justice, Civilian Clemency," 59), that occurred when the most respected fighter in a platoon led its members to rape and murder children. Loyalty to one's comrades must be joined with a *nomos* of honor. Even when attempts are made to make war a business, the honor culture remains as a demand. See Mateo Taussig-Rubbo, "Outsourcing Sacrifice: The Labor of Private Military Contractors," *Yale Journal of Law and the Humanities* 21 (2009): 101.

55. Quoted in French, *Code of the Warrior*, 12.

56. *American Military Culture in the Twenty-first Century*, 85, item 70.

57. Interview with H.

58. Interview with K.

59. A service member who does not want to remain in service is not as likely to receive clemency. See, e.g., United States v. Hundley, 56 M.J. 858 (N.M. Ct. Crim. App. 2002) ("although appellant's desire for a discharge cannot transform an inappropriate sentence into a just one, it is 'a strong indication of a lack of rehabilitative potential and a significant factor for consideration'").

60. I would not advocate wholesale borrowing of military process as a "reform" for civilian sentencing processes or vice versa. The hierarchical approach to mercy in the military context makes sense given the chains of responsibility that link commanders and commanded, the fact that each is at risk from the others' decisions in a way not always true for civilians, and the fact that each knows a great deal about the others and works closely with them.

61. Interview with R. See also Lieutenant Colonel W. G. "Scotch" Perdue, "Weighing the Scales of Discipline: A Perspective on the Naval Commanding Officer's Prosecutorial Discretion," *Naval Law Review* 46 (1999): 69.

62. Uniform Code of Military Justice, Article 15.

63. *2005 Annual Report to the Committees on Armed Services and Secretary of Defense*, appendix, available at http://www.armfor.uscourts.gov/annual/FY05AnnualReport.pdf.

64. Interview with H. See also Elizabeth Lutes Hillman, *Defending America: Military Culture and the Cold War Court-Martial* (Princeton: Princeton University Press, 2005), 25–26 ("The centralized authority that military officers sought to preserve [under the new Uniform Code of Military Justice, or UCMJ] was not necessarily wielded in malevolent fashion; commanders could use their discretion to excuse as well as to punish. After a court-martial concluded the UCMJ permitted the officer who ordered the trial to unilaterally reduce, but not enhance, the sentence of a convicted service member. An accused person who had served in combat, performed well in an elite unit, or had a long record of meritorious service was likely to benefit from the intervention of a senior officer, even if convicted of a crime under the UCMJ").

65. John Braithwaite, *Restorative Justice and Responsive Regulation* (New York: Oxford University Press, 2002), 30–31 ("The idea of the pyramid is that our presumption should

always be to start at the base of the pyramid, then escalate to somewhat punitive approaches only reluctantly and only when dialogue fails, and then escalate to even more punitive approaches only when the more modest forms of punishment fail").

66. The convening authority may not be the same commander who brought or "preferred" the charges. The convening authority is usually at least two steps up the chain of command from the defendant. The convening authority does not play any role as investigating officer, judge, or prosecutor and plays no role in the trial itself. Lower-ranking commanders may convene summary or special courts-martial but do not have the authority to convene a general court-martial. If a lower-ranking commander believes a general court-martial is appropriate, he or she must send the case up the chain of command. Service members can elect a general court-martial instead of more summary dispositions, if they choose, though the sentencing risks are much greater.

67. See, e.g., United States v. Bauer, 1998 CCA LEXIS 44 (N.M. Ct. Crim. App. 1998) (sentence given by judge after plea was reduced to reflect pretrial agreement reached with convening authority [CA]); United States v. Muse, 1995 CCA LEXIS 87 (1995) (sentence of twenty years reduced to thirteen per pretrial agreement with CA); United States v. Washington, 1996 CCA LEXIS 475 (N.M. Ct. Crim. App. 1996) (pretrial agreement suspended all but three years of a twenty-five-year sentence for raping stepdaughter; defendant had twenty-one years of "stellar" performance as a chief petty officer). In some circumstances, a pretrial agreement may be reached without a plea of guilty—if the defendant agrees to stipulated facts, for example. See David A. Schleuter, *The Military Criminal Justice System: Practice and Procedure,* 5th ed. (Charlottesville: LexisNexis, 1999), 376 ("Promises by the convening authority usually relate to withdrawing charges, referring less serious charges, referring charges to a particular court, instructing the prosecutor not to present evidence on certain charges, or providing some sort of sentence relief such as suspension of a portion of the sentence . . . Although pretrial agreements usually involve a promise by the accused to plead guilty, there is nothing to prevent the parties from reaching an agreement involving a plea of not guilty or even a conditional plea of guilty").

68. United States v. Clemons, 16 M.J. 44 (CMA 1983) (Everett, C. J., concurring, arguing that military character and record should be more generally admissible even under the new rule, because, citing Wigmore, military personnel are subject to closer supervision and more record-keeping than civilians); United States v. Kahakauwila, 19 M.J. 60, 61 (CMA 1984) (error to exclude military character as evidence in conviction for drug sale) (Opinion for the Court by Everett, C. J., citing, with approval, the more expansive good-character rule of common law: "The military rule is taken from the Federal Rules of Evidence. However, the peculiar nature of the military community makes similar interpretation inappropriate"); United States v. Weeks, 20 M.J. 22 (CMA 1985) (error to equate military character with general good character—former is admissible in case involving drug sale); United States v. Belz, 20 M.J. 33 (CMA 1985) (held that general military character could be admissible in defense of a drug charge, since it had been held admissible in defense of "conduct unbecoming" based on similar facts); United States v. Court, 24 M.J. 11 (CMA 1987) (error to restrict introduction of entire military record especially when charged with "conduct unbecoming an officer"); United States v. Hurst, 29 M.J. 477, 481–82 (CMA 1990) (error to restrict introduction of officer effectiveness re-

ports in child abuse case because "the location of the offenses on base, their abusive and degrading nature and their deleterious impact on the military family clearly call into question appellant's character as a military officer"). See also "Symposium on the Military Rules of Evidence," *Military Law Review* 130 (1990): 1, 3 (comments of retired justice Robinson O. Everett: military courts "obliterated" the civilian limitation on character evidence to a relevant "trait," despite the intention of the drafters and the language of the rule, because of unique circumstances of military culture).

69. Military service is a "discouraged factor" for sentencing departures under the guidelines. See U.S.S.G. § 5H1.11 (service "not ordinarily relevant"). I have found no pre-*Booker* federal criminal case that granted a departure on this ground, and several cases overturned departures. See, e.g., United States v. Miller, 94 Fed. Appx. 121 (3d Cir. 2004) (overturning downward departure for military service); United States v. Jared, 50 Fed. Appx. 259 (6th Cir. 2002) (reversing a downward departure for military service); United States v. Coble, 11 Fed. Appx. 193 (4th Cir. 2001) (same); United States v. Given, 164 F.3d 389, 395 (7th Cir. 1999) (same); United States v. Miller, 146 F.3d 1281 (8th Cir. 1998) (military performance not relevant though defendant had received a Bronze Star in Vietnam); United States v. Lawrence, 1997 WL 563134 (4th Cir. 1997) (overturning departure) (unpublished opinion); United States v. Winters, 105 F.3d 200, 209 (5th Cir. 1997) (same); United States v. Ellis, 1997 U.S. Dist. LEXIS 7362 (E.D. Penn. 1997) (refusing to depart for military service); United States v. Rybicki, 96 F.3d 754 (4th Cir. 1996) (reversing departure for a Vietnam veteran who had saved a civilian during My Lai); United States v. Pittman, 1993 U.S. App. LEXIS 21851 (4th Cir. 1993) (with no showing that military service was extraordinary, there is no error in failing to consider it). United States v. Pipich (688 F.Supp. 191 (D. Md. 1988)) granted a downward departure for military service, based on a long history of respect for those with exemplary military service, but this case was decided before the Sentencing Commission amended the guidelines to make military service a discouraged factor.

Post-*Booker*, some courts are finding a conflict between the guidelines' rule discouraging departures based on military service (U.S.S.G. § 5H1.11) and the guidelines enabling statute that directs courts to consider a defendant's history and circumstances (18 U.S.C. § 3553(a)(1)). See United States v. Ranum, 353 F.Supp.2d 984 (E.D. Wisc. 2005); United States v. Long, 425 F.3d 482, 488–89 (7th Cir. 2005) (post-*Booker*, district courts can consider "discouraged factors" including military and community service). One case, United States v. Nellum (2005 U.S. Dist. LEXIS 1568 (N.D. Ind. 2005)), granted a downward departure based, in part, on military service ("The defendant is also an Army veteran, who was honorably discharged. Under the guidelines, Nellum's military service is not ordinarily relevant in arriving at an appropriate sentence. See U.S.S.G. § 5H1.11. Yet, this Court finds it very relevant that a defendant honorably served his country when considering his history and circumstances [18 U.S.C. § 3553(a)(1)]"). Other courts continued to deny these departures. See United States v. Tabor, 365 F.Supp.2d 1052, 1061–62 (D. Neb. 2005) (remanded for resentencing on other grounds); United States v. Turner, 2005 U.S. Dist. LEXIS 6368 (N.D. Ind. 2005). However, as the plight of veterans becomes more salient to us, military service is becoming a more acceptable departure ground or ground for leniency. See Linda Greenhouse, "Selective Empathy," *New York Times,* December 3, 2009, questioning the fairness in the Supreme Court's decision to overturn a death sentence in *Porter v. McCollum* and not in *Bobby v. Van Hook,* based primarily on the former's claim that military service evidence had been withheld from the jury instead of the childhood abuse evidence withheld in the *Van Hook* case.

70. Interview with B, 2003. One marine sergeant reports, "If you are willing to volunteer and you have a good attitude, the Marines takes care of you, they reward you" (interview with J).

71. See United States v. Thomas, 38 C.M.R. 655 (Army Bd. of Rev. 1968) (court-martial appended clemency recommendation to life sentence in part on ground that "idea of committing the offenses concerned originated with the accused's patrol leader . . . and probably would not have occurred without his encouragement and guidance").

72. Interview with B.

73. United States v. Weatherspoon, 44 M.J. 211, 213 (CAAF 1996) ("for over 4 decades, the President has provided for, and this Court has recognized, the power of a court-martial to recommend clemency to the convening authority, contemporaneously with announcement of the sentence"); United States v. Strom, 5 C.M.R. 769 (Air Force Bd. of Rev. 1952) (members of court-martial appended recommendations of clemency to the sentence).

74. United States v. Smith, 20 CMR 477 (Army Bd. of Rev. 1955).

75. Schleuter, *Military Criminal Justice System,* 777–81.

76. United States v. Raistrick, 1998 CCA LEXIS 268 (A.F. Ct. Crim. App. 1998) (defendant convicted of sodomy with his ten-year-old stepson; court sent the case back for clemency reconsideration by CA because counsel failed to ask for full extent of clemency options defendant wanted; court held that counsel's failure met standard of "colorable showing of possible prejudice" because appellant "had many years of good service, had shown remorse for his actions and believed individuals at Lajes Field and his family would have requested clemency consideration if contacted"); United States v. Frueh, 35 M.J. 550 (Army Ct. Crim. App. 1992) (setting aside CA's approval of the sentence because defense counsel failed to submit clemency application: "A defense counsel has a responsibility to review a case after the trial and to raise all legal issues and clemency matters with the convening authority which may assist his client"; waiver of right to submit matters regarding clemency should in future be signed by both lawyer and client); United States v. Washington, 1996 CCA LEXIS 475 (N.M. Ct. Crim. App. 1996) (defense counsel must submit clemency petition even if unlikely to result in more clemency than pretrial agreement, especially where clemency requested was reduction to E-3 rather than E-1 in order to help support family); United States v. Washington, 1996 CCA LEXIS 483 (N.M. Ct. Crim. App. 1996) (case returned to CA even though "relatively lenient sentence" because counsel did not submit fiancee's letter asking for clemency on the ground that she has no support for defendant's newborn child).

77. See United States v. Manibo, 1990 CMR LEXIS 252 (N.M. Ct. Crim. App. 1990) (staff judge advocate recommended clemency, but CA did not grant it); United States v. Guerrero, 2001 CCA LEXIS 131 (2001) (staff judge advocate on behalf of CA offered clemency if defendant would take polygraph); United States v. Clear, 34 M.J. 129 (CMA 1992) (CA's decision set aside because staff judge advocate did not advise CA of trial judge's recommendation of clemency).

78. See United States v. Tu, 30 M.J. 587 (Army Ct. Crim. App. 1990) ("When taking

final action on the findings and sentence, the convening authority considers legal error in his quasi-judicial capacity and must therefore apply appropriate legal standards of review . . . Clemency is a matter of executive grace and the convening authority therefore acts in his executive capacity . . . When serving in this latter function, the convening authority's discretion is plenary and he has complete discretion to disapprove findings of guilty and any portion or all of an adjudged sentence . . . Thus, the convening authority's final action in a court-martial may require him to apply independent and ofttimes inconsistent standards" (citations omitted)).

79. United States v. Myers, 46 C.M.R. 719, 720 (Army Bd. of Rev. 1972).

80. United States v. Cook, 46 M.J. 37, 39 (CAAF 1997); United States v. Wilson, 9 U.S.C.M.A. 223, 26 C.M.R. 3, 6 (CMA 1958) ("it is while the case is at the convening authority level that the accused stands the greatest chance of being relieved from the consequences of a harsh finding or a severe sentence"); United States v. Sorrell, 47 M.J. 432, 434 (CAAF 1998) (Sullivan, J., dissenting) ("Our clemency process is too important a step in our military justice system to have even the hint of anything irregular as part of the process").

81. See note 76.

82. Interview with B. Published and "unpublished" but electronically available examples of posttrial grants of clemency by a convening authority include D'Agnese v. United States Naval Clemency and Parole Board, 2006 U.S. Dist. LEXIS 33284 (D. Kans. 2006) (noting that CA had reduced sentence from twenty years to twelve years); United States v. Rocha, 2005 CCA LEXIS 361 (N-M 2005) (CA reduced nine-month sentence to two hundred days, but staff judge advocate's delay forced defendant to serve out entire sentence; court of appeal further reduced confinement to one hundred days so that defendant could seek an adequate monetary remedy from another court); United States v. Fagan, 59 M.J. 238 (CAAF 2004) (CA had reduced thirty-month sentence to twenty months in case involving distribution of marijuana, larceny, and forgery); United States v. Jenkins, 62 M.J. 582 (N-M 2005) (CA reduced twelve-year sentence for rape to nine years); United States v. Phillips, 2006 CCA LEXIS 61 (CAAF 2006) (CA reduced fine); United States v. Rountree, 2005 CCA LEXIS 347 (N-M 2005) (CA disapproved hard labor without confinement); United States v. Gaines, 61 M.J. 689 (N-M 2005) (CA reduced two years to twelve months); United States v. Griggs, 2005 CCA LEXIS 183 (N-M 2005) (reducing ninety-day sentence to time served); United States v. Robbins, 60 M.J. 607 (N-M 2004) (CA disapproved one month of confinement and one month of pay forfeiture); United States v. Myers, 46 C.M.R. 719 (Army Bd. of Rev. 1972) (CA reduced bad-conduct discharge to four months of confinement at hard labor); United States v. Huggins, 1998 CCA LEXIS 93 (N.M. Ct. Crim. App. 1998) (CA reduced bad-conduct discharge and reduction to pay grade E-1 by suspending bad-conduct discharge for twelve months and reducing pay grade only to E-3); United States v. Sorrell, 47 M.J. 432 (CAAF 1998) (CA reduced sentence by six months); United States v. Freeman, 2000 CCA LEXIS 199 (A.F. Ct. Crim. App. 2000) (CA reduced sentence from bad-conduct discharge, confinement for ten months, forfeiture of one thousand dollars per month for ten months, and reduction to E-1 to bad-conduct discharge, confinement for eight months, forfeiture of $959 per month for ten months, and reduction to E-1); United States v. Strom, 5 C.M.R. 769 (Air Force Bd. of Rev. 1952) (CA suspended a dishonorable discharge and all but six

months of confinement and forfeitures); United States v. Rogers, 1998 CCA LEXIS 244 (A.F. Ct. Crim. App. 1998) (CA allowed defendant to enter return-to-duty program instead of receiving immediate bad-conduct discharge); United States v. Henson, 58 M.J. 529 (Army Ct. Crim. App. 2003) (for larceny, eighteen months reduced to ten months by CA); United States v. Lentz, 54 M.J. 818 (N.M. Ct. Crim. App. 2000) (for wife and child abuse and for adultery, CA granted clemency from eighteen to twelve years). One examination of sentences and clemency for service members in the Vietnam era is Solis's "Military Justice, Civilian Clemency" (arguing that stateside parole boards exercised more clemency than military panels convened abroad during wartime). His statistics show that court-martial sentences were reduced by the convening authority in fourteen of the twenty-seven cases he examined. The most dramatic exercise of clemency was reducing a life sentence to one year. Five other life sentences were approved; nine others were reduced to between twenty and forty years.

83. See, e.g., United States v. Baur, 1998 CCA LEXIS 44 (N.M. Ct. Crim. App. 1998) (plea bargain included waiving automatic forfeitures "with the understanding that the funds would be used for the benefit of appellant's wife and two children"); United States v. Craft, 1999 CCA LEXIS 226 (A.F. Ct. Crim. App. 1999) (CA disapproved adjudged forfeitures and waived for three months the mandatory forfeiture for appellant's spouse and children "based on a letter written by appellant's wife"). See also Gary Solis, *Son Thang*, 278–79 ("Here was the hidden price of a court-martial conviction and perhaps its cruelest cost. In punishing the serviceman his family is penalized as well . . . It is a matter that every military judge considers when deciding upon a sentence").

84. 10 U.S.C. § 866c requires a court of appeals to affirm only that sentence that should be approved. United States v. Craft, 1999 CCA LEXIS 226 (A.F. Ct. Crim. App. 1999) (reducing confinement by one month because CA did not consider clemency materials); United States v. Griffith, 2000 CCA LEXIS 253 (N.M. Ct. Crim. App. 2000) (reducing dishonorable discharge to bad-conduct discharge because CA did not have opportunity to act on clemency petition); United States v. King, 21 C.M.R. 365 (Army Bd. of Rev. 1956) (reducing dishonorable discharge, total forfeiture, and confinement at hard labor for one year to bad-conduct discharge, total forfeitures, and confinement at hard labor for nine months, for sleeping on guard duty; no error, but "we do not foreclose ourselves at this appellate level from our duty and obligation to make our own independent evaluation and determination of the appropriateness of the sentence"); United States v. Haynes, 44 C.M.R. 713 (Navy Bd. of Rev. 1971) (eliminating bad-conduct discharge for attempted larceny, on ground that court-martial was misinformed of its right to recommend an administrative discharge "both in law and in grace"); United States v. Chollet, 30 M.J. 1079 (C.G. Ct. Crim. App. 1990) (eliminating bad-conduct discharge for wrongful cocaine use on ground that record was not clear and that court really thought an administrative discharge more appropriate); United States v. Triplett, 56 M.J. 875 (Army Ct. Crim. App. 2002) (reducing confinement from fifteen to ten years because sentence was disproportionately more severe than co-accuseds); United States v. Doss, 57 M.J. 182 (CAAF 2002) (court of appeal reduced sentence because lawyer failed to present evidence of mental distress at sentencing, but Court of Appeals for the Armed Forces revised because court of appeal should have remanded instead). But see United States v. Ransom, 56 M.J. 861 (Army Ct. Crim. App. 2002) (sentence of co-accused was highly dis-

parate but difference was rational). The court may not consider a civilian sentence in determining appropriateness: see United States v. Hutchinson, 57 M.J. 231 (CAAF 2002).

85. United States v. Healy, 26 M.J. 394, 395 (CMA 1988). See also United States v. Fagan, 59 M.J. 238 (CAAF 2004) (overturning Army Court of Appeals' reduction of sentence from twenty to nineteen months because court had not held the required fact-finding hearing to determine whether the defendant's claims of ill treatment in prison were valid; court had no general clemency authority absent a finding of legal right); United States v. Miller, 18 M.J. 599 (N.M. Ct. Crim. App. 1983) (trial judge's recommendation for clemency does not undermine the appropriateness of the sentence—the two are distinct; a sentence may be considered not excessive, even when the trial judge believes clemency should be recommended); United States v. Johnson, 58 M.J. 509, 514 (N.M. Ct. Crim. App. 2003) (refusing to reduce sentence because it was appropriate for the crime; "appellant's argument on appeal is simply a plea for clemency, which is the prerogative of the CA and not the appellate courts"); United States v. Emerson, 20 C.M.R. 434 (Army Bd. of Rev. 1955) (refusing to change dishonorable discharge (suspended) to bad-conduct discharge in order to give effect to CA's desire to keep appellant from losing all his pay during confinement; appellate court cannot give effect to illegal attempts at clemency by altering a sentence without a basis in justice). Other examples are found in retired colonel Jack Crouchet's *Vietnam Stories*, 197–205, 57–69 (remembering two cases in which service members were extended clemency by the appellate process: one for refusing to go into combat—after having served faithfully in other firefights—and the other for taking part in a prison riot).

86. United States v. Healy, 26 M.J. 395.

87. Again, there is a significant difference here from constitutional rights in civilian practice. The courts will generally not inquire into the pardon process. See Ohio Adult Parole Authority v. Woodard, 523 U.S. 272 (1998).

88. Schleuter, *Military Criminal Justice System*, 33–34.

89. See Major Dennis L. Phillips, "The Army's Clemency and Parole Program in the Correctional Environment: A Procedural Guide and Analysis," *Army Lawyer*, 1986, 18.

90. Interview with B.

91. See Department of Defense Instruction 1325.7 7/17/2001, as amended June 10, 2003 ("6.10.4.3. Return-to-Duty Programs. Each Service is authorized to establish policies and procedures for prisoner return-to-duty programs. The scope of these programs shall be determined by available resources, facilities, personnel, and the needs of the Service. Prisoners shall be evaluated under their Service regulations for suitability for the program and provided appropriate opportunities to improve potential for return to duty").

The U.S. Air Force return-to-duty program is run at Bolling Air Force Base in Washington, D.C. A. J. Bosker reports, "Candidates must attend individual and group counseling plus develop a personal rehabilitation plan. A treatment team, comprised of a social worker, a psychologist, substance abuse and mental health technicians, military training leaders and a chaplain, regularly evaluates candidates. They meet each week to assess each candidate's progress in individual and group therapy, seminars, military training and other treatment programs. When a candidate completes all phases of the program, a board is convened from among the Air Force members at the Charleston

Brig. They consider each candidate's judgment, impulse control and coping skills, acceptance of responsibility, potential for future misconduct and promise to contribute to the Air Force" ("CSAF Witnesses Air Force Return-to-Duty Program," October 28, 2002, http://www.af.mil/news/story.asp?storyID=102802506).

92. I do not use the technical term *war crimes* here because "war crimes" carrying the death penalty under domestic law are not and cannot be prosecuted under catchall provisions of the Uniform Code of Military Justice. See Major Mynda Ohman, "Integrating Title 18 War Crimes into Title 10: A Proposal to Amend the Uniform Code of Military Justice," *Air Force Law Review* 57 (2005): 1 (the UCMJ does not contain its own category of war crimes, and though it allows prosecution of any federal crime through a catchall provision, crimes carrying the death penalty must be defined within the UCMJ itself). I also wish to avoid the knotty legal questions of just when a murder or assault crosses over to the technical definition of "war crime."

93. Pantano (*Warlord*) explains that the bodies of the Iraqis he killed were buried in the middle of a combat zone; they could not at first be exhumed for examination. See also Tim Whitmire, "Short Sentences, Dismissals, Show Wartime Murder Prosecutions Hard," Associated Press, June 5, 2005. On the many difficulties in finding and transporting witnesses and preserving evidence in Vietnam, see Gary Solis, *Marines and Military Law in Vietnam: Trial by Fire* (Washington, D.C.: U.S. Government Printing Office, 1989).

94. American jurisprudence for qualified immunity has already made this choice based in "positive law," granting qualified immunity to any officer whose actions do not violate "clearly established law." Ironically, those officers guilty of outrageous acts of cruelty that are so beyond the pale as to have no precedent may be the ones who are exonerated. For examples, see Linda Ross Meyer, "When Reasonable Minds Differ," *New York University Law Review* 71 (1996): 1467.

95. Hannah Arendt, *Eichmann in Jerusalem: A Report on the Banality of Evil* (New York: Penguin, 1961), 14–16.

96. Ibid.

97. See, e.g., Dexter Filkins, "The Fall of the Warrior King," *New York Times Magazine,* October 23, 2005.

98. Interview with H. Private First Class Justin Watt, whose concern began the investigation into the Mahmoudiya rape/murders, "felt obligated to say something . . . out of a sense of loyalty to the friends who had fought in Iraq and died. 'We'd come through hell together and there were a lot of good men who died . . . And this happened for what? We're just trying to do a little good over here'" (Paul von Zilbauer, Qais Mizher, Ali Adeeb, "Soldier Who Testified on Killings Says He Feared for His Life," *New York Times,* August 8, 2006). See also the letter of reprimand issued in United States v. Islas, 2000 CCA LEXIS 239 (N.M. Ct. Crim. App. 2000) ("the extent of your selfishness is nothing less than an embarrassment to the Naval service, the Marine Corps and to your family"); United States v. Court, 24 M.J. 11 (CMA 1987) (Cox, J., dissenting in part as to remand for harmless error finding: "Because of my strong feelings, I am simply unwilling to allow the concept of 'an officer and a gentleman' to erode on my watch"); United States v. Brisky, 2001 CCA LEXIS 68 (N.M. Ct. Crim. App. 2001) (no judicial bias shown by judge's reference to "our Marine Corps' ethics" and "our ethics").

99. On Son Thang, Solis (*Son Thang*, 12) reports, "The infantrymen of 1/7 contended with considerably more than forty-two identified enemy battalions. The Marines' opponents included a Vietnamese civilian population that was not exactly sitting out the war—the civilians often were the enemy. According to Marine historians, it was a war 'of snipers, ambushes, and old women who planted booby traps—... Throughout the summer of 1969, 1/7 was engaged in virtually continuous heavy combat.'"

On Mahmoudiya, Robert F. Worth, Carolyn Marshall, and Kirk Semple report, "In February, soldiers were ordered to spend up to 30 days at a time at the checkpoint—eating and sleeping there—instead of the routine three-to-five-day rotation . . . The checkpoints south of Baghdad are deadly, and the one the accused men were at was among the worst . . . On December 10, about three months before the rape, an Iraqi man in civilian clothing walked up to it, greeting and shaking hands with one of the soldiers on duty, according to relatives and lawyers of men in the unit. The Iraqi then raised a pistol and shot two sergeants in the head, fatally wounding them. Seconds later, Private Spielman shot and killed the attacker. Mr. Green, who was also at the scene, threw one of the wounded sergeants onto the hood of a Humvee and struggled to keep him alive during a frantic ride back to base." ("The Reach of War: Accusations; G.I. Crime Photos May Be Evidence," *New York Times*, August 5, 2006, A8).

Haditha was an area of intense insurgent activity, where a roadside bomb killed fourteen Marines on August 8, 2005. On November 19, the day the marines allegedly killed twenty-four civilians in their homes and car, including seven women and three kids, a lance corporal was killed by another roadside bomb. See Gayle S. Putrich, "A Dozen Marines May Face Courts-Martial for Alleged Iraq Massacre," *Marine Times*, May 25, 2006.

On Xuan Ngoc, Solis (*Marines and Military Law*, 54) quotes testimony of a navy psychiatrist: "War in Vietnam is one where the enemy is usually unseen until he chooses to make himself known, while the Marines are forced to repeatedly expose themselves to attack and ambush. Civilians often shelter and aid the enemy and give rise to very strong resentment from the Marine troops, especially when it is clear that the civilians can prevent the death of numerous Marines by providing information about the presence of enemy troops and the location of booby traps and mines. This is a situation that caused PFC Potter to feel appropriately angry and frustrated and to look forward to raiding a village."

On Abu Ghraib, see the reports reprinted in *The Torture Papers: The Road to Abu Ghraib*, ed. Karen J. Greenberg and Joshua L. Dratel (New York: Cambridge University Press, 2005). According to the Fay-Jones Report of August 23, 2004, the brigade in Abu Ghraib was "severely underresourced" because it "had to conduct tactical counter-insurgency operations while also executing its planned missions" (988). According to the Taguba Report, "In addition to being severely undermanned, the quality of life for Soldiers assigned to Abu Ghraib (BCCF) was extremely poor . . . There were numerous mortar attacks, random rifle and RPG attacks, and a serious threat to Soldiers and detainees in the facility. The Prison complex was also severely overcrowded" (433–34). See also Marian Blasberg and Anita Blasberg, "The Prisoner and the Guard: A Tale of Two Lives Destroyed by Abu Ghraib," *Der Spiegel* (English edition), September 26, 2005 (Abu Ghraib felt like living in hell; it was over one hundred degrees, there was constant shelling, prisoners were abusive, guards were abusive, it was filthy and rat-infested, hours were long, and there was no place else to go).

100. On My Lai, Hammer (*Court-Martial of Lieutenant Calley*, 245) reports, "When Calley arrived in Vietnam, he had had forty-five men in his platoon; by the eve of the attack on My Lai(4), he was down to twenty-seven men, and of his casualties, 'I would say ninety-five per cent with mines, booby traps.'"

On Son Thang, Solis (*Son Thang*, 23) reports, "Any combat death affects the entire company to some degree. The loss of Sgt. Jerry E. Lineberry [killed along with twelve others in an enemy ambush] was particularly disheartening. Lineberry, an eight-year Marine and the platoon sergeant of B Company's second platoon, was competent and well-liked, a spark plug around whom younger Marines rallied."

Violence in Abu Ghraib escalated after prisoners with weapons injured a female soldier and a prisoner shot at a guard. See Blasberg and Blasberg, "The Prisoner and the Guard."

In Mahmoudiya, a civilian had recently murdered two sergeants and the defendants had tried to keep them alive (see n. 99). Worth, Marshall, and Semple ("Reach of War") report, "All told, between September and June, at least 17 members of the battalion were killed, 8 of them from Company B, and dozens more were seriously wounded. In February, morale took another hit when a fire broke out in the abandoned factory being used as makeshift barracks . . . Fire destroyed most soldiers' personal items."

In Haditha, fourteen marines had been killed by a roadside bomb three months before the alleged murders, and a lance corporal had been killed by a roadside bomb just before the murders. See Bing West, "The Road to Haditha," *Atlantic Monthly*, October 2006, 98.

101. On Mahmoudiya, Worth, Marshall, and Semple ("Reach of War") report, "At the time, the men's squad leader and the overseeing platoon commander—both highly respected leaders—were on leave . . . 'I know none of that would have happened if he was around,' [a fellow sergeant told reporters]."

In Son Thang, a recently demoted private, Herrod, was put in charge of the "killer team," even though he had never commanded before and even though he was outranked by another member of the team (Solis, *Son Thang*).

Lines of command were confused in Abu Ghraib; no one wore any insignia, so no one knew who was supposed to give orders and who was supposed to follow them. Military police were under the impression that military intelligence wanted the abuse to happen. According to the Fay-Jones Report, the "MI Brigade Commander did not assign a specific subordinate unit to be responsible for interrogations at Abu Ghraib and did not ensure that a military intelligence chain of command at Abu Ghraib was established. The absence of effective leadership was a factor in not sooner discovering and taking actions to prevent both the violent/sexual abuse incidents and the misinterpretation/confusion . . . The perception that non-DOD agencies had different rules regarding interrogation and detention operations was evident" (*Torture Papers*, 990). Blasberg and Blasberg ("The Prisoner and the Guard") report, "There was chaos in the camp, a state of lawlessness."

102. In Son Thang, the company commander, Ambort, reported that he had "reminded [Herrod and his team] of the nine people that we had killed on the 12th of Feb-

ruary and I reminded him of Whitmore, who had died that day. I said, 'Don't let them get us any more. I want you to pay these little bastards back'" (Solis, *Son Thang*, 27).

In Quang Nam on February 8, 1968, a company that had lost five men in a firefight the night before rounded up nineteen women and children and shot them all. See Nick Turse and Deborah Nelson, "Civilian Killings Went Unpunished: Declassified Papers Show U.S. Atrocities Went Far Beyond My Lai," *Los Angeles Times*, August 6, 2006.

On My Lai, Hammer (*Court-Martial of Lieutenant Calley*, 189) reports, "Medina started out with words similar to, you all know what happened in a mine field a couple of miles from here. Well, tomorrow you're going to have a chance to get back at them . . . When we came through the next day he didn't want to see anything living but GIs."

In Abu Ghraib, violence against prisoners began before, but escalated after, prisoners with weapons injured a female soldier, and riots and shooting occurred (*Torture Papers*, Taguba Report).

103. See *Dellums Committee Hearings*, 165–66: "These men were rather bitter, like their friends had been killed, and they went back and threw the old woman and the child down the well and threw two grenades in on top of them." Soldiers killed thirty women and children in a village near where a favorite member of the platoon had just been blown up by a hidden explosive device (ibid., 186–92).

104. For a moving article comparing the experience of war criminal and victim, see Blasberg and Blasberg, "The Prisoner and the Guard."

105. The kidnapping, murder, and mutilation of two soldiers at the dangerous Mahmoudiya checkpoint was asserted to be revenge for the rape and murder of an Iraqi girl and her family by Steven D. Green and other members of his unit. Their actions were allegedly prompted by the murder of their officer by an Iraqi civilian pretending friendship. Green was given an honorable discharge for a personality disorder, then arrested by civilian federal criminal authorities, the first to be tried under a 2000 statute that allows federal trial of citizens who commit crimes overseas. He was tried in Kentucky for capital rape/murder, but the sentencing jury hung, resulting in a life sentence. The life sentence is reportedly "likely to anger Iraqis" who "had asserted that only a death penalty could satisfy the family and fellow villagers" (James Dao, "Ex-Soldier Gets Life Sentence for Iraq Murders," *New York Times*, May 21, 2009).

106. Erving Goffman, *Asylums: Essays on the Social Situation of Mental Patients and Other Inmates* (New York: Anchor Press, 1961).

107. *Dellums Committee Hearings*, 18.

108. Ibid., 127.

109. Ibid., 47.

110. Arendt, *Eichmann in Jerusalem*, 135–37.

111. *Dellums Committee Hearings*, 277.

112. Ibid., 37.

113. Sack, *Lieutenant Calley*, 106.

114. *Dellums Committee Hearings*, 161.

115. Ibid., 188.

116. Ibid., 98.

117. Ibid., 198.

118. Lieutenant Colonel Dave Grossman, *On Killing: The Psychological Cost of Learn-*

ing to Kill in War and Society (New York: Little, Brown, 1996), 223 ("The killer can be empowered by his killing, but ultimately, often years later, he may bear the emotional burden of guilt that he has not buried with his acts").

119. *Dellums Committee Hearings,* 220.

120. Grossman, *On Killing,* 160–64 (comparing Nazi propaganda of a "master race" to our own "body count" mentality in Vietnam: "If your propaganda machine can convince your soldiers that their opponents are not really human but are 'inferior forms of life,' then their natural resistance to killing their own species will be reduced ... The adolescent soldier against whom such propaganda is directed is desperately trying to rationalize what he is being *forced* to do, and he is therefore predisposed to believe this nonsense").

121. Solis, *Son Thang,* 103.

122. Pantano, *Warlord,* 46.

123. *Dellums Committee Hearings,* 273.

124. Ibid., 51.

125. Quoted in Bing West, "The Road to Haditha," *Atlantic Monthly,* October 2006, 98.

126. Pantano, *Warlord,* 110–13.

127. Ibid., 256.

128. John Crawford, *The Last True Story I'll Ever Tell: An Accidental Soldier's Account of the War in Iraq* (New York: Penguin, 2005), 154. See also "Iraq Soldier Given Life Rape Sentence," *Guardian,* November 17, 2006 (James Barker pled guilty to the rape of a fourteen-year-old girl and to conspiring in the murder of her parents and her six-year-old sister. He stated, "I want the people of Iraq to know that I did not go there to do the terrible things that I did ... I do not ask anyone to forgive me today. To live there, to survive there, I became angry and mean. I loved my friends, my fellow soldiers, and my leaders, but I began to hate everyone else in Iraq").

129. *Dellums Committee Hearings,* 68–69.

130. See Sack, *Lieutenant Calley,* 74–75; Pantano, *Warlord,* 255–56; Crawford, *Last True Story,* 197; *Dellums Committee Hearings,* 192 ("Someone who supposedly wears one face during the day, and agrees with us, and feeds us, and then at night he tries to kill us. You know, who is the enemy? Apparently the whole Vietnamese people are the enemy. That's the way I saw it and that's the way I was trained to treat them, and that's the way it was"). Calley reported, "I realized, I've been foolish. I had been asking everyone where the VC were: I had been talking to VC myself! That is why everyone said: 'I don't know.' They weren't about to tell me, 'I surrender.' At last it had dawned on me, 'These people, they're all the VC'" (Sack, *Lieutenant Calley,* 78–79). See also Belknap, *Vietnam War on Trial,* 57 (low morale of Charlie Company just before My Lai).

131. *Dellums Committee Hearings,* 252.

132. Sack, *Lieutenant Calley,* 28, 74.

133. Belknap, *Vietnam War on Trial,* 57.

134. *Dellums Committee Hearings,* 56.

135. Solis, *Son Thang,* 103.

136. Ironically, even Adolf Eichmann was concerned when he saw German soldiers shooting down women and children. He described his conversation with a local SS com-

mander, "'Well, it is horrible what is being done around here; I said young people are being made into sadists. How can one do that? Simply bang away at women and children? That is impossible. Our people will go mad or become insane, our own people" (Arendt, *Eichmann in Jerusalem*, 88–89).

137. Pantano (*Warlord*, 357) argues that no war can be fought "clean" and that our insistence that it be clean is hypocritical: "You are paid to follow orders, to do what you are told. You are paid to accomplish the mission. No, we don't care how, just get out there and do it. Well, we didn't really mean, 'we don't care how.' We just meant we didn't want to know how. Because if we know how, then we have to do something about it." See also Blasberg and Blasberg, "The Prisoner and the Guard"; C. J. Chivers, "Medic Tends a Fallen Marine, With Skill, Prayer, and Anger," *New York Times*, November 2, 2006, A1 ("I would like to say that I am a good man … but seeing this now, [his friend felled by sniper fire] what happened to Smith, I want to hurt people. You know what I mean?").

138. See Benedict Carey, "When Death Is on the Docket, the Moral Compass Wavers," *New York Times*, February 6, 2006 (finding "moral disengagement" prevalent in guards who were on execution teams; even counselors who were "highly morally engaged" when they first joined the execution staff found their engagement eroded over time: "After they had been involved in 10 executions, the counselors' scores on the disengagement scale almost matched the executioners'"); Samuel H. Pillsbury, "Speaking the Language of Evil," in *Minding Evil: Explorations of Human Iniquity*, ed. Margaret Sönser Breen (New York: Rodopi, 2005), 55, 67 (arguing that "moral indifference" is evil and that sentencing structures like California's three-strikes law that require "moral indifference" to all aspects of the person of the defendant are insidious and cruel).

139. Josh White, Charles Lane, and Julie Tate, "Homicide Charges Rare in Iraq War: Few Troops Tried for Killing Civilians," *Washington Post*, August 28, 2006, A1.

140. It looks as though Sergeant Williams tried to implicate falsely his own commander in order to reduce his own sentence, then later recanted ("Midwest: Kansas: Soldier Recants Iraq Accusation," *New York Times*, November 18, 2005).

141. David Finkel and Christian Davenport, "Records Paint Dark Portrait of Guard: Before Abu Ghraib, Graner Left a Trail of Alleged Violence," *Washington Post*, June 5, 2004, A1.

142. Pantano, *Warlord*, 220.

143. *Dellums Committee Hearings*, 196.

144. Arendt, *Eichmann in Jerusalem*, 256.

145. Pantano, *Warlord*, 44.

146. Calley's counsel made this point at his trial: "It's all right for the air corps to bomb cities; it's all right for the artillery to tear down houses and wreck the lives of the inhabitants. But it is wrong for the infantry" (Hammer, *Court-Martial of Lieutenant Calley*, 337).

147. An analysis of the theories of command responsibility is beyond the scope of this book. Suffice it to say that actual prior knowledge or actually illegal orders (our present scheme) is too little; vicarious responsibility is too much. Perhaps we could draw on the innovations of tort law—a presumption of vicarious responsibility with a burden of proof on the defendant to prove affirmative efforts to prevent atrocities. I leave all of that for another day.

148. Arendt, *Eichmann in Jerusalem*, 278.

149. See Shai Lavi, "Crimes of Action, Crimes of Thought: Arendt on Reconciliation, Forgiveness, and Judgment," in *Thinking in Dark Times: Hannah Arendt on Ethics and Politics*, ed. Roger Berkowitz, Jeffrey Katz, and Thomas Keenan (New York: Fordham University Press, 2010), 233–34 ("It is precisely the capability of judgment that is absent in thoughtless evil, and it is only through an act of judgment that this wrong can be corrected" [referring to Arendt's work]).

150. "Iraq Soldier Given Life Rape Sentence," *Guardian*, November 17, 2006.

151. Grossman, *On Killing*, 156–76 (discussing means of increasing emotional distance in war in order to make it easier to kill).

152. Raimond Gaita, *A Common Humanity: Thinking about Love and Truth and Justice* (New York: Routledge, 1998), xvii.

153. George P. Fletcher, "The Storrs Lectures: Liberals and Romantics at War: The Problem of Collective Guilt," *Yale Law Journal* 111 (2002): 1541–42.

154. Wiesenthal, *Sunflower*, 146 (comment by Matthew Fox).

155. See also Nir Eisikovits, "'I Am the Enemy You Killed, My Friend': Rethinking the Legitimacy of Truth Commissions," *Metaphilosophy* (2006), reprinted in *Genocide's Aftermath: Responsibility and Repair*, ed. Claudia Card and Armen T. Marsoobian (London: Blackwell, 2007) ("sympathizing with an enemy requires acquiring detailed knowledge about the way she lives," and "the willingness to collect such information depends on something like political generosity").

156. Wiesenthal, *Sunflower*, 37.

157. Wiesenthal, *Sunflower*, 246 (comment by Albert Speer).

158. Fortuoff Video Archive for Holocaust Testimonies.

159. *Dellums Committee Hearings*, 236.

CONCLUSION

1. Alexandre Dumas, *The Count of Monte Cristo*, trans. Robin Buss (New York: Penguin, 1996).

2. Trisha Olson, "Of Claiming the Law: The Distress of the Wanderer," *Margins* 1 (2001): 451. Jon Elster, "Norms of Revenge," *Ethics* 100 (1990): 862, 872 (the "devastating feeling of shame experienced by the man who fails to avenge an insult and who is constantly reminded that he is less than a man"); Thomas J. Scheff, "Community Conferences: Shame and Anger in Therapeutic Jurisprudence," *Revista Juridica Universidad de Puerto Rico* 67 (1998): 97 ("The victim, especially, is likely to feel the shame of helplessness, impotence, betrayal, and/or violation in response to the offense against him or her. However, this shame is usually not acknowledged—by the victim or others—but masked by the more visible emotion of anger"); Arnold Barnes and Paul H. Ephross, "The Impact of Hate Violence on Victims: Emotional and Behavioral Responses to Attacks," *Social Work* 39 (1994): 247.

3. Marianne Constable reminds me that this would be Kafka's answer: the punishment finds the crime.

4. See Scheff, "Community Conferences."

5. Robert C. Solomon (*The Passions: Emotions and the Meaning of Life* [Indianapo-

lis: Hackett, 1993], 228) says "anger registers our displeasure that the world does not obey our expectations, and displays our desire to punish those who would not obey our demands." Anger is a defense against shame; see Scheff, "Community Conferences." See also Robert C. Solomon, "Justice v. Vengeance," in *The Passions of Law*, ed. Susan Bandes (New York: New York University Press, 1999), 140–41 ("the criminal justice system is the codification and implementation of just this primal need for not only social but cosmic stability" and "a felt need to put the world back into balance").

6. See the discussion in chapters 3 and 4 and, e.g., Michael S. Moore, "The Moral Worth of Retribution," in *Responsibility, Character, and the Emotions*, ed. Ferdinand Schoeman (Cambridge: Cambridge University Press, 1987), 179–219; G. W. F. Hegel, *Philosophy of Right*, trans. T. M. Knox (Oxford: Clarendon, 1952); Herbert Morris, "A Paternalistic Theory of Punishment," *American Philosophy Quarterly* 18 (1981): 263, reprinted in *A Reader on Punishment*, ed. Anthony Duff and David Garland (New York: Oxford University Press, 1994).

7. Jean Hampton, "Correcting Harms versus Righting Wrongs: The Goal of Retribution," *UCLA Law Review* 39 (1992): 1659–1702.

8. See Solomon, "Justice v. Vengeance," 141.

9. The pun remains in both English and French (*comte* and *compter*).

10. As the captain of a smuggling vessel explains, "It's not their faults if they're bandits, it's the fault of the authorities . . . they are being hunted down because they . . . kill[ed] an enemy" "as if revenge wasn't in a Corsican's nature" (267).

11. Olson, "Of Claiming the Law," 475.

12. For example, Dantès saves the firm and honor of his loyal employer, Morell, when he is about to be bankrupt. As a result, his son, Maximilien, resolves to rescue someone on each anniversary of this family miracle. Beside Villefort's son, the innocent victims of Dantès' revenge are Villefort's in-laws and Noirtier's valet.

13. See Linda Ross Meyer, "Catastrophe: Plowing Up the Ground of Reason," in *Law and Catastrophe*, ed. Austin Sarat (Stanford: Stanford University Press, 2007).

14. Friedrich Nietzsche, *Thus Spoke Zarathustra*, in *The Philosophy of Nietzsche*, trans. T. Common (New York: Modern Library, 1950), 1–368, 155.

15. Jeffrie Murphy comes to this view of revenge and retribution in his more recent work: "One is always corrupted when one would presume to occupy a role best reserved for the gods. As mere humans, with radically finite knowledge, it is perhaps better for us to admit that we are not totally clear about what we are up to here" ("Moral Epistemology, the Retributive Emotions, and the 'Clumsy Moral Philosophy,' " in Bandes, *Passions of Law*, 159).

16. Villefort's full name is *Villefort-Noirtier*, but he refuses to use his father's name, in order to avoid his father's Bonapartist affiliations. Villefort's name means "fortress," and Dumas tells us that "he occupied an impregnable fortress . . . his post as crown prosecutor" (471).

17. J. M. Coetzee, *Disgrace* (New York: Penguin Putnam, 1999), cited, by page number, in text.

18. Quoted in James Kirwan, *Sublimity* (New York: Routledge, 2005), 138.

19. Cathy Caruth, *Unclaimed Experience: Trauma, Narrative, and History* (Baltimore: Johns Hopkins University Press, 1996), 56.

Bibliography

Alexander, Larry, and Emily Sherwin. *The Rule of Rules: Morality, Rules, and the Dilemmas of Law.* Durham: Duke University Press, 2001.

Alfieri, Anthony V. "Mercy Lawyers." *North Carolina Law Review* 82 (2004): 1297.

Ammar, Douglas. "Forgiveness and the Law—a Redemptive Opportunity." *Fordham Urban Law Journal* 27 (2000): 1583.

Anselm of Canterbury. *Proslogion.* In *A Scholastic Miscellany: Anselm to Ockham,* ed. Eugene R. Fairweather. Philadelphia: Westminster Press, 1956.

Arendt, Hannah. *Eichmann in Jerusalem: A Report on the Banality of Evil.* New York: Penguin, 1961.

Arendt, Hannah. *The Human Condition.* New York: Anchor Books, 1958.

Arendt, Hannah. *Lectures on Kant's Political Philosophy,* ed. Ronald Beiner. Chicago: University of Chicago Press, 1982.

Arendt, Hannah. *The Life of the Mind.* New York: Harcourt, 1978.

Austin, James, Dana Coleman, Johnette Peyton, and Kelly Dedel Johnson. "Reliability and Validity Study of the LSI-R Risk Assessment Instrument, Final Report to the Pennsylvania Board of Probation and Parole." January 9, 2003.

Axelrod, Robert. *The Evolution of Cooperation.* New York: Basic Books, 2006.

Ayres, Ian. *Supercrunchers: Why Thinking by Numbers Is the New Way to Be Smart.* New York: Bantam, 2007.

Baker, Anthony V. "Slavery and Tushnet and Mann, Oh Why? Finding 'Big Law' in Small Places." *Quinnipiac Law Review* 26 (2008): 691.

Bandes, Susan. "When Victims Seek Closure: Forgiveness, Vengeance, and the Role of Government." *Fordham Urban Law Journal* 27 (2000): 1599.

Banner, Stuart. *The Death Penalty: An American History.* Cambridge, Mass.: Harvard University Press, 2002.

Barkow, Rachel E. "The Ascent of the Administrative State and the Demise of Mercy." *Harvard Law Review* 121 (2008): 1333–65.

Barnes, Arnold, and Paul H. Ephross. "The Impact of Hate Violence on Victims: Emotional and Behavioral Responses to Attacks." *Social Work* 39 (1994): 247.

Barnes, Harry Elmer. *The Story of Punishment.* Boston: Stratford, 1930.

Belknap, Michael. *The Vietnam War on Trial: The My Lai Massacre and the Court-Martial of Lieutenant Calley.* Lawrence: University Press of Kansas, 2002.

Beloof, Douglas Evan. "The Third Model of Criminal Process: The Victim Participation Model." *Utah Law Review,* 1999, 289.

Bennett, Christopher. *The Apology Ritual: A Philosophical Theory of Punishment.* Cambridge: Cambridge University Press, 2008.

Berkowitz, Roger. *The Gift of Science: Leibnitz and the Modern Legal Tradition.* New York: Oxford University Press, 2005.

Bibas, Stephanos, and Richard A. Bierschbach. "Integrating Remorse and Apology into Criminal Procedure." *Yale Law Journal* 85 (2004): 114.

Blackstone. *Commentaries on the Laws of England.* Book IV. Chicago: University of Chicago Press, 1979.

Braithwaite, John. *Restorative Justice and Responsive Regulation.* New York: Oxford University Press, 2002.

Braithwaite, John, and Philip Pettit. *Not Just Deserts: A Republican Theory of Criminal Justice.* New York: Oxford University Press, 1990.

Brewer, Scott. "Exemplary Reasoning: Semantics, Pragmatics, and the Rational Force of Legal Argument by Analogy." *Harvard Law Review* 109 (1996): 923.

Brien, Andrew. "Utilitarianism and Retributivism." *Philosophia* 24 (1995): 493.

Bronsteen, John, Chris Buccafusco, and Jonathan Masur. "Happiness and Punishment." *University of Chicago Law Review* 76 (2009): 1037.

Brown, Edmund (Pat), with Dick Adler. *Public Justice, Private Mercy: A Governor's Education on Death Row.* New York: Weidenfeld and Nicolson, 1989.

Burns, Robert P. *A Theory of the Trial.* Princeton: Princeton University Press, 1999.

Burton, Steven J. *Judging in Good Faith.* Cambridge: Cambridge University Press, 1992.

Buss, Sarah. "Appearing Respectful: The Moral Significance of Manners." *Ethics* 109 (1999): 795–826.

Calabresi, Guido. *A Common Law for the Age of Statutes.* Boston: Harvard University Press, 1982.

Campos, Paul. "The Paradox of Punishment." *Wisconsin Law Review,* 1992, 1931.

Card, Claudia. "On Mercy." *Philosophical Review* 81 (1972): 182.

Carroll, Lewis. *Through the Looking Glass.* New York: Random House, 1946.

Caruth, Cathy. "Trauma and Experience." in *Trauma: Explorations in Memory,* ed. Cathy Caruth. Baltimore: Johns Hopkins University Press, 1995.

Caruth, Cathy. *Unclaimed Experience: Trauma, Narrative, and History.* Baltimore: Johns Hopkins University Press, 1996.

Cassell, Paul G. "Barbarians at the Gates? A Reply to the Critics of the Victims' Rights Amendment." *Utah Law Review,* 1999, 479.

Celermajer, Danielle. *The Sins of the Nation and the Ritual of Apologies.* New York: Cambridge University Press, 2009.

Celeste, Richard F. "Executive Clemency: One Executive's Real Life Decisions." *Capital University Law Review* 31 (2003): 139–40.

Coetzee, J. M. *Disgrace.* New York: Penguin Putnam, 1999.

Constable, Marianne. "Genealogy and Jurisprudence: Nietzsche, Nihilism, and the Social Scientification of Law." *Law and Social Inquiry* 19 (1994): 551.

Constable, Marianne. *Just Silences: The Limits and Possibilities of Modern Law.* Princeton: Princeton University Press, 2005.

Constable, Marianne. "On the (Legal) Study Methods of Our Time: Vico Redux." *Chicago Kent Law Review* 83 (2008): 1303, 1323.

Cox, H. "Repentance and Forgiveness: A Christian Perspective." In *Repentance: A Comparative Perspective,* ed. A. Etzioni. Lanham, Md.: Rowman and Littlefield, 1997.

Crawford, John. *The Last True Story I'll Ever Tell: An Accidental Soldier's Account of the War in Iraq.* New York: Penguin, 2005.

Crouchet, Jack. *Vietnam Stories: A Judge's Memoir.* Boulder: University Press of Colorado, 1997.

Cuneo, Michael. *Almost Midnight: An American Story of Murder and Redemption.* New York: Broadway Books, 2004.

Culbert, Jennifer L. *Dead Certainty: The Death Penalty and the Problem of Judgment.* Stanford: Stanford University Press, 2008.

Cusac, Anne-Marie. *Cruel and Unusual: The Culture of Punishment in America.* New Haven: Yale University Press, 2009.

Dan-Cohen, Meir. *Harmful Thoughts: Essays on Law, Self, and Morality.* Princeton: Princeton University Press, 2002.

Dan-Cohen, Meir. "Responsibility and the Boundaries of the Self." *Harvard Law Review* 105 (1992): 959.

Dan-Cohen, Meir. "Revising the Past: On the Metaphysics of Forgiveness, Repentance, and Pardon." In *Forgiveness, Mercy, and Clemency,* ed. Austin Sarat and Nasser Hussein. Stanford: Stanford University Press, 2007.

Davidson, Donald. "Actions, Reasons, and Causes." In *Essays on Actions and Events.* New York: Oxford University Press, 1980.

The Dellums Committee Hearings on War Crimes in Vietnam: An Inquiry into Command Responsibility in Southeast Asia. Citizens Commission of Inquiry. New York: Vintage, 1972.

Derrida, Jacques. "On Forgiveness." In *Forgiveness and Cosmopolitanism.* New York: Routledge, 2001.

Digeser, P. E. "Justice, Forgiveness, Mercy, and Forgetting: The Complex Meaning of Executive Pardoning." *Capital University Law Review* 31 (2003): 161.

Digeser, P. E. *Political Forgiveness.* Ithaca: Cornell University Press, 2001.

Dolinko, David. "Some Naive Thoughts about Justice and Mercy." *Ohio State Journal of Criminal Law* 4 (2007): 349, 354.

Dostoevsky, Fyodor. *The Brothers Karamazov.* Norton Critical Edition. New York: W. W. Norton, 1976.

Dostoevsky, Fyodor. *Crime and Punishment,* trans. Jessie Coulson. Oxford: Oxford University Press, 1980.

Dressler, Josh. "Hating Criminals: How Can Something That Feels So Good Be Wrong?" *Michigan Law Review* 88 (1990): 1448.

Dreyfus, Hubert. *Being-in-the-World: A Commentary on Heidegger's "Being and Time,"* Division I. Cambridge, Mass.: MIT Press, 1991.

Duff, R. A. "Justice, Mercy, and Forgiveness." *Criminal Justice Ethics* 9 (1990): 51.

Duff, R. A. *Punishment, Communication, and Community.* Oxford: Oxford University Press, 2001.

Duff, R. A. *Trials and Punishments.* Cambridge: Cambridge University Press, 1986.

Dumas, Alexandre. *The Count of Monte Cristo,* trans. Robin Buss. New York: Penguin, 1996.

Dworkin, Ronald. *Law's Empire.* Cambridge, Mass.: Harvard University Press, 1986.

Dworkin, Ronald. *Taking Rights Seriously.* Cambridge, Mass.: Harvard University Press, 1977.

Edlin, Douglas E. *Judges and Unjust Laws: Common Law Constitutionalism and the Foundations of Judicial Review.* Ann Arbor: University of Michigan Press, 2008.

Eisenberg, Melvin Aron. *The Nature of the Common Law.* Boston: Harvard University Press, 1988.

Eisenberg, Theodore, Stephen P. Garvey, and Martin T. Wells. "But Was He Sorry? The Role of Remorse in Capital Sentencing." *Cornell Law Review* 83 (1998): 1599.

Eisikovits, Nir. "'I Am the Enemy You Killed, My Friend': Rethinking the Legitimacy of Truth Commissions." *Metaphilosophy* (2006). Reprinted in *Genocide's Aftermath: Responsibility and Repair,* ed. Claudia Card and Armen T. Marsoobian. London: Blackwell, 2007.

Eisikovits, Nir. *Sympathizing with the Enemy: Reconciliation, Transitional Justice, Negotiation.* Boston: Brill, 2010.

Eliot, T. S. "Tradition and the Individual Talent." In *The Sacred Wood and Major Early Essays.* Mineola, N.Y.: Dover, 1998.

Elster, Jon. *Closing the Books: Transitional Justice in Historical Perspective.* Cambridge: Cambridge University Press, 2004.

Elster, Jon. "Norms of Revenge." *Ethics* 100 (1990): 862.

Enright, Robert D., and Bruce A. Kittle. "Forgiveness in Psychology and Law: The Meeting of Moral Development and Restorative Justice." *Fordham Urban Law Journal* 27 (2000): 1621.

Euripides. *Alcestis.*

Farnsworth, Ward. "The Economics of Enmity." *University of Chicago Law Review* 69 (2002): 211.

Fish, Stanley. "Normal Circumstances, Literal Language, Direct Speech Acts, the Ordinary, the Everyday, the Obvious, What Goes without Saying, and Other Special Cases." In *Is There a Text in This Class? The Authority of Interpretive Communities.* Cambridge, Mass.: Harvard University Press, 1982.

Feeley, Malcolm. *The Process Is the Punishment.* New York: Russell Sage, 1979.

Feinberg, Joel. "The Expressive Function of Punishment." In *A Reader on Punishment,* ed. Anthony Duff and David Garland, 71–91. New York: Oxford University Press, 1994.

Felman, Shoshana. "Education and Crisis." In *Trauma: Explorations in Memory,* ed. Cathy Caruth. Baltimore: Johns Hopkins University Press, 1995.

Fletcher, George P. *Loyalty: An Essay on the Morality of Relationships.* New York: Oxford University Press, 1993.

Fletcher, George P. "The Place of Victims in the Theory of Retribution." *Buffalo Criminal Law Review* 3 (1999): 51.

Fletcher, George P. "The Storrs Lectures: Liberals and Romantics at War: The Problem of Collective Guilt." *Yale Law Journal* 111 (2002): 1499, 1551.

Fletcher, George P. *With Justice for Some: Victims' Rights in Criminal Trials.* Reading: Addison Wesley, 1995.

Frank, Robert H. *Passions within Reason: The Strategic Role of the Emotions.* New York: W. W. Norton, 1988.

French, Shannon E. *The Code of the Warrior: Exploring Warrior Values Past and Present.* Lanham, Md.: Rowman and Littlefield, 2005.

Freud, Sigmund. *Beyond the Pleasure Principle.* New York: W. W. Norton, 1961.

Gaita, Raimond. *A Common Humanity: Thinking about Love and Truth and Justice.* New York: Routledge, 1998.

Gaita, Raimond. *The Philosopher's Dog: Friendships with Animals.* New York: Random House, 2005.

Galanter, Marc, and David Luban. "Poetic Justice: Punitive Damages and Legal Pluralism." *American University Law Review* 42 (1993): 1393.

Garvey, Stephen P. "Punishment as Atonement." *UCLA Law Review* 46 (1999): 1801.

Garvey, Stephen P. "Questions of Mercy." *Ohio State Journal of Criminal Law* 4 (2007): 321.

Garvey, Stephen P. "Restorative Justice, Punishment, and Atonement." *Utah Law Review,* 2003, 303.

Gendreau, Paul, Tracy Little, and Claire Goggin. "A Meta-Analysis of the Predictors of Adult Offender Recidivism: What Works." *Criminology* 34 (1996): 575, 576.

Goffman, Erving. *Asylums: Essays on the Social Situation of Mental Patients and Other Inmates.* New York: Anchor Press, 1961.

Greenberg, Karen J., and Joshua L. Dratel, eds. *The Torture Papers: The Road to Abu Ghraib.* New York: Cambridge University Press, 2005.

Grossman, Lieutenant Colonel Dave. *On Killing: The Psychological Cost of Learning to Kill in War and Society.* New York: Little, Brown, 1996.

Guyer, Paul. *Kant and the Claims of Taste.* Cambridge: Cambridge University Press, 1997.

Hadley, Michael L. "Spiritual Foundations of Restorative Justice." In *Handbook of Restorative Justice,* ed. Douglas Sullivan and Larry L Tifft. New York: Routledge, 2008.

Hamlin, Alan P. "Rational Revenge." *Ethics* 101 (1991): 374.

Hammer, Richard. *The Court-Martial of Lieutenant Calley.* New York: CM&G Press, 1971.

Hampton, Jean. "Correcting Harms versus Righting Wrongs: The Goal of Retribution." *UCLA Law Review* 39 (1992): 1659.

Hampton, Jean. "The Moral Education Theory of Punishment." In *Punishment,* ed. A. J. Simmons et al., 112–42. Princeton: Princeton University Press, 1995.

Hampton, Jean, and Jeffrie Murphy. *Forgiveness and Mercy.* Cambridge: Cambridge University Press, 1988.

Harcourt, Bernard. *Against Prediction: Profiling, Policing, and Punishing in an Actuarial Age.* Chicago: University of Chicago Press, 2006.

Harel, Alon, and Gideon Parchomovsky. "On Hate and Equality." *Yale Law Journal* 109 (1999): 507.

Hart, H. L. A. *The Concept of Law.* Oxford: Clarendon, 1961.

Hart, H. L. A. *Punishment and Responsibility: Essays in the Philosophy of Law.* Oxford: Clarendon, 1968.

Hay, Douglas. "Property, Authority, and the Criminal Law." In *Albion's Fatal Tree: Crime and Society in Eighteenth-Century England.* New York: Pantheon, 1975.

Hegel, G. W. F. *Philosophy of Right,* trans. T. M. Knox. Oxford: Clarendon, 1952.

Hegel, G. W. F. "Who Thinks Abstractly?" In *Texts and Commentary,* trans. Walter Kaufmann. New York: Anchor Books, 1966.

Heidegger, Martin. *Being and Time,* trans. John Macquarrie and Edward Robinson. New York: Harper and Row, 1962.

Heidegger, Martin. "Dialogue on Language." In *On the Way to Language,* trans. Peter D. Hertz, 44–46. New York: Harper and Row, 1982.

Heidegger, Martin. "Letter on Humanism," trans. E. Lohner. In *Philosophy in the Twentieth Century,* ed. William Barrett and Henry D. Aiken, 3:270–302. New York: Random House, 1962.

Heidegger, Martin. *Nietzsche: Will to Power as Art,* trans. David Farrell Krell. San Francisco: Harper and Row, 1979.

Heidegger, Martin. "Origin of the Work of Art." In *Poetry, Language, Thought,* trans. A. Hofstadter. New York: Harper and Row, 1971.

Heidegger, Martin. *The Question Concerning Technology, and Other Essays,* trans. W. Lovitt. New York: Harper Perennial, 1982.

Hestevold, H. Scott. "Disjunctive Desert." *American Philosophical Quarterly* 20 (1983): 357.

Hillman, Elizabeth Lutes. *Defending America: Military Culture and the Cold War Court-Martial.* Princeton: Princeton University Press, 2005.

Hurd, Heidi. "The Morality of Mercy." *Ohio State Journal of Criminal Law* 4 (2007): 389.

Inbau, Fred E., John E. Reid, Joseph P. Buckley, and Brian C. Jayne. *Criminal Interrogation and Confessions.* 4th ed. New York: Aspen, 2004.

Janicik, Doug. "Allowing Victims' Families to View Executions: The Eighth Amendment and Society's Justifications for Punishment." *Ohio State Law Journal* 61 (2000): 935.

Jankelevitch, Vladimir. *Forgiveness,* trans. Andrew Kelley. Chicago: University of Chicago Press, 2005.

Johnson, Carla Anne Hage. "Entitled to Clemency: Mercy in the Criminal Law." *Law and Philosophy* 10 (1991): 109.

Kadish, Sanford, and Stephen Schulhofer. *Criminal Law and Its Process: Cases and Materials.* 6th ed. New York: Little, Brown, 1995.

Kadish, Sanford, Stephen Schulhofer, and Carol Steiker. *Criminal Law and Its Process: Cases and Materials.* New York: Aspen, 2007.

Kahan, Dan. "What Do Alternative Sanctions Mean?" *University of Chicago Law Review* 63 (1996): 591.

Kahan, Dan. "What's Really Wrong with Shaming Sanctions?" *Texas Law Review* 84 (2006): 2075.

Kant, Immanuel. *The Critique of Judgment,* trans. J. H. Bernard. Amherst, N.Y.: Prometheus, 2000.

Kant, Immanuel. *Critique of Pure Reason,* trans. Norman Kemp Smith. New York: St. Martin's Press, 1965.

Kant, Immanuel. *Fundamental Principles of the Metaphysic of Morals,* trans. T. K. Abbott. Buffalo: Prometheus, 1987.

Kant, Immanuel. *The Philosophy of Law,* trans. W. Hastie. Edinburgh: T. T. Clark, 1887.

Kershnar, Stephen. "Mercy, Retributivism and Harsh Punishment." *International Journal of Applied Philosophy* 14 (2000): 209.

Knowles, John. *A Separate Peace.* New York: Bantam, 1960.

Kobil, Daniel. "How to Grant Clemency in Unforgiving Times." *Capital University Law Review* 31 (2003): 227.

Kobil, Daniel. "Mercy in Clemency Decisions." In *Forgiveness, Mercy, and Clemency,* ed. Austin Sarat and Nasser Hussain. Stanford: Stanford University Press, 2007.

Kobil, Daniel T. "The Quality of Mercy Strained: Wresting the Pardoning Power from the King." *Texas Law Review* 69 (1991): 569.

Kolber, Adam J. "The Subjective Experience of Punishment." *Columbia Law Review* 109 (2009): 182.

Krystal, Henry. "Trauma and Aging." In *Trauma: Explorations in Memory,* ed. Cathy Caruth. Baltimore: Johns Hopkins University Press, 1995.

Lakoff, George. *Women, Fire, and Dangerous Things: What Categories Reveal about the Mind.* Chicago: University of Chicago Press, 1987.

Lamb, Sharon. "The Psychology of Condemnation: Underlying Emotions and Their Symbolic Expression in Condemning and Shaming." *Brooklyn Law Review* 68 (2003): 929.

Lardner, George, Jr., and Margaret Colgate Love. "Mandatory Sentences and Presidential Mercy: The Role of Judges in Pardon Cases, 1790–1850." *Federal Sentencing Reporter* 16 (2002): 212.

Lavi, Shai. "Crimes of Action, Crimes of Thought: Arendt on Reconciliation, Forgiveness, and Judgment." In *Thinking in Dark Times: Hannah Arendt on Ethics and Politics,* ed. Roger Berkowitz, Jeffrey Katz, and Thomas Keenan. New York: Fordham University Press, 2010.

Leo, Richard A. "Criminal Law: Inside the Interrogation Room." *Journal of Criminal Law and Criminology* 86 (1996): 266.

Levi, Edward H. *An Introduction to Legal Reasoning.* Chicago: University of Chicago Press, 1962.

Levinas, Emmanuel. *Existence and Existents,* trans. Alphonso Lingis. Pittsburgh: Duquesne University Press, 2001.

Levinas, Emmanuel. *Otherwise than Being, or Beyond Essence,* trans. Alphonso Lingis. Pittsburgh: Duquesne University Press, 1998.

Levinas, Emmanuel. *Totality and Infinity: An Essay on Exteriority,* trans. Alphonso Lingis. Pittsburgh: Duquesne University Press, 1969.

Lewis, C. S. *The Four Loves.* New York: Harcourt Brace, 1960.

Liddell, H. G., and Robert Scott. *An Intermediate Greek-English Lexicon.* Oxford: Clarendon, 1986.

Lincoln, Abraham. *Lincoln: Speeches and Writings,* ed. Don E. Fehrenbacher. New York: Library of America, 1989.

Lipkin, Robert Justin. "Punishment, Penance, and Respect for Autonomy." *Social Theory and Practice* 14 (1988): 87.

Long, Leonard. "Rethinking Selective Incapacitation: More at Stake than Controlling Violent Crime." *UMKC Law Review* 62 (1993): 107.

Louw, Dirk J. "The African Concept of *Ubuntu* and Restorative Justice." In *Handbook of Restorative Justice,* ed. Douglas Sullivan and Larry L. Tifft, 161–73. New York: Routledge, 2008.

Love, Margaret Colgate. "Of Pardons, Politics, and Collar Buttons: Reflections on the President's Duty to Be Merciful." *Fordham Urban Law Journal* 27 (2000): 1483.

Love, Margaret Colgate. "The Pardon Paradox: Lessons of Clinton's Last Pardons." *Capital University Law Review* 31 (2003): 185.

Manderson, Desmond. *Proximity, Levinas, and the Soul of Law.* Montreal: McGill-Queens University Press, 2007.

Manderson, Desmond. *Songs without Music: The Aesthetic Dimensions of Justice.* Berkeley: University of California Press, 2000.

Markel, Dan. "Against Mercy." *Minnesota Law Review* 88 (2004): 1421.

Markel, Dan. "Are Shaming Sanctions Beautifully Retributive?" *Vanderbilt Law Review* 54 (2001): 2151.

Martel, James R. *Love Is a Sweet Chain: Desire, Autonomy, and Friendship in Liberal Political Theory.* New York: Routledge, 2001.

Mathiesen, T. "General Prevention as Communication." In *A Reader on Punishment,* ed. Anthony Duff and David Garland, 221–37. New York: Oxford University Press, 1994.

May, Larry. *Sharing Responsibility.* Chicago: University of Chicago Press, 1992.

McBride, Keally. *Punishment and Political Order.* Ann Arbor: University of Michigan Press, 2007.

McCune, Pat. Book review. *Michigan Law Review* 89 (1991): 1661.

McEwan, Ian. *Atonement.* New York: Anchor Books, 2003.

Meyer, Jeffrey A. "Authentically Innocent: Juries and Federal Regulatory Crimes." *Hastings Law Journal* 59 (2007): 137.

Meyer, Linda Ross. "Catastrophe: Plowing Up the Ground of Reason." In *Law and Catastrophe,* ed. Austin Sarat. Stanford: Stanford University Press, 2007.

Meyer, Linda Ross. "Is Practical Reason Mindless?" *Georgetown Law Journal* 86 (1998): 647.

Meyer, Linda Ross. "Nothing We Say Matters: Teague and New Rules." *University of Chicago Law Review* 61 (1994): 423.

Meyer, Linda Ross. "Unruly Rights." *Cardozo Law Review* 22 (2000): 1.

Meyer, Linda Ross. "When Reasonable Minds Differ." *New York University Law Review* 71 (1996): 1467.

Meyer, Linda Ross. "Why Barbara, Celarent, Darii, and Ferio Flunk Out of Law School: Comment on Scott Brewer, 'On the Possibility of Necessity in Legal Argument.'" *John Marshall Law Review* 34 (2000): 77.

Miller, Marc. "The Foundations of Law: Sentencing Equality Pathology." *Emory Law Journal* 54 (2005): 271.

Minow, Martha. *Between Vengeance and Forgiveness: Facing History after Genocide and Mass Violence.* Boston: Beacon Press, 1999.

Minow, Martha. "Breaking the Cycles of Hatred." In *Breaking the Cycles of Hatred: Memory, Law, and Repair.* Princeton: Princeton University Press, 2002.

Moore, Kathleen Dean. *Pardons: Justice, Mercy, and the Public Interest.* New York: Oxford University Press, 1989.

Moore, Michael S. "The Independent Moral Significance of Wrongdoing." *Journal of Contemporary Legal Issues* 5 (1994): 237.

Moore, Michael S. "The Moral Worth of Retribution." In *Responsibility, Character, and the Emotions,* ed. Ferdinand Schoeman, 179–219. Cambridge: Cambridge University Press, 1987.

Morris, Herbert. "Murphy on Forgiveness." *Criminal Justice Ethics* 7 (1988): 15.

Morris, Herbert. "Nonmoral Guilt." In *Responsibility, Character, and the Emotions,* ed. Ferdinand Schoeman. Cambridge: Cambridge University Press, 1987.

Morris, Herbert. "A Paternalistic Theory of Punishment." *American Philosophy Quarterly* 18 (1981): 263. Reprinted in *A Reader on Punishment,* ed. Anthony Duff and David Garland. New York: Oxford University Press, 1994.

Morris, Herbert. "Persons and Punishment." In *On Guilt and Innocence: Essays in Legal Philosophy and Moral Psychology,* 31–88. Berkeley: University of California Press, 1976.

Murphy, Jeffrie G. "The Case of Dostoevsky's General—Some Ruminations on Forgiving the Unforgivable." *Monist* 92 (July 2009).

Murphy, Jeffrie G. "Forgiveness, Mercy, and the Retributive Emotions." *Criminal Justice Ethics* 7 (1988): 3.

Murphy, Jeffrie G. *Getting Even: Forgiveness and Its Limits.* New York: Oxford University Press, 2003.

Murphy, Jeffrie G. "Legal Moralism and Retributivism Revisited." *Proceedings and Addresses of the American Philosophical Association* 80 (2006): 45.

Murphy, Jeffrie G. "Marxism and Retribution." Reprinted in *A Reader on Punishment,* ed. R. A. Duff and D. Garland. New York: Oxford University Press, 1994.

Murphy, Jeffrie G. "Mercy and Legal Justice." In *Forgiveness and Mercy,* by Jean Hampton and Jeffrie G. Murphy. Cambridge: Cambridge University Press, 1988.

Murphy, Jeffrie G. "Moral Epistemology, the Retributive Emotions, and the 'Clumsy Moral Philosophy.'" In *The Passions of Law,* ed. Susan Bandes. New York: New York University Press, 1999.

Murphy, Jeffrie G. "Remorse, Apology, and Mercy." *Ohio State Journal of Criminal Law* 4 (2007): 423.

Murphy, Jeffrie G. "Shame Creeps through Guilt and Feels Like Retribution." *Law and Philosophy* 18 (1999): 327.

Natapoff, Alexandra. "Snitching: The Institutional and Communal Consequences." *University of Cincinnati Law Review* 73 (2004): 645.

Nietzsche, Friedrich. *On the Genealogy of Morals,* trans. Walter Kaufmann and R. J. Hollingdale. New York: Vintage, 1967.

Nietzsche, Friedrich. *Twilight of the Idols,* trans. R. J. Hollingdale. New York: Penguin, 1979.

Nonet, Philippe. "In the Matter of *Green v. Recht.*" *California Law Review* 75 (1987): 363.

Nonet, Philippe. "Sanction." *Cumberland Law Review* 25 (1994): 489.

Nonet, Philippe. "What Is Positive Law?" *Yale Law Journal* 100 (1990): 667.

North, Joanna. "The 'Ideal' of Forgiveness: A Philosopher's Exploration." In *Exploring Forgiveness,* ed. Robert D. Enright and Joanna North. Madison: University of Wisconsin Press, 1998.

Nussbaum, Martha C. "Equity and Mercy." In *Sex and Social Justice.* New York: Oxford University Press, 2000.

Nussbaum, Martha C., and Dan M. Kahan. "Two Conceptions of Emotion in the Criminal Law." *Columbia Law Review* 96 (1996): 270.

O'Driscoll, Lyla H. "The Quality of Mercy." *Southern Journal of Philosophy* 21 (1983): 229.

Ohman, Major Mynda. "Integrating Title 18 War Crimes into Title 10: A Proposal to Amend the Uniform Code of Military Justice." *Air Force Law Review* 57 (2005): 1.

Oleson, J. C. "The Punitive Coma." *California Law Review* 90 (2002): 829.

Olson, Trisha. "Of Claiming the Law: The Distress of the Wanderer." *Margins* 1 (2001): 451.

Olson, Trisha. "Of the Worshipful Warrior: Sanctuary and Punishment in the Middle Ages." *St. Thomas Law Review* 16 (2004): 473.

Osiel, Mark J. "Obeying Orders." *California Law Review* 86 (1998): 939.

Osiel, Mark J. *Obeying Orders: Atrocity, Military Discipline, and the Law of War.* Piscataway, N.J.: Transaction, 2002.

Pantano, Ilario, with Malcolm McConnell. *Warlord: No Better Friend, No Worse Enemy.* New York: Threshold Editions, 2006.

Payne, Leigh A. *Unsettling Accounts: Neither Truth nor Reconciliation in Confessions of State Violence.* Durham: Duke University Press, 2008.

Perdue, Lieutenant Colonel W. G. "Scotch." "Weighing the Scales of Discipline: A Perspective on the Naval Commanding Officer's Prosecutorial Discretion." *Naval Law Review* 46 (1999): 69.

Pillsbury, Samuel H. "Crimes of Indifference." *Rutgers Law Review* 49 (1996): 105.

Pillsbury, Samuel H. *Judging Evil: Rethinking the Law of Murder and Manslaughter.* New York: New York University Press, 2000.

Pillsbury, Samuel H. "Speaking the Language of Evil." In *Minding Evil: Explorations of Human Iniquity,* ed. Margaret Sönser Breen. New York: Rodopi, 2005.

Ponzio, Julia. "Politics Not Left to Itself." In *Levinas, Law, Politics,* ed. Marinos Diamantides, 35–48. New York: Routledge-Cavendish, 2007.

Rainbolt, George W. "Mercy: An Independent, Imperfect Virtue." *American Philosophical Quarterly* 27 (1990): 169.

Rapaport, Elizabeth. "Retribution and Redemption in the Operation of Executive Clemency." *Chicago-Kent Law Review* 74 (2000): 1501.

Raz, Joseph. *Practical Reason and Norms.* Oxford: Oxford University Press, 1990.

Rogat, Yosal. "The Judge as Spectator." *University of Chicago Law Review* 31 (1964): 213.

Rotman, E. "Beyond Punishment." In *A Reader on Punishment,* ed. Anthony Duff and David Garland, 284–305. New York: Oxford University Press, 1994.

Rowling, J. K. *Harry Potter and the Prisoner of Azkaban.* Danbury: Scholastic, 2001.

Rubenfeld, Jed. *Freedom and Time: A Theory of Constitutional Self-Government.* New Haven: Yale University Press, 2001.

Sachs, David. "How to Distinguish Self-Respect from Self-Esteem." *Philosophy and Public Affairs* 10 (1981): 346–60.

Sack, John. *Lieutenant Calley: His Own Story as Told to John Sack.* New York: Viking, 1971.

Sandel, Michael J. *Liberalism and the Limits of Justice.* 2nd ed. Cambridge: Cambridge University Press, 1998.

Sarat, Austin. *Mercy on Trial: What It Means to Stop an Execution.* Princeton: Princeton University Press, 2005.

Sarat, Austin. "When Memory Speaks: Remembrance and Revenge in *Unforgiven.*" In *Breaking the Cycles of Hatred: Memory, Law and Repair,* ed. Martha Minow. Princeton: Princeton University Press, 2002.

Sarat, Austin, and Nasser Hussain. "On Lawful Lawlessness: George Ryan, Executive Clemency and the Rhetoric of Sparing Life." *Stanford Law Review* 56 (2004): 1307.

Scalia, Antonin. "The Rule of Law Is a Law of Rules." *University of Chicago Law Review* 56 (1989): 1175.

Schauer, Frederick. "Is the Common Law Law?" *California Law Review* 77 (1989): 455.

Scheff, Thomas J. "Community Conferences: Shame and Anger in Therapeutic Jurisprudence." *Revista Juridica Universidad de Puerto Rico* 67 (1998): 95.

Schlager, Melinda D., and David J. Simourd. "Validity of the Level of Service Inventory—Revised (LSI-R) Among African American and Hispanic Male Offenders." *Criminal Justice and Behavior* 34 (April 2007): 545.

Schleuter, David A. *The Military Criminal Justice System: Practice and Procedure.* 5th ed. Charlottesville: LexisNexis, 1999.

Shane, Peter M. "Presidents, Pardons, and Prosecutors: Legal Accountability and Separation of Powers." *Yale Law and Policy Review* 11 (1993): 361.

Shanor, Charles, and Marc Miller. "Pardon Us: Systematic Presidential Pardons." *Federal Sentencing Reporter* 12 (2001): 139.

Shklar, Judith. *Faces of Injustice.* New Haven: Yale University Press, 1992.

Sigler, Mary. "Mercy, Clemency, and the Case of Karla Faye Tucker." *Ohio State Journal of Criminal Law* 4 (2007): 455.

Simmonds, N. E. "Judgment and Mercy." *Oxford Journal of Legal Studies* 13 (1993): 52.

Simon, Jonathan. *Governing through Crime: How the War on Crime Transformed American Democracy and Created a Culture of Fear.* New York: Oxford University Press, 2007.

Simons, Kenneth W. "Retributivists Need Not and Should Not Endorse the Subjectivist Account of Punishment." *Columbia Law Review Sidebar* 109 (2009): 1.

Sitze, Adam. "Keeping the Peace." In *Forgiveness, Mercy, and Clemency,* ed. Austin Sarat and Nasser Hussain. Stanford: Stanford University Press, 2007.

Slaughter, Marty. "Levinas, Mercy, and the Middle Ages." In *Levinas, Law, Politics,* ed. Marinos Diamantides, 49–65. New York: Routledge-Cavendish, 2007.

Slaughter, Marty. "Sublime Mercy." *Journal of Law, Culture, and Humanities* 6 (2010).

Slobogin, Christopher. "Dangerousness and Expertise Redux." *Emory Law Journal* 56 (2006): 275.

Smart, Alwynne. "Mercy." *Philosophy* 43 (1968): 345.

Smith, George H. "Of the Certainty of Law and the Uncertainty of Judicial Decisions." *American University Law Review* 23 (1889): 699.

Smith, Steven D. *Law's Quandary.* Cambridge, Mass.: Harvard University Press, 2007.

Solis, Gary. *Marines and Military Law in Vietnam: Trial by Fire.* Washington, D.C.: U.S. Government Printing Office, 1989.

Solis, Gary D. "Military Justice, Civilian Clemency: The Sentences of Marine Corps War Crimes in South Vietnam." *Transnational Law and Contemporary Problems* 10 (2002): 59.

Solis, Gary. *Son Thang: An American War Crime.* Annapolis: Naval Institute Press, 1997.

Solomon, Robert C. "Justice v. Vengeance." In *The Passions of Law,* ed. Susan Bandes. New York: New York University Press, 1999.

Solomon, Robert C. *The Passions: Emotions and the Meaning of Life.* Indianapolis: Hackett, 1993.

Statman, Daniel. "Doing Without Mercy." *Southern Journal of Philosophy* 32 (1994): 331.

Stauffer, Jill. "Productive Ambivalence: Levinasian Subjectivity, Justice, and the Rule of Law." In *Essays on Levinas and Law: A Mosaic,* ed. Desmond Manderson. New York: Palgrave, 2009.

Stauffer, Jill. "Seeking the Between of Vengeance and Forgiveness: Martha Minow, Hannah Arendt, and the Possibilities of Forgiveness." *Theory and Event* 6 (2002): 1.

Sterba, James. "Can a Person Deserve Mercy?" *Journal of Social Philosophy* 10 (1979): 11.

Strasser, Mark. "Some Reflections on the President's Pardon Power." *Capital University Law Review* 31 (2003): 141.

Strauss, David A. "Common Law Constitutional Interpretation." *University of Chicago Law Review* 63 (1996): 877.

Stroud, Jonathan. *The Amulet of Sarakand.* New York: Mirimax/Hyperion, 2003.

Sullivan, Dennis, and Larry L. Tifft, eds. *Handbook of Restorative Justice.* New York: Routledge, 2008.

Sunstein, Cass R. "On Analogical Reasoning." *Harvard Law Review* 106 (1993): 741.

Sverdlik, Stephen. "Justice and Mercy." *Journal of Social Philosophy* 16, no. 3 (1985): 36.

Tait, David. "Pardons in Perspective: The Role of Forgiveness in Criminal Justice." *Federal Sentencing Reporter* 13 (2001): 134.

Tamanaha, Brian. *Law as a Means to an End: Threat to the Rule of Law.* New York: Cambridge University Press, 2006.

Tasioulas, John. "Repentance and the Liberal State." *Ohio State Journal of Criminal Law* 4 (2007): 487.

Taussig-Rubbo, Mateo. "Outsourcing Sacrifice: The Labor of Private Military Contractors." *Yale Journal of Law and the Humanities* 21 (2009): 101.

Thomas, Clarence. "Crime and Punishment—and Personal Responsibility." *National Times* 31 (September 1994).

Tutu, Archbishop Desmond. Foreword to *Exploring Forgiveness,* ed. Robert D. Enright and Joanna North. Madison: University of Wisconsin Press, 1998.

Twambley, P. "Mercy and Forgiveness." *Analysis* 36 (1976): 84.

Ullmann-Margalit, Edna, and Cass R. Sunstein. "Inequality and Indignation." *Philosophy and Public Affairs* 30 (2002): 337.

Umbreit, Mark S. *Victim Meets Offender: The Impact of Restorative Justice and Mediation.* Monsey, N.Y.: Criminal Justice Press, 1994.

Utz, Pamela J. *Settling the Facts.* Toronto: Lexington, 1978.

Waldorf, Lars. "Rwanda's Failing Experiment in Restorative Justice." In *Handbook of Restorative Justice,* ed. Dennis Sullivan and Larry Tifft. New York: Routledge, 2008.

Walker, Margaret Urban. *Moral Repair: Reconstructing Moral Relations after Wrongdoing.* New York: Cambridge University Press, 2006.

Walker, Nigel. "The Quiddity of Mercy." *Philosophy* 70 (1995): 27–37.

Wechsler, Herbert. "Toward Neutral Principles of Constitutional Law." In *Principles, Politics, and Fundamental Law.* Cambridge, Mass.: Harvard University Press, 1961.

Weinrib, Lloyd L. *Legal Reason: The Use of Analogy in Legal Argument.* New York: Cambridge University Press, 2005.

Whitman, James Q. *Harsh Justice: Criminal Punishment and the Widening Divide between America and Europe.* New York: Oxford University Press, 2003.

Wiesenthal, Simon. *The Sunflower: On the Possibilities and Limits of Forgiveness.* New York: Schocken, 1998.

Williams, Bernard. *Moral Luck.* Cambridge: Cambridge University Press, 1981.

Willis, Clint, ed. *Semper Fi: Stories of the United States Marines from Boot Camp to Battle.* New York: Scribner, 2003.

Wilson, J. Q. "Penalties and Opportunities." In *A Reader on Punishment,* ed. Anthony Duff and David Garland, 174–209. New York: Oxford University Press, 1994.

Winter, Steven. "Transcendental Nonsense, Metaphoric Reasoning, and the Cognitive Stakes for Law." *Pennsylvania Law Review* 137 (1989): 1105.

Wittgenstein, Ludwig. *Philosophical Investigations,* trans. G. E. M. Anscombe. New York: Macmillan, 1953.

Zaibert, Leo. *Punishment and Retribution.* Burlington, Vt.: Ashgate, 2006.

Zimring, Frank, and Gordon Hawkins. *Incapacitation: Penal Confinement and the Restraint of Crime.* New York: Oxford University Press, 1995.

Zion, James W., and Robert Yazzie. "Navajo Peacemaking: Original Dispute Resolution and a Life Way." In *Handbook of Restorative Justice,* ed. Douglas Sullivan and Larry L. Tifft, 151–60. New York: Routledge, 2008.

Index